Counter Revolu ...ies

The History of Shopping in Dundee

Authors Jack Searle and Craig Muir

This book is dedicated to the memory of Dennis Collins,
a true Dundonian, a keen historian, and a good and ever helpful friend.

First published in the United Kingdom in 2017 by
Dundee Civic Trust

© 2017 Dundee Civic Trust

This book was written and produced by

Authors Jack Searle with Craig Muir
Designed by Craig Muir

Publisher Dundee Civic Trust

ISBN 978-0-9548579-5-0

Printed in Dundee by Winter & Simpson

To find out about all our publications, please visit
www.dundeecivictrust. co.uk
There you can subscribe to our newsletter, browse or
download our current catalogue, and buy any titles
that are in print.

Contents

Preface

For many years shopping was an important part of the social and commercial life of the United Kingdom. Annie S. Maxwell, writing enthusiastically about shopping in Dundee on the occasion the visit of the British Association to the city in 1912 commented that, "Every woman loves shopping, most of all shopping of what can be called a personal kind. … The big drapery and furnishing establishments of Dundee fairly charm the money from the pockets of its womenfolk. Up to date? Of course they are. No high handed indifferent methods here, but pleasant ready service."

Although shopping remained a popular pastime for the remainder of the century it could mean different things to different people as the two examples below can confirm.

In the late 1960s shortly after I came to Dundee my wife and I heard about a collection of Celtic Crosses in a museum at St Vigeans near Arbroath. We decided to go and have a look. The museum was housed in a row of single storey cottage buildings and to see the crosses one had to get the key from the occupant of the end cottage, have a look at the museum and then return the key.

When we returned I noticed that the keeper of the key had an English accent and inquired where he came from. "I'm from Gloucestershire", he replied. "Really", I said, "and how did you get to live here?"

"Well", he replied, "I was in the Royal Naval Air Service and was posted to the seaplane base at Leuchars. When I was off duty I used to go into Dundee. On one occasion I happened to go into D. M. Brown's department store where, at the bottom of a rather grand staircase, shoppers were regularly entertained by a string trio. I rather fancied the young lady playing the violin. She was local, I was hooked, and that was that".

As a second and somewhat less enthusiastic example, I recently became aware that a park seat in Chester has a brass plaque on it bearing the following inscription:-

"This bench is dedicated to the men who have lost the will to live whilst following their partners around the shoe shops of Chester."

But like it or hate it there is little doubt that shopping has played an important social and economic role in the life of Dundee, and that healthy shopping centre remains vital to its attractiveness as a place to live, work, study and visit.

However, going by the results of surveys of young people, it would seem that the future of shopping as a face to face activity is by no means assured.

As Annie S. Maxwell somewhat prophetically said in 1912 "An easy and luxurious method of shopping is by telephone. Shopping by post is another institution of modern times and one which contains great possibilities for development in Dundee and elsewhere". It seems that she was all too right.

Introduction

This book is the story of how shopping grew to become a major leisure activity in the 20th century with particular reference to Dundee. A useful definition of shopping is that it is "an activity in which a customer browses the available goods and services presented by one or more retailers with the intent to purchase a suitable selection of them". However, a moment's reflection might well lead one to conclude that this definition is somewhat one sided being written purely from the view of the customer. I felt that it would be remiss not to take the opportunity presented by this introduction also to give some idea of the story of shopping viewed from the point of view of those behind the counter.

Throughout the middle ages there were virtually no shops as we know them, retailing being carried on by craftsmen from their workshops or by itinerant traders and salespeople. These were almost entirely male and those who were female were almost always the wives or partners of male traders.

Although some merchants were held in high regard due to their great wealth, working in retailing was not at this time a way to increase one's social status. Indeed, anybody who was involved with retailing was generally held in low esteem right up to the end of the 19th century.

During this period retailing was commonly regarded as an occupation associated with "greed, pettiness, and narrow mindedness". In these circumstances, it is not altogether surprising that in 1686 shopkeepers were referred to as "home traders, who we call shopkeepers, add to their own wealth by buying cheaper and selling dearer", and who were people who make "no contribution to the wealth of the nation".

For most people starting a shop was an difficult and expensive matter. As a consequence, early shop owners quite often had more than one occupation, while others slowly moved from being itinerant traders to become stall holders before at last taking the step of setting up their own premises.

In the early shops, only the shopkeeper and his or her immediate family members were involved in selling goods. In 1720 Daniel Defoe, who in his early life had been a trader selling wool, wine, and hosiery, remarked on the importance to shop owners of having an able wife. As, at this time, there were no regulated prices for non-food goods, shop owners had to have a good idea of the market and to be skilled negotiators thereby emphasising the advantage of keeping things in the family.

But as the 18th century went on shops began to grow in size and shop assistants began to be employed. The aim of many of these was to branch out on their own. At first this was relatively easy but by the mid eighteenth century to start a shop successfully a significant amount of cash was required. A contemporary assessment was that £100 was required to set up in even a basic retail business. To set up a drapers could cost as much as £1,000. This for most shop assistants was a high hurdle and meant loans - either from relatives, friends, or commercial sources. For some lucky individuals, it was a legacy that gave them their opportunity to own their own shop.

For the owners of shops selling non-perishable goods it was essential to develop both knowledge of goods available and of trends in fashion. To keep up with such matters they would often send their sons to be apprenticed in large stores in major cities before coming back to take part in the family business.

In 1747 shop assistants had to know their place. A contemporary urged the male (which they nearly all were) shop assistant employed in the fashion trade "to speak fluently - but not elegantly - to entertain the ladies and to be master of a handsome Bow and Cringe". Daniel Defoe, commented that "The best shopkeepers do not think it below them to stand cap in hand at the door (of their shop) to ask their customers to come in."

As shops became larger and particularly with the emergence of department stores the social status of those at the top of the retail tree rose significantly, and the owners of some of the large department stores joined the social elite. A measure of this is that some of these were knighted like Sir James Maple, the owner of a large London furniture store, and Sir Alfred James Newton, the Chairman of Harrods. Even many of those that were not officially recognised still acquired a high status. like for example Harry Selfridge, who was known as "The Earl of Oxford Street".

These large retail establishments focused on selling goods made primarily with middle and upper class women in mind. The fact that these women were, by and large, more comfortable dealing with female assistants led to the employment of large numbers of working class women who worked behind the counters. Many women also laboured in the tailoring workshops associated with these stores.

Consequently, whilst in the early 19th century it was considered slightly dubious for a girl to be serving behind a counter, in the space of a few years, the female workforce could be numbered in tens of thousands. Sometimes there were genuine opportunities for the woman with some clerical skills to gain some advancement but most who started on the shop floor stayed there for the rest of their working lives.

As early as the 1840s, the working conditions for shop assistants became an issue for reformers. Although the working conditions were much better than those found in industry at the time, many shop assistants were exploited by their employers. Whether this was the case depended very much on the particular stores in which they worked.

In some stores assistants worked a fourteen hour day, six days a week with only short breaks for lunch. In addition to "smiling and serving" they were also required to stand, which turned the day into an exhausting ordeal. The introduction of gas lighting around the middle of the century made matters worse by enabling shops to extend opening times, and with it the shop assistants' working day. The issue of working conditions in shops was identified by social reformers as early as 1840. It was later taken up by the Early Closing Association, which sought to shorten hours and put an end to Sunday trading. The consequent lobbying by the Association eventually secured an hour long break for lunch and in 1852 the working week was cut to 60 hours by Act of Parliament.

The conditions continued to arouse public concern and in 1895 an article entitled the "The Ethics of Shopping" written by a well known philanthropist, Lady St Helier, condemned the exploitation and physical conditions that ruined the health of young women assistants.

Stirred to action, in 1899 the Government passed the Seats for Shop Assistants Act. Whilst this did result in a rash of inventions for temporary seating which would not impede the sale of goods, the measure made very little difference for there were no provisions for the enforcement of the Act.

In the latter part of the century the growth of mass production and the increase in the range of goods, now imported from all over the world, meant that the level of skills and knowledge required of the ordinary shop assistants was still maintained and the need for specialists such as window dressers steadily grew. The shopping magnates became aware of both public concern about working conditions and of the need for assistants to work as a team, and began to introduce leisure and social clubs for their employees. By the 1880s management trainee courses for women started to become available in many of the larger stores.

Although the large department stores dominated most city centres in 1900 over 90% of trade was still in the hands of independent stores where the personal skills of the proprietor could make or break a business. This meant that both owners and shop assistants still had to be very careful not to offend customers in any way, as for the former this could lead to loss of trade whilst for the latter it could lead to instant dismissal.

For shop and store owners and for shop assistants the 20th century was to be a turbulent time. At first there was an air of stability and things went on much as before. In the period up to 1914 retailing continued to expand and the army of shop assistants continued to increase. The growth of retail chains continued and some middle class ladies began to order goods by telephone.

The start of the First World War changed all that. The commencement of the war first affected those in provision shops who had to deal with large numbers of people attempting to stockpile food of all kinds. The supply of some goods, like sugar, became very scarce and shop owners and assistants found themselves having to discriminate between customers.

The scarcity of goods also led to rampant inflation and the balance of power between the sellers of food and the customer being quite reversed, the latter being dependent upon the informal rationing schemes operated by the former. The introduction in 1917 of the regulation of food prices and the rationing of some foodstuffs by the newly created Ministry of Food emphasised this changed relationship. However, shortages were such that shop assistants had to deal with many unsatisfied customers some of whom could be quite abusive and who, in some cases, reverted to violence.

At the start of the war many of the larger stores encouraged their male staff to join the forces just as they had in peacetime encouraged them to join the Territorials. By the spring of 1915 over 250,000 shop assistants had joined up. The attitude of shop owners changed as the war went on because of the growing shortages of staff. Many more women began to be employed although employers firmly resisted paying them male wage rates. Some shops lost female staff who went to work in munition factories. Nevertheless, the proportion of women working in clothing shops increased from 55% in July 1914 to 71% by October 1917. As women began to occupy more senior jobs employers responded by starting training schemes for their new female staff.

The sharp wartime decline in the sale of luxury goods led to difficult times for the major department stores and many laid off staff, but despite this, the shortage of experienced staff did lead to some significant improvement in staff working conditions. In 1916 the Government introduced the regulation of shop opening hours and although these were not particularly stringent, some large London based department stores decided that for the duration of the war they would close altogether on Saturdays.

Although things began to return to normal after the end of the war, there was no immediate change as for a while goods continued to be scarce. Some things, however, had changed forever for although many of the women engaged during the war were discharged to make way for men returning from service in the forces, the proportion of women working in shops continued to increase.

By 1921 the short post war boom was over and many shop workers began to find themselves affected by short term working and staff cuts. However, the depression which followed the 1929 financial crash affected not only shop workers but also shop owners throughout the whole retail industry. Quite apart from that the large drapery stores and department stores were being affected by the growth of the multiple store chains such as Marks & Spencer and C & A Modes who, throughout the interwar period, began to make inroads into the markets previously dominated by them.

Some shop assistants benefited from the "quality service" strategy adopted by many independent traders as they struggled to compete with the multiple chains. Staff welfare was improved, training schemes introduced and benefit schemes established. Staff magazines were produced urging staff to improve their performance.

Staff conditions were also improved as a result of government action. The Shops Act of 1934 brought about better sanitary facilities for workers and introduced a 48 hour week for most who worked in retailing. In 1937 Sunday closing came into force for most shops, the principal exemptions being in respect of those working in cafes and ice cream parlours.

But just as things were settling down shops assistants in larger stores began to be provided with a new staff facility - air raid shelters - a preliminary to the commencement of the Second World War. Unlike in the First World War the Government was quick to act to introduce rationing, and the range of goods rationed was much greater than in the previous war.

As in the First World War the effects of rationing foodstuffs led to considerable problems for those owning and working in provision shops and created ill feeling between them and their customers. Rationed goods were no longer displayed as before the war, but hidden away below counters. Large queues formed whenever un-rationed goods of any kind were available. One shop assistant described working in a butchers at this time as "like being under siege".

Male shop workers quickly found themselves subject to conscription and whilst the recruitment of women as shop assistants was greatly expanded to fill the gap, in 1941 single women were also required to register. As a result, many shop assistants left to work in agriculture, in munitions and armament factories while others joined the armed forces. The retailing industry was forced to employ more married women and in more senior positions, and to persuade male staff about to retire, to stay on.

Fuel shortages, and the blackout led to shorter working hours and this improvement in shop workers' conditions lasted well into the post war period. Another change that persisted was the increase in female employment in the retailing industry. Put simply, many men chose not to return to their former jobs and went to work in industry, commerce and transport which tended to be better paid and freer from petty regulation.

More change was to come in the post war period. The percentage of women shop assistants increased from 66% in 1951 to 75% by 1961, and in some sectors, such as variety chain stores, 98% of shop assistants were female. However, there was little increase in the number of females in more senior jobs. It is interesting to note that the one remaining bastion of male employees in retailing was the Cooperative movement, where for many years the preponderance of shop assistants were male.

As the economy expanded labour became much more mobile and shop owners found it more and more difficult to retain staff. Staff attitudes had often changed, and a take it or leave it attitude which had entered retailing in the years of wartime shortages still prevailed. Indeed, in the postwar period it was commonly complained that shop assistants had become too independent and lacked commitment to customers and employers alike. There was little doubt that the emancipation of women during the war made them much less inclined to take on unpaid duties, and less tolerant of the petty regulations on dress and behavior still to be found in larger stores.

Despite the growth of the economy new trends in retailing started to create insecurity for many of those employed in shops. For instance, the introduction of self service began to remove large numbers of jobs in grocery shops. At first progress was slow but by the mid1960s there were more than 20,000 self-service stores in operation. The increasing availability of branded goods in both food and non-food sectors gradually led to a de-skilling of many shop assistants jobs as they were moved from behind the counters to the monotony of jobs at check-outs.

However, the steady growth in the economy led to an explosion in the number and range of goods for sale. This disguised the fact that many shops were being absorbed into chains of stores who required an ever increasing volume of sales per employee. In addition many small independent shops began to go out of business with a consequent reduction in the numbers employed in them. Between 1957 and 1966 the number of workers in small independent shops in the UK dropped by around 160,000. This was a trend which was to continue to the present time.

As the 20th century moved towards its end, the deregulation of retailing increased and in 1994 the opening of shops on Sunday was permitted. The new trends on the high street did little to help the prospects for jobs in retailing. There was a growth of ethnic shops but nearly all of these only employed family members. The increasing number of charity shops which began to appear tended to use volunteers rather than employ shop assistants.

As the Millennium loomed many superstores were open on a 24 hour basis and short time contracts for shop assistants were commonplace. This was not altogether surprising for the superstores now had to compete with online retailers, many of whose employees were on such contracts.

The 21st century saw the final indignity for many sales assistants as they were replaced by self service check outs and others found themselves on zero hours contracts. Even worse, the global growth of online shopping began not only to remove shop assistants but also the very shops in which they worked.

As 2020 approaches, it rather looks that shop assistants have become an endangered species and that the importance of shopping as a leisure activity is beginning to wane. In these circumstances, I felt it important that some kind of record of the way in the story of shopping in Dundee should be set down.

Turning to the book, it is in two parts, the first of which is a history of shopping in Dundee set in the context of the wider development of retailing and covering the period from the Middle Ages up to the year 2000. This is strongly focused on shopping in the city centre and does not deal directly with the sub-centres such as Lochee, the Hilltown, and Broughty Ferry, or out of centre shopping except insofar as these had a direct effect upon retailing in the city centre.

The second part of the book is a description of some aspects of Dundee as a shopping centre when it was in its prime, which I would define as the mid 1950s.

This includes the histories of some of the major stores in Dundee and of a number of the smaller retailers of the time, together with a list of all the shops to be found in the major shopping streets of Dundee city centre in 1955.

This list is confined to the main shopping streets within the central area of Dundee, roughly defined as the area lying within the current line of the Inner Ring Road. Attached to each entry in the list is some basic information about the shops, and/or owners, and in some cases the memories of some of those who remember them. It is hoped that this list will give a feel for the varied nature of the shops to be found in the city centre of the time.

No book on this subject could cover everything but it is hoped that this account may stir memories amongst its readers, of times when going shopping in Dundee was a pleasurable and important part of their lives.

1 Medieval Times

The buying and selling of goods is an activity that has existed from times immemorial. Initially most trading was done by barter. When coins became available as a means of exchange, the retailing of goods became part of daily life. At the centre of cities in ancient Greece was the agora that acted as a meeting and market place where merchants had stalls to sell their wares. In Roman towns and cities the forum performed a similar function. Nearer home a purchasing list from the period around 100 AD has been discovered at Vindolanda, a Roman settlement near Hadrian's Wall.

In northern Europe, apart from the development of markets there was little development in retailing until the Middle Ages when most settlements were still very small and fairly self-contained. For those people outside a wealthy minority a subsistence economy was the rule and food was either grown, or bartered locally. Other goods could be obtained from the homes of specialist makers or travelling merchants. As hamlets and villages grew into towns and cities they increasingly began to be dependent for their needs on the surrounding countryside and on trading.

By the early Middle Ages, with the ending of Viking attacks and better climatic conditions, a northern European trading area, extending from the Baltic to the British Isles, had begun to grow around the North Sea.

North Sea Trading Area

Town Charters

Markets began to be held in the larger settlements where farmers from the surrounding hinterland could bring in and sell their produce. Where a town was located on the coast, fishermen would display their wares on the nearest beach.

The rapid growth of population in the 11th century arising from an increase in food production and the stabilisation of medieval society, led to an increase in the number and size of towns. Monarchs swiftly realised that this could be used to their advantage. By granting charters to towns the monarch could weaken the power of the nobles and, at the same time, win the townspeople's support for the king.

The charters granted to towns by the monarch generally gave the inhabitants extensive financial and legal powers. The town was given management of its own finances and, for its part, paid its taxes in a lump sum to the king. It was also generally given the right to elect its own officials to administer these powers.

Charters almost always gave the towns the right to hold regular markets and fairs. This was an important matter as most medieval towns relied upon the taxation of goods bought and sold within the town to generate income. Progress was rapid and between 1200 and 1349 around 1200 new markets were established in Britain.

Although in medieval times the power to hold and regulate markets and fairs was in the grant of the Crown, in some places it was in the hands of the religious authorities. Certainly the dates of fairs were often associated with the dates of religious celebrations as in the case of Glasgow Fair. This had originated in 1190 when Bishop Jocelin gained the permission of King William the Lion to hold a fair within the boundaries of Glasgow Cathedral. Other fairs that were known to be in existence in Scotland in mediaeval times were Aberdeen (1274) and Dumbarton (1226).

London Bridge circa. 1250

Most markets only had temporary stalls but permanent shops began to appear in larger settlements and particularly in London where, in 1209, King John licensed the building of houses and shops on London Bridge.

In the 1200s in some of the larger towns in England, retailers of related goods began to group together, as in St Martin's Seld in Soper (Shopkeeper) Lane, in London. This housed 21 small plots and 30 chests for traders specialising in gloves and leather goods. The relatively high rents to be had from shops soon began to attract investors, an example from the 1200s being the twenty-two shops built on a speculative basis in Church Street in Tewkesbury.

Dundee

Things were much less advanced in Scotland in medieval times. Roads were primitive, even where they actually existed and rivers became natural highways that were important for the development of mediaeval towns. Dundee, as a small fishing settlement located on the estuary of the River Tay, had easy access to the North Sea and was therefore well positioned to thrive at the local, national and European levels by importing and exporting goods.

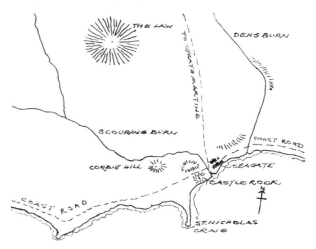

Dundee circa. 1000

In the 12th century King David 1 of Scotland created the first Royal Burghs. Royal Burghs were settlements where one could normally find the manufacture of clothes, shoes, dishes and pots, joinery and foodstuffs such as bread and ale. Other foods such as milk, eggs meal, corn, fruit and vegetables came in from the hinterland and were mainly available on market days. The charter confirming Dundee as a Royal Burgh is no longer extant and its precise date is unknown but as it was granted by King David it would have been some time before 1153. However, the charter would certainly have conferred rights and privileges relating to trade within the burgh boundary.

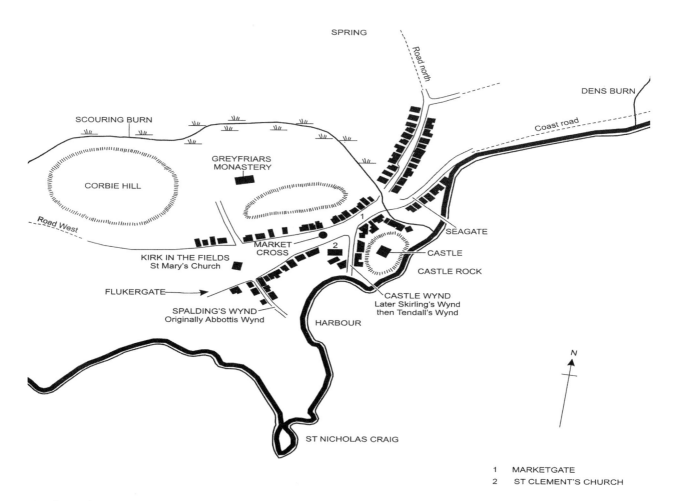

SPRING

Road north

DENS BURN

SCOURING BURN

Coast road

GREYFRIARS
MONASTERY

CORBIE HILL

Road West

SEAGATE

CASTLE

KIRK IN THE FIELDS
St Mary's Church

MARKET
CROSS

CASTLE ROCK

FLUKERGATE

CASTLE WYND
Later Skirling's Wynd
then Tendall's Wynd

SPALDING'S WYND
Originally Abbottis Wynd

HARBOUR

N

ST NICHOLAS CRAIG

1   MARKETGATE
2   ST CLEMENT'S CHURCH

Dundee 13th Century

More importantly in the late 12th century King William the Lion gave land lying on both sides of the River Tay that included Dundee to his brother David, Earl of Huntingdon. David was also a member of the English Court and in 1191 persuaded King John of England to grant a charter to the Burgesses of Dundee. This gave them the right to trade free of all taxes with his lands in France and England, but not London, and underlined Dundee's involvement in trading abroad.

The authority to hold a market was generally bestowed by the Crown and in Scotland markets were mostly under the control of the burghs. Particular care was taken to ensure that locations and dates of fairs and markets in particular regions did not clash. Places that did not get a Royal Charter were at a distinct disadvantage as was later shown in 1327 when David II issued an edict "prohibiting the villages of Coupar Angus, Kettins, Kirriemuir, and Alyth from holding markets", this rule being reaffirmed in 1358.

The rights set out in the Royal Charters empowering the Burghs were often confirmed or amended when a new monarch took the throne. Significantly the one part of Dundee's Royal Charter that was not amended in later confirmations was the extent of the area over which the Burgh had rights. In today's terms this was bounded by Tay Street in the west, the south wall of the Howff in the north, St Roques Lane in the east, and on the south by the then shoreline of the Tay estuary. This left the area to the north of the town, which was later to become home to the Hilltown, outwith the control of the burgh authorities.

Dundee was a prosperous settlement long before it was given its charter, but its chartered status and its favourable location on sea and river ensured that after 1199 the growth of the burgh accelerated. It began to attract trade that had previously gone to Montrose, St Andrews, and Perth. Within Dundee woollen goods and guns were made and exported but they were made and sold not in shops, but in the homes of the makers on a one to one basis, or acquired from travelling agents who visited the homes of the wealthy.

By the 13th century trade was being attracted to Dundee from Europe and particularly the Baltic ports such as Lubeck. When, in around 1250, Mathew Paris of St Albans drew his map of Britain, the town of Dundee had become sufficiently important to be named on the map.

The year of the first fair known to be held in Dundee, St Mary's Fair or The First Mary's Fair, is unknown but was held on 15 August to coincide with the day of The Assumption of the Virgin, or St Mary's Mass. It is however likely that its foundation was associated with the creation of the burgh in 1190. A second fair, the Latter Mary Fair, was held on 8 September. the Nativity of the Virgin.

In medieval times fairs were often held on the ground around churches and in Dundee the early Fairs were probably held in St Mary's kirkyard. This was helpful to the church as the revenue raised could be used to fund building works and maintenance.

The town and its trade continued to grow and in 1458 King James II granted Dundee a charter which allowed another fair to take place. This was initially scheduled to take place over the eight days from 13 November but in 1491 the date was changed to 23 November to coincide with the feast of St Clement.

In 1503 Parliament passed an Act forbidding fairs to be held in kirkyards. Whilst in some towns this was disregarded, it is known that at sometime before the 1550s St Mary's Fair had been relocated to the west end of the High Street.

The increase in the number and size of fairs and markets was closely related to the growth of urban areas for these were increasingly dependent upon the produce of their hinterlands for the supply of perishable goods and food.

However there was an important difference between fairs and markets. Fairs were occasional, if regular. events which would attract traders and entertainers from considerable distances. Markets on the other hand were the principal means by which food supplies came into the mediaeval town. They were also the means by which the burgh authorities attempted to regulate and increase the amount of food available and to ensure that there was some equity in the distribution of supplies in time of scarcity.

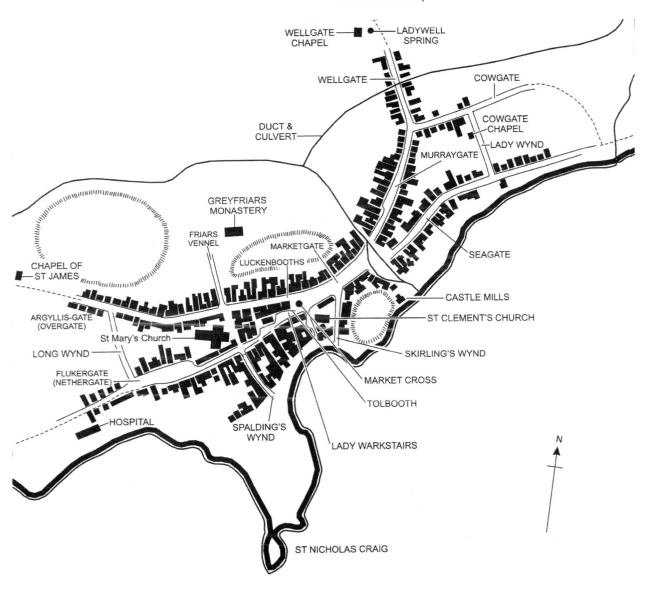

Dundee 15th Century

To administer these powers there had to be some kind of focal point and this, in Scotland, was the Tollbooth. This generally consisted of a council chamber, a courthouse, and a jail. As was often the way in Scottish towns, Dundee's markets took place in a wider part of the High Street where they were located around the Mercat Cross, the focus for the selling or bartering of goods. The Cross, a symbol of municipal status, was built by the burgh authorities close to the Tollbooth.

In 1325 King Robert I consented to the establishment of a new Tollbooth in the High Street in Dundee at a point east of St Mary's in the Fields around which the town continued to be concentrated until the 1400s. In 1363 the Tron, a weighing beam used in Scotland to check weights and measures, was set up at the west end of the High Street - Marketgait, reinforcing the street as the focus for the buying and bartering of goods in the Burgh.

Not all goods were sold on the street. Some things, particularly luxury goods, could be purchased at the harbour warehouses where timber, wine and other luxury goods were being imported for the numerous religious establishments in the area around the Tay and for the landed gentry of Angus and northern Fife. Such items were also sold to the wealthy in Dundee. In 1311 supplies for Dundee Castle were ordered from Tomas Tresk, a merchant living in Dundee, and timber and coal were being sold from warehouses at the harbour.

But successful though fairs and markets were in the mediaeval period, the problem was that the would be customer could only buy goods when the market or fair was taking place. A permanent location for sales was clearly better for the customer but the shopkeeper required enough potential customers at that place to give him a living the whole year round. This meant that shops could only survive in larger towns, or at a location with a densely populated hinterland. Although some goods were sold from houses in Dundee shops were very few in number for most of the period.

Shopping in Medieval Dundee

During this period the town was still very small and streets were unpaved. As most of the population had not the means to buy anything more than food and they had few furnishings and possessions, people in Dundee would not have recognised the concept of shopping as we know it. The average diet was based on oatmeal and, in the winter, kail and root vegetables. Protein could be got from the plentiful supplies of fish, sometimes hawked around the town, sometimes bought or bartered on the shore, where fishermen laid out their wares on planks.

On market days and fairs a wider range of food and goods could be purchased from farmers and travelling packmen using the backs of carts, temporary stalls and benches to sell their goods. Markets were lively, and often rowdy, occasions when farmers and others would come in from the surrounding countryside to hire labour and to sell cattle and horses. Farm wives would sell eggs, butter and other farmhouse produce. As the market place was unpaved and open to the weather and livestock were bought and sold in the marketplace, shopping could be a wet, smelly and dirty experience.

For most people the best opportunity to buy a wider range of non perishable goods was at the St Mary's Fair and the Latter Fair. The goods sold at these fairs were generally fairly basic, but with Dundee having a harbour imported goods were among the things on sale. For example, in 1264 cloths and furs for King Alexander III were purchased at Dundee market. However, conditions at the fairs were no better than that at the market.

The better off Dundonians had houses in the town with gardens attached to them that were used to grow fruit and vegetables, and, quite often, to keep chickens, pigs and goats. Such retailers as there were generally operated from their own houses where they sold a fairly narrow range of items at the door. The goods sold might be made on the premises, or in a nearby workshop while others such as smoked fish were processed by the retailer. Some merchants would buy goods in bulk, preserve them by drying or salting them, and then divide the wholesale bulk into small portions for the final consumer. However, the range of goods was small and the nearest things to shops, as we know them, were the houses of specialist craftsmen or the warehouses by the shore.

2 The Early Modern Period 1500 - 1713

The Early Modern Period ran from 1500 to 1713 and was a time of global exploration by Europeans that resulted in new and exotic goods becoming available for sale, first for the rich and then gradually to the better off classes.

In comparing developments in England and Scotland it should be borne in mind that the better climate and more fertile lands of the former resulted in a significantly greater agricultural surplus. In Scotland agriculture was still mainly at a subsistence level leaving all but the very rich with little choice other than to make their basic clothes and furniture themselves. As a result, England at this time had much larger towns than Scotland, and many more of them and the proportion of the population that lived in towns was much larger than in Scotland. Inevitably this meant that north of the border, up until Georgian times the development of retailing – a very urban occupation - trailed in the wake of the situation obtaining in the south of England.

As towns and cities grew in size their function as trading centres increased. The wider range and larger amounts of goods available for sale led to innovations in the way that goods were sold. London, in the 16th century, was easily the largest city in the United Kingdom, and as might be expected, the home to most innovations in shopping. After 1500 streets composed almost wholly of shops began to appear in the capital, and by the late 1560s shopping galleries began to be opened in London.

In 1609 Robert Cecil opened the New Exchange in the Strand. This had been designed by Inigo Jones as a building housing a number of shops, targeted on the upper classes. The King was present at its formal

The New Exchange

Our Lady Warkstairs

opening at which imported exotic luxury items were for sale. Noise was kept to a minimum and beggars and vagrants were strictly excluded.

Throughout the period the number of shops in Britain continued to increase and it has been estimated by the pioneer statistician Gregory King that by 1700 there were about 40,000 shopkeepers in England and Wales. These employed around 180,000 working in shops, many of which had become specialised in the goods they sold.

Dundee

Conditions in Dundee at the start of the sixteenth century were much less sophisticated than in the south of England. At the start of the 1500s the streets were still, for the most part crooked, narrow and of irregular width. They were by now paved with water-worn cobblestones that presented a durable but uneven surface. Unlikely though it seems, it was in this period that a baker was allowed by the burgh authorities to build his oven under the High Street on condition that he properly restored the road above.

The development of the town westwards from the original settlement on the shore had resulted in a wide High Street that connected the Seagate and the Murraygate, the major roads into the city centre from the east, to the Overgate and the Nethergate which came in from the west. The High Street was thus the marketplace in which most civic activity took place, from the buying and selling of goods, the holding of markets and fairs and informal bartering.

Dundee in the 1600s

In the early part of the period most streets had only frontage development, but as the town became more congested, the gardens at the rear of many of the properties started to be built upon. This reduced their capacity to produce fruit and vegetables thereby increasing the need for places where such produce could be bought. As a result, in Windmill Brae in the Overgait front gardens had begun to be built over to provide booths or shops. By 1508 the building known as Our Lady Warkstairs, on the north side of High Street, (opposite to where Crichton Street now runs), had an arcaded front, some of which had been filled in to create enclosed shops. Hucksters, or sellers of small wares used any corners or spaces they could find to sell their goods.

The manner of the sale of goods and the taxing of transactions were matters of great importance to the burgesses of Dundee as tax revenues from retail sales, together with harbour dues, provided most of the funds required to run the burgh. When in 1511 James IV signed the Burgh charter confirming all previous burgh rights and obligations, it included powers to levy all stand keepers in order to pay for the cleansing of streets and marketplaces. One penny was paid on each load of victual (meal), salt, fish butter and eggs.

Interestingly the burgesses were also given powers in the Charter to fine any owner of a horse left standing on the street the sum of one penny – perhaps the first example of parking fines in Dundee.

Important though the burgesses were in the control of Dundee, an important role was also played by the trade guilds. The merchant guilds had a monopoly of buying and selling of goods within the liberties of the burgh. No un-free man could sell eggs, mussels, butter, cheese, fish and salt. None could use the steps of the Mercat Cross to sell their wares as these were reserved for farmer's wives to sell their produce.

As the century went on, more and more of the membership of the Guildry were also burgesses and though until 1590 the Guildry was independent of the Burgh Council, after that date it became practically the same body of men.

The Dundee burgesses were keen to encourage people from the surrounding areas to come into the town and when the fairs were held the ordinary restrictions imposed upon un-free traders were removed. This was very successful and in order to accommodate the increasing numbers of stalls. the Dundee burgesses tried changing the location of the First Fair from the confined west end of the Marketgait to the open churchyard of St Mary's Church.

The buyers of food and other goods increasingly looked to the Burgh Council to regulate retailers and to see that customers got fair measures of the goods they purchased. The burgesses took the question of profiteering seriously and prohibited the activities of middlemen at all markets. Transactions were strictly to be between the producers or makers and the consumers of goods. Those persons buying goods to sell on to others could be fined by the Council. In September 1521 one Janet Howller was fined for doing just that and a Robert Stewart had his goods appropriated for the same offence.

A meal market for the selling of oatmeal and grain was the first of the institutions created by the burgesses. This was operated by the Baker's incorporation and was located in the Nethergate roughly opposite where the City Churches stand today. To its west lay the Greenmarket where vegetables and herbs could be bought.

The regulation of the prices of basic foodstuffs was a matter of great importance to all Dundonians and therefore of the Burgh Council who regularly took action to regulate the price of bread. This they did on six occasions between 1520 and 1523. To ensure that food was fairly shared they also rationed grain in times of food shortages.

To enforce trading regulations within the burgh the council appointed meat and bread inspectors. In addition, as the sale of wine was confined to the burghs, official wine-tasters were now employed as town officials.

It is important to remember that these regulations still only applied to the area bounded by Tay Street on the west, the lands of Greyfriars on the north, St Roques Lane in the east, and on the south by the shore. This meant that in Rotten Row (the then name for the Hilltown) traders could operate free from regulation. This was much resented by the burgh traders and a guard was often stationed at the Wellgate to prevent the entrance into the burgh of unauthorised goods made by the large numbers of weavers and bonnet makers in the Hilltown.

In the 1560s the council undertook a number of measures designed to improve the centre of Dundee. The paving of the Cowgate eastwards from the Murraygate was undertaken, pigs were banned from being kept in any of the town's closes and wynds as was the keeping of middens in the streets of Dundee. At the same time a new flesh house or meatmarket was put in place at east end of the Hiegate (approximately where the former Clydesdale Bank building stands today).

Dundee was not only a centre for the trade of food, it was also home to a great number of craftsmen. In 1587 it was recorded that craftsmen operating in the burgh included smiths, sword slippers, guard makers, cutlers, gun-makers, goldsmiths, pewter workers and lorimers (metal workers who made spurs and other equine accessories}. Most of these worked and sold their goods from their own homes but an alternative for both makers and customers appeared in 1513 when, in the Wooden Land, on the north side of Argyllisgait (later to become the Overgate), shoemakers could hire benches by the week to make, and sell their goods.

In common with most other Scottish towns, Dundee had a tollbooth that served as the centre for the administration of the town. This housed a council

The Wooden Land

meeting chamber, a court house and a jail. In the early 1500s the tollbooth in Dundee stood on the north side of Marketgait at the east end of Our Lady Warkstairs. However, this location had been found so inconvenient and the site so small that it was decided in the early 1500s to erect a new tollbooth in the upper part of St Clement's Churchyard (roughly where the mouth of the City Square is today situated).

For the first time the Burgh Council decided that shops should be part of a public building and accordingly a number of booths for traders were incorporated on the ground floor. After the under-vaulting and the walls of seven booths on the ground floor had been completed, work on the building was stopped. The cause for the stoppage is unknown but it may have been due to an interdict by the church authorities as the site was partly on land owned by the church.

The building remained unfinished until, in 1522, the Council let several of the unfinished booths to traders on the condition that they roofed the shells. This work was carried out but unfortunately, in 1548, as a result of the wars of religion, the town was occupied by the English who burned down the tollbooth and with it the traders' booths.

Improving the town centre

The burgh council then turned its mind to what in retrospect were to be two very persistent problems for traders and shoppers using the centre of Dundee. These were the cleansing of the streets in the centre and the removal of congestion.

Going shopping in the town at this time could be a less than pleasant experience as household middens, although formally forbidden, were still commonplace, and most refuse was just dumped upon the streets. The conditions in the High Street were particularly bad as quite apart from the piles of domestic waste encountered, there was animal dung everywhere due to the regular holding of horse markets on the thoroughfare and the constant driving of livestock to the slaughterhouse located at the east end of the street.

This did not reflect well upon the reputation of the Burgh or those responsible for its administration. As a consequence, a number of decrees were issued by the Burgh Council requiring private middens or dumps to be removed from the streets on pain of a fine or imprisonment. These measures were less than successful. Consequently, when in 1591, a new hangman was appointed he was also made the towns first public street cleaner. Accordingly, the

Council resolved that each quarter of the town be patrolled by constables and larger fines imposed on those who emptied their closets into the street or into the kirkyard. This did not cure the problem and even in the 1660s the councillors were still trying to ensure adequate street cleaning

As the town grew, so did the level of congestion in the town centre and by 1562 the High Street had become a very busy place. The use of the area around the tollbooth in the High Street for the holding of markets and fairs had grown and the large number of traders laying out their wares there were still causing obstruction. Furthermore, additional traffic was being generated by Provost Pierson's huge warehouse at what is now the bottom of Crichton Street (later known as the Provost's Mansion or the Custom House) that had recently been built to accommodate imported goods.

Provost Pierson's Warehouse

In response the Council resolved that merchants could not sit at the market cross on the "Hie gait" to sell their wares, but only at their doors or windows, or at the heads of the closes where they lived. The Council also decided that no markets be opened before 11.00am.

Municipal Enterprise

The Burgh Council was not solely concerned with regulating others –it was also determined to take direct action to improve the town as a centre for commerce. When in 1564, Queen Mary gifted to the burgh the lands and buildings belonging to the Greyfriars in Dundee, the Burgh Council saw this as an opportunity to make further improvements to the town centre. A new Flesh market was built utilising stones from the Greyfriars Howff. It was located in the High Street opposite Castle Street and had 12 booths, eight of which had lofts.

The Mercat Cross

In 1566 the Council found it necessary to bring in regulations to control the sale of fish. From then on fish were only to be sold in the Fish market and none of the fish purchased could be sold on to others, whether the fish were dried or fresh. The fish concerned included salmon, porpoises, herring and whiting.

In an attempt to improve the efficiency of the market place in 1568 the Meal Market was moved from the Marketgait to the Overgait near to St Salvador's Close. This was eventually found to be inconvenient and in 1589 it was shifted back to its previous location.

A measure of the Burgh council's aspirations was to be seen in 1586 when a new Market Cross was commissioned. The Council was determined to get the best and chose as its designer John Myles, the King's Master Mason for Scotland.

A time of setbacks
Dundee had suffered considerable damage earlier in the century due to the hostilities associated with Henry VII's 'Rough Wooing' of Scotland in the 1540s.

Further damage was sustained in the subsequent wars of religion, during which the town was attacked by both the English and the Scots.

These turbulent times prompted the Council to ask for royal approval to build a town wall. This was not only to give some protection to the burghers of Dundee against attack but also to properly control the passage of goods into and out of the town. Permission for the works to go ahead was granted in 1591.

Whilst the last decade of the 16th century was a difficult time for Dundee, the 17th century was in many ways worse. In 1606 there was an outbreak of bubonic plague in the town that ran on for two years. Whilst the town did make a recovery from this, a catastrophic failure of crops in the years 1621 to 1624 led to a serious famine in the country and a sharp decline in the supplies of food for sale in Dundee.

The Union of the Crowns of England and Scotland in 1603 had great implications for Dundee as it eventually led to the involvement of Scotland in the wars of religion that so affected the prosperity and progress of the town during the following century.

The prospect of religious change creating civil disturbance prompted Charles I to attempt to bolster up his popular support by granting charters to a number of towns in Scotland. Thus it was that in 1641 a new Royal Charter was given by King Charles I to the Burgh of Dundee "to be the chief and principal burgh within the Sheriffdom of Forfar, wherein there is great trade of Merchandise".

If this was a high point for the town, it was not to last for the very next year the town was attacked and sacked by the forces of the Marquis of Montrose.

The inevitable commercial setback that this entailed was worsened by the commercial ambitions of the Viscount Scrimgeour who obtained a Royal Charter for the Baronial Burgh of Hilltown of Dudhope. This gave the new Baronial Burgh the liberty of holding a weekly market and two fairs each year in the Hilltown. More importantly being outside the Dundee Burgh area all its shop owners and traders were free from local taxes. Whilst the Hilltown was not initially a serious competitor to the shop owners within the burgh limits, it was effectively Dundee's first out of town shopping centre and was able to produce goods free from regulation and at lower prices.

In 1648 as Dundee recovered from the depredations brought down upon it by the Marquis of Montrose there was another outbreak of bubonic plague in the city. Fortunately, this was the last occasion when plague occurred in Dundee but it was not to be the last of the burgh's misfortunes for it was followed in 1651 by the siege and sack of the city by General Monck.

However in 1669 an act was passed enabling the establishment of two new markets in Dundee. The first of these was to held for eight days starting on the first Tuesday in July and the second from the first Tuesday in October. The date of the latter was later altered to the first Tuesday after 11 July and became known as the Stobb Fair.

The town once again recovered and after this set of calamities a period of stability and prosperity ensued. However, there were setbacks from time to time such as the serious failure of crops in 1689 that forced the Burgh Council to intervene in the grain market in order to stop profiteering.

By the late 1600s the growth in the economy and population of the town had increased the size of the annual fairs and the number of itinerant traders attending them. Such were the numbers that traders in small wares had begun to use "cadgers", men who used trains of packhorses to transport the trader's goods to fairs. Such developments meant that shoppers could by then find a far wider range of goods at the fairs.

Another mark of the increased prosperity of the town was the growth in the trade passing through the harbour. Despite the fact that the tribulations of the latter part of the sixteenth century resulted in the population number dropping from 12,000 in 1639 to 8,250 in 1690, the period from 1660 to 1697 saw the number of ships and cargos entering Dundee Harbour increase more than fourfold.

As the century came to an end there was one more bright spot for the burgh when the Burgh Council in 1697, by agreement with Sir Robert Mill, took over control of the Barony of the Hilltown and thereby brought the trade from whole of the urban area under their authority.

Shopping in the Early Modern Period
Going to buy goods in Dundee during this period was not a pleasant task for the sensitive, particularly when it was raining. The streets of Dundee were still poorly paved and pretty filthy, due in large part to

Trading in the High Street

Harbour Circa 1700

the absence of any kind of sewage system but also to the presence in the town of many horses and of livestock being driven to the shambles that was still located next to the High Street. Consequently, the well-to-do were often seen wearing shoes with very thick wooden soles designed to keep their feet above the glaur - a medieval equivalent of platform soles.

The shopping experience was significantly improved when in 1642 the cattle market was removed to Fairmuir, but the town centre was still a crowded and malodorous place. When among the crowds attending the annual fairs one had to be wary of pickpockets and of the violent incidents that could, and did, occur.

Although the selling of food and other goods was still concentrated on stalls and booths set up on market days, permanent booths had now begun to appear around the marketplace. These were not shops as we know them today, but much more open affairs. An observer of the time commented:- "Many of the houses had wooden fronts supported by pillars within which were open piazzas, sometimes used as the workshops of craftsmen and often the booths of merchants". Although there were now many more booths where goods could be bought, these were still mostly small and unpretentious.

At that time there were few lucken or locked booths, the goods being usually displayed upon benches within the open fronts and sometimes on permanent stone erections in the street. These displays were often seen as obstructions, and were, on occasions, removed by the Burgh officials.

If basics were required, then oatmeal could be bought in the High Street from the traders congregated in the Meal Market. Meat was available for the better off from the butcher's stalls at the Fleshmarket, and fish, both fresh and dried, could be bought in the Burgh Fish Market.

The records kept of harbour dues for the period from 1550 to 1556 give some idea of the range of goods being sold in Dundee. One ship from Flanders unloaded 40,000 strings of onions, 24 barrels of apples, 2 tons of Spanish iron, quantities of English cloth, 10 tuns of wine from Gascony, glass, playing cards, 6 reams of paper and 60 stones of wax. And at around the same time a Dundee trader named Robert Jack bought quantities of velvet, worsted, silk satins, sewing silk, silk ribbons and other small items from one James Findloson (sic). However, oranges and exotic fruit were virtually unknown and sugar was uncommon due to its price.

As the period went on more goods became available and although stealing had gone on since times immemorial, a mark of the better range and quality of shops was that, in 1699, shoplifting became a criminal offence.

3 THE GEORGIAN TOWN 1713 - 1840

In Britain this period was one of rapid urban growth and the development of what was known as 'the middling' classes. Shopping as we know it today emerged during the eighteenth century and was linked to the growth of disposable income. The expansion of the British Empire was accompanied by the increasing availability of a wide range of luxury goods including tea, cotton, tobacco and silks. As an instance, sugar consumption doubled in the first half of the eighteenth century.

Important developments included the marketing of goods for individuals, as opposed to items for the household, and the new role of goods as status symbols, this being emphasised by more rapid changes in fashion. New ways of selling were adopted, a good example of which was to be seen in the actions of the pottery magnate Josiah Wedgwood who pioneered the use of marketing to influence the direction of the current taste and fashion. In 1774 Wedgwood moved his London shop to the fashionable Portland House in Soho where he hoped to improve his sales. There, alongside his high-class ceramics showrooms, he included a self-selection department where manufacturer's seconds could be purchased.

As the period went on the idea developed that shopping could be a leisure occupation rather than a simple necessity. Thus, when in 1791, John Lackington opened his Temple of the Muses in London – a massive book and print shop - it included an 'experience' store where people could peruse the stock. There were also two rooms to be used for relaxation.

The Temple of the Muses

The Soho Bazaar

This trend towards shopping as a leisure activity was assisted by the introduction in 1773 of plate glass manufacture. The London tailor Frances Place was the first to instal plate glass windows in his shop in Charing Cross. This innovation was quickly adopted by other retailers and similar display windows were soon to be seen in streets throughout the capital.

At the other end of the spectrum there were grass roots developments in retailing. In 1761 the Fenwick Weavers Society bought a sack of oatmeal and sold the contents to its members at low cost, starting the very earliest known consumers' co-operative. Later in 1796 the Birmingham Flour and Bread Company set itself up as a consumer co-operative on a large scale to provide 'honest bread at a low price'.

The latter part of this period saw the first steps taken on the path to the development of department stores, namely the opening of bazaars. These were made up of a large space surrounded by galleries and lit from above, where space was let out to traders offering a variety of products. This had already been anticipated in France where in 1786 the Galleries du Bois with 120 shops opened as the world's first shopping mall.

In 1816 John Trotter opened the Soho Bazaar, the first true bazaar, in Soho Square, London. Within its interior, counters topped with mahogany were provided and rented on a daily basis, to some 200 female traders. As the century went on bazaars were developed in a number of British cities, a typical example being the Western Exchange near London's Bond Street.

The Western Exchange off Bond Street London—opened 1817

Shopping arcades were another development of the Georgian period. The first English glass-roofed arcade was the Royal Opera Arcade that was opened in 1817. The very next year saw the opening of Burlington Arcade in London.

A notable trend was the evolution of specialist shops, particularly drapers, into showrooms stocking a range of goods. These large stores were described as warehouses or emporia and were the forerunners of the department store. Such ideas quickly spread to the provinces and in 1831 the Kendall Milne department store opened in Manchester with free entry, price-marked goods, and fixed prices.

In Scotland, the first part of the period was characterised by towns just trying to cope with circumstances but in the latter part of the 18th century the rapid growth of population and an improving economic environment led to a general movement by local authorities to improve and regenerate their town centres. Dundee was an active participant in this movement.

Dundee

At the start of the period the predominant economic and social centre of Dundee was still the public market place in the High Street.

Until the eighteenth century the development of Dundee as a shopping and trading centre had occurred in a spasmodic and unguided way but in the Georgian period the Burgh Council and the Guildry became active agents in the improvement of trading conditions in the town centre. To this end they made a series of decisions and pursued policies that were to provide the foundations for the commercial centre that can still be seen today.

As the weekly markets and annual fairs grew and took up more space the burgh authorities started to become ambivalent about them. The markets and fairs were desired for the trade and taxes that they generated. However, the disturbance they created and the insanitary nature of the meat and livestock market where animals were slaughtered on the public street, together with the the violence which often occurred was increasingly unwelcome. It did not help that food riots often took place in the marketplace in times of scarcity or famine.

By the 18th century the provision of better market facilities began to be the focus of the Burgh Council's attention. The initial approach was to remove some of the dirtier and smellier parts of the market, such as the meat and livestock sales, to locations away from the marketplace.

The Council realised that before Dundee could take forward any improvements to the town it had to improve its financial circumstances. To this end in the early 1700s a decision was made by the Council to exempt small amounts of linen sold in Dundee from custom charges. By 1720 this had led to the regional trade in linen being concentrated in the city, stimulating its growth and emphasising the role of Dundee as a regional trading centre. The result was a steady increase in the wealth of its citizens.

As a consequence, Dundee became a city with aspirations, and the Burgh Council embarked on a programme of works designed to upgrade the town and to encourage its growth. The first of these was to build a new Townhouse or tollbooth. The Council employed William Adam, one of the most prominent architects of the time, to design the new townhouse. This, the Council decided, was to be located on the south side of the High Street alongside the Market Place. Significantly, in 1731 when the Town House was completed it featured at ground level, set back behind an arcade, a row of shops, including a bank and a post office. These shops were in the latest fashion and had small bow windows made up of small panes of glass.

The Town House with shopping arcade

The erection of the splendid new Tollbooth only served to underline the shortcomings of Dundee's existing commercial centre. At this time, most of the buildings in the centre were wooden fronted and many had become run down. Rents were low and shops were small. To deal with this state of affairs the Dean of Guild, in 1735 was charged with identifying ruinous buildings on the frontages of the main streets and compelling the owners to repair and improve them or to face compulsory acquisition by the town. This policy was determinedly pursued by the Burgh Council with some success, for in 1775 a contemporary account noted that, "Murraygate may be said to be almost new built from end to end."

An article in a short-lived Dundee newspaper, the Dundee Weekly Intelligencer, commented that, "Open air markets possess all the features of a country fair and are resorted to by roughs and perilous characters of both sexes. The hucksters and jostlers that prevail and the rude and offensive language that assails the ears on all hands, prevent the more respectable inhabitants from frequenting these places." As the burgh councillors were part of that middle class it was not surprising that they were well aware of these feelings.

The availability of water for traders and for the horses of both traders and customers was an important matter for any shopping centre in Georgian times. In 1743 four new wells, all supplied from the Ladywell reservoir at the foot of the Hilltown, were installed by the Burgh Council in the town centre. These were the Dog Well in the Murraygate, St Clements Well in the High Street, the Burnhead Well in the Seagate and the Overgate Well in Tally Street.

The lack of lighting was another matter of concern and in 1752 the Burgh Council decided to introduce civic street lighting and, to that end, purchased a quantity of lamp standards from London. By 1768 there were some fifty eight street lights operating in the city centre.

The growth in trade meant more shops and that in turn generated a demand for more storage facilities. To cater for this in 1756 the Town Council invested in the construction of three new warehouses. These were to be built alongside the harbour to facilitate trade and to produce an income for the burgh.

In the 1760s a contemporary description of Dundee refers to "its increasing wealth', and as shops and customers increased in numbers and sophistication, the contrast between the internal environment of the stores and condition of the public streets became ever more apparent. It was not therefore surprising that in 1767 a meeting took place between the Guildry, and a number of city merchants to discuss this matter. It was decided to establish a committee to pursue the improvement of streets. To facilitate these the post of City Architect was created and a native Dundonian, Samuel Bell, was appointed to oversee improvements to the centre of the city.

At first the committee acted to improve what existed. The clearing of the filth that accumulated on the city centre streets had been identified as a matter needing attention as early as 1560. However, in spite of the regular attempts by the authorities to resolve the problem by the issuing of decrees and the imposition of fines to stop people dumping

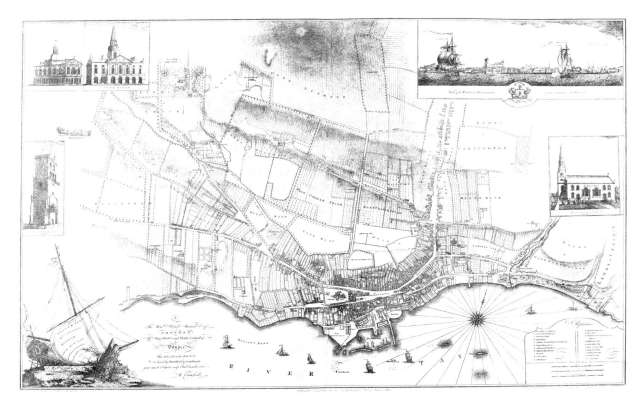

Dundee - 1776 Crawford plan

rubbish in the streets, the situation remained unsatisfactory. In 1773 the Council decided bite on the bullet and to spend public money to employ scavengers to clear and sweep the streets. However, this was only on a random basis, and it was not until 1778 that regular cleaning of streets was introduced in Dundee.

A related problem confronting the Burgh Council was that the main shopping and trading area of the town – the High Street – was still home to some unpleasant activities that had been established in the middle ages and which detracted from the town's image. Chief among these was the town's outdated slaughterhouse.

The Council also felt that the temporary stands erected every Friday on the High Street by Fleshers to sell meat seemed no longer appropriate for a town with Dundee's ambitions. So it was that in 1775 the Town Council decided to sell the Flesh Shambles at the head of the Murraygait and to construct a new Fleshmarket. This was built on a site lying roughly where the Gilfillan Church stands today.

The new building was rectangular and divided into two squares. One was to be called the Town Market and to be owned by the Flesher Trade of Dundee. The other was to be owned by the Council and to be called the Country Market and used by fleshers from outwith Dundee. The building was divided into stalls and had a well at its west end to facilitate the

cleansing of the Market. The slaughtering of animals was to be removed from the town centre altogether and a site was chosen for a new slaughterhouse on Craig Pier near the ferry berth.

However, the Dundee Fleshers were not happy with the new arrangements, partly because rents were raised by 50%, and in an attempt to halt the proposed measures, raised an action against the Town Council. In August 1776, the Lords of Session sitting in Edinburgh, decided in favour of the Council, and the fleshers were forced to decamp to the new Flesh Market.

The Council disposed of the site of the old Flesh Market to the Nine Trades who decided that the ground would be cleared and resolved that a large new Trades Hall would be erected to designs by the architect, Samuel Bell. The new Trades Hall was opened in 1776 by the Convenor and the Deacons of the Nine Trades with some ceremony, including a procession from the Hospital with a band and drums. The Hall itself was located on the first floor level so that shops could be incorporated on the ground floor level.

By 1776 the authority's programme of improvements was beginning to bear fruit and a contemporary observer noted that Dundee's "markets were well supplied with Beef, Mutton, and other meats not only on market days but all other days of the week except the Sabbath. Fresh fish could be bought on

Trades Hall with bow window shops

any day and there were two market days every week, these being held on Tuesday and Thursday."

With ships arriving in the Harbour from America, the Mediterranean, Holland, France, Russia, Denmark, and Sweden, Dundee was now a busy town. Home produced goods were in plentiful supply as well as a wide range of goods from abroad now available in its increasing number of shops. Locally produced food and goods could be bought at the town's weekly markets and the fairs that took place in July, August, September and October of each year

Congestion

Unfortunately, the increase in trade did not come alone. The consequent congestion of the central streets caused by traders and shoppers going about their business became a problem that, in different forms, was to worry the municipal administrators for the next two centuries. The congestion had a number of causes.

The most obvious of these and the subject of constant complaint from traders was that the medieval street pattern could no longer cope with the ever increasing traffic of goods to and from the harbour. This particularly emphasised the shortcomings of the streets connecting the shore

with the High Street. None of the existing pends and wynds was wide enough for two carts or carriages to pass each other. To deal with this problem it was decided to create three new streets – Crichton Street, Castle Street and Tay Street.

In 1777 the Council bought and demolished Dr Crichton's mansion to allow the start of the construction of the street that still bears his name. It was, however, to take four years to complete. Moreover, the initial plans for a broad straight street were not carried through, largely due to the influence of Provost Riddoch who became leader of the Burgh Council in 1777, a post that he held for most of the period up to 1814.

In January 1795 following a proposal made in 1794 by Provost Riddoch the Town Council bought land to enable the new Castle Street to connect the Market place with the harbour. Instructions were given to Samuel Bell the architect to prepare a scheme for buildings with ground floor shops and two upper storeys to be occupied by dwelling houses.

Although the construction of the carriageway of the upper part of Castle Street had largely been completed by 1793, some of the feus that had been created were still not occupied by permanent buildings - a situation that was to persist for decades to come. Part of the problem was that although partly constructed, Castle Street was still not properly connected to the harbour at its southern end. This was due to the lack of agreement between the Burgh Council and the owner of a former timber yard at the bottom of the proposed street. The Town Council spent the next eleven years arguing over compensation for this piece of land owned by none other than Provost Riddoch.

The streets were also congested due to the encroachment on the pavements and carriageways by the traders themselves. "Before shops were introduced moveable booths, in which the merchant displayed his goods, were set up in front of his dwelling. These became to be erected permanently in front of the house and encroaching on the carriageway. These booths could be as much as ten or twelve feet in front of the house". Although the Council recognised the problem no action was taken due to a combination of political and financial self interest.

However, in 1777 the Council decided to remove the Mercat Cross from the High Street to ease the flow of traffic. At the same time the Council decided to install new paving in the narrows of the Nethergate and to raise the paving levels around the Town House.

Dundee 1847 - Charles Edward

They also decided to deal with one other cause of congestion that was under their own control. This was the town's Meal Market that was still located in the Nethergate and, as the busiest of the burgh's markets, was the cause of much congestion. A decision was therefore made by the Council in 1782 to remove the Meal Market from the High Street and relocate it to a site lying beside the fish market – roughly just south of where the Caird Hall stands today.

The site made available by the relocation of the Meal Market was used to construct the Union Hall. This was originally erected in 1783 as an English Episcopal Chapel designed by Samuel Bell, but reflecting its prominent location in the retailing centre of Dundee, its ground floor consisted of shops that were let to traders of various kinds. One of these shops was occupied by John Croome, a haberdasher and wholesale merchant. Two of the other shops were, unsurprisingly, given the previous use of the site, occupied by meal merchants.

In the late 1780s the provision of adequate supplies of water in the central area reared its head again. On this occasion the maintenance of the facilities was the issue and in July 1788, John Flight, a hammerman, made an offer to keep the public fountain pipes and wells in proper order for 3 pounds, 10 shillings yearly to be paid six monthly. This was approved by the Council on 27 July of that year.

In 1799 it was reported that retail shops were found in every street and corner and food was to be had in great abundance at all times. Melons, cucumbers, sour milk and asparagus were being sold in the streets. The design of shops had become changed, with bow windows now very much the fashion. These facilitated window-shopping that had now become a leisure activity for those with money, and perhaps more so, for those without.

The 19th century

If by the end of the eighteenth century the Council felt to be in control of matters, they were to be sorely abused of this notion by the developments that were to take place in the first decades of the nineteenth century.

The greatest of these was the growth of the population of Dundee. In the first half of the 19th century this was nothing short of dramatic, rising from 30,000 in 1821 to 64,000 in 1841. This was combined with two other factors, rising prosperity, which meant that that there was much more money around, and the development of railways and steam ferries that had enlarged and increased Dundee's grip upon its hinterland in Angus, eastern Perthshire and north-east Fife.

The Burgh Council responded to the rapid increase in population and trade with a range of measures to further improve the town centre. It first acted to alleviate the shortcomings of the existing streets, particularly with the restrictions the narrow parts

Union Hall 1783 with ground floor shops

of the High Street, the Nethergate and the Seagate imposed upon the movement of goods and shoppers around the city centre.

Whilst the narrows of the Nethergate were described in 1802 as a bottleneck in an increasingly busy street, the narrows of the Murraygate were even more congested. This clearly required action and in 1809 the Burgh Council sponsored an Act of Parliament to enable the widening of the Murraygate.

The Act was passed in 1810 but intentions were one thing – actions quite another. The widening only took place in 1871 – over 60 years after the passing of the enabling legislation. This was in spite of problems of congestion so severe that in 1823 the occupants of Murraygate served a petition on the Council to prohibit the leaving of carts in the thoroughfare. By 1840 congestion caused by the fish cadgers and fish barrows was such that it was impossible to enter the shops on either side of the narrows, but still another 30 years were to go by before the Murraygate was widened.

But all this expenditure on the city centre was not to the liking of all Dundonians. Much of the cash spent on city improvements was coming from the harbour taxes imposed by the Burgh Council. The shipping interests in Dundee felt that the Burgh

Council, while spending heavily on improving the commercial centre of the town, had given less than adequate attention to the expansion of the harbour, upon which so much of the town's prosperity depended. In 1815 their lobbying of the Government was successful and the Council's powers over the Harbour were taken from them and given to a new independent Harbour Trust.

The loss of the Harbour revenues was a setback for the Burgh Council and the return from commercial rents of properties in the new streets became an even more essential part of their plans for urban development. Thus, when in 1808 the new Theatre Royal opened in Castle Street it incorporated a row of shops at ground level. Similarly, when in 1824 Union Street was laid out by David Neave the design incorporated commercial premises at ground level. When in 1826 the Thistle Hall (which was built by the Masons but also functioned as a public hall) opened in Union Street as the burgh's principal venue for assemblies it boasted a row of elegant new shops on the ground floor.

Despite losing its harbour revenues the Burgh Council continued its efforts to improve Dundee. The first decision to be taken was to improve the administration of the town. In Scotland at this time

Thistle Hall, Union Street incorporating shops

a common way of progressing the improvement of conditions prevailing in town centre streets was by the establishment of police committees or commissioners. These were given powers, among others things for watching, lighting and street cleansing. Dundee, as a progressive town, instituted its Police and Fire Commission in 1824, a high proportion of its members being shop owners. For its own part the Burgh Council decided in the light of the great increase in the burgh's population, to enlarge the town centre.

When it came to the expansion of the town centre the burgh had only one real option. The centre had already been extended to the east and west, and was bounded on the south by the harbour and the river. Unsurprisingly the council decided that the Meadowlands, lying to the north of the town centre, and up to then used largely for recreation, should be developed as an extension to the centre. Accordingly, in 1824 the Council instructed William Burns to draw up recommendations for three new streets designed to connect the existing town with the Meadowlands. These were to be of buildings four storeys in height and all were to have shops on the ground floor. In the event only one of these streets, Reform Street, was to be built.

The actual creation of Reform Street was a long drawn out affair and it was only in 1834 that the first feus became available in Reform Street. Although there was considerable local scepticism about the building of this new thoroughfare - it was nick-named Weathercock Street by its detractors – it turned out to be a great success and sites soon began to be taken up.

Nevertheless, the markets and fairs were still being held in the High Street where they were sources of major congestion and general rowdiness. Accordingly, in 1824 the Burgh Council decided that

visiting fairs, which by now had declined as major retailing events and had become much more venues for travelling entertainments, were to be relocated to a site north of the Overgate.

Whilst this improved things, the regular street markets with its "Cheap Jacks" selling household utensils, tools, watches and bridles and saddles from their carts remained on the High Street causing congestion and arousing the resentment of established traders. The rowdiness on both sites remained a cause of complaint by both the growing number of permanent shop owners and the burgeoning middle class. How ill equipped the Burgh authorities were to deal with this is illustrated by the fact that in 1853 Dundee had a population of around 55,000 and only six constables to keep order.

The Council was also aware that the drastic increase in the population of the city raised issues that went far beyond the expansion of the town centre and it raised a parliamentary bill that resulted in 1831 in the expansion of the city boundaries.

At the end of the Georgian period the town authorities could look back with some satisfaction at the way in which they had been active agents in turning what had been a mediaeval town into a thriving industrial city. However, they must have reflected upon the fact that their concentration on the development of the town centre, rather than the harbour, had resulted in their power over the harbour being lost.

Shopping in Georgian Dundee

At the start of the Georgian period shops sold their goods through openings in walls where the shutters could be arranged to form a counter on the façade. Shoppers did not, by and large, get to enter the premises but gradually access into the shops became possible. Shops generally opened only during daylight hours and where they were lit, it was by candles. As time went by oil lamps were increasingly used to provide lighting inside shops. In the streets the amount of lighting provided by oil lamps had steadily increased. In 1826 a gas supply was introduced and by 1830 gas lights were to be seen in the Seagate and were progressively being installed further west.

An indication of the appearance of the town to the would-be shopper towards the end of the Georgian period can be found in Dundee Delineated published in 1821.

"The High Street or Cross or Market Place is a spacious rectangle 360 feet long by 100 feet wide. The houses around it are built in free stone, in general pretty regular in front and of a moderate height. The shops with which it is completely surrounded are every day getting more commodious, tasteful and some of them, highly ornamental. From the great square running to the west is the Luckenbooths. The house in the corner fronting the High Street is now possessed by an extensive upholstery ware room".

"Greengrocers and fruit sellers (are) daily occupied in the High Street and the marketplace. Hot pies and bridies were sold by itinerant street sellers, while oysters and fish could be bought on the thoroughfares."

The town was well supplied with fish and butcher meat. The fishermen now sold their fish in the Fish Market on boards or "stocks" that were supplied by the burgh authorities. The Butcher Market situated in Butcher Row had long been the place for the supply of butcher meat to the inhabitants, but it was beginning to fall into disuse, several butchers having given up using the market stalls and removed to shops in other positions in the town to carry on their trade.

"The Butter Market was well frequented by the country dames and lasses … Burly farmers in boots and tops (could) be seen on a good cart horse wending their way into town on a market day, the gude wife comfortably perched on a pad behind her jolly lord – he to dispose of his corn, and she to sell her hens, butter, and eggs."

At this time the majority of the shops in the centre of Dundee were still small and unpretentious. The best shops were located along the north side of the High Street. As examples of the goods for sale could be seen in their small-paned bow windows, window-shopping was now possible. With the lighting provided by oil lamps on the streets and within the shops candles and oil lamps one could even shop after it became dark. If one entered the shops, the items for sale would be seen on the shelves behind the counter. Items of interest would be shown, one at a time, to the potential customer.

The floors of the shops were generally above ground level and access was by two or three steps that projected into the footpath, often resulting in a dangerous obstruction to pedestrians. Part of the stock was kept and shown in a sub-basement or cellar, which resulted in the steps giving access terminating in the middle of the footpath. These arrangements caused much annoyance to one John

MacIntosh, who provided a sedan chair service for the better off. He complained to the Burgh Council that the steps in the pavement resulted in his operatives either falling into the open steps, or stumbling over the sloping wooden structures that covered them at night.

By the end of the period a wide range of shops were located in the streets of Dundee. A good example was the Murraygate where one could find fourteen merchants of various kinds, three booksellers, eleven grocers, four vintners, a slater, a reed maker and a saddler.

Shops were now also located in the eastern end of the Overgate. These included that of W Gilruth, who sold everything from house furnishings to jewellery and cutlery. Boots could be bought at William Chalmers, the holder of a royal warrant

Shoppers would probably have avoided the demolition and road works on the north of the square where works were still in hand for the building of the new Reform Street. This was soon to become the town's most fashionable street and many clothing shops had already opened in the southern part of the street even as building was still in progress beyond Bank Street.

A variety of shops were now to be found in the High Street and the Nethergate. In one of the shops beneath the Trades Hall, Mr Rogers sold clothes for children from his Baby Linen Warehouse. Shoes could be ordered at any one of a number of shoemakers located in the High Street and ladies could get their corsets made in the premises of Jane Divine in Thorter Row. In the Nethergate ironmongery and fireplaces could be purchased from Alexander Lawson and seeds and plants from William Laird.

At the top of Crichton Street one could visit one of the many tobacconists now to be found in the town where not only tobacco, matches and pipes but also candles made on the premises could be bought. From here it was just a short stroll down the narrow Crichton Street to the Greenmarket and the Fishmarket and across to the bottom of Castle Street where the Exchange Coffee House had been erected in 1828.

In the more fashionable Union Street, travellers from Fife could be seen who had just disembarked from one of the steam ferries recently introduced on the route from Craig Pier to Woodhaven. As they looked into the new shops beneath the Thistle Hall they were perhaps reflecting on how much the town had changed in recent years.

4 THE VICTORIAN CITY 1837 to 1901

At a national level this period was characterised by a massive increase in population and wealth, and a rapid expansion of urban areas. The introduction of both long distance and local railways, and steam-powered ships greatly facilitated the movement of goods, people and ideas. In factories the use of steam-powered machines greatly facilitated the mass production of cheaper goods of all kinds. Extremely important for the industrialised production of clothes was the creation in 1850 of the first commercially viable sewing machine.

There were number of other technological advances during this period that had significant implications for retailing. The introduction in 1858 of the Mason Preserving Jar and the canning of food on a commercial basis enabled a wide range of food to be sold throughout the year. The patenting of of the humble coat hanger in 1869 revolutionised the way in which clothes could be stored and presented, while the use of cardboard transformed packaging.

Mason Glass Jars

In 1883 the cash register (originally a device designed to prevent pilfering by shop staff) was introduced and this, along with the development of pneumatic tubes for the movement of cash and receipts within shops and stores, gave improved security and control. The increasing availability of elevators and lifts was particularly important as it facilitated the development of multi-storied shops at a time when stores were growing in size. All of these developments had profound and far-reaching implications for the retailing industry throughout the UK.

Early cash Register

The first NCR cash registers in Britain were being used by 1886 while in 1898 Harrods installed the first escalator in the UK (in this case, a moving belt). So exciting was this thought to be that staff were on hand with smelling salts in case any of the escalator users fainted.

With more people to cater for and an increased range of goods to sell the number of shops greatly increased, as did their size. As shops grew larger and sold an increasingly wide range of goods their owners began to reorganise the way in which the store was set out and goods displayed. This period saw the development of the first bazaars and department stores. In Newcastle Bainbridge's drapery and fashion store opened in 1838 and by 1849 had developed into the world's first department store with 23 separate departments. Most of the early department stores grew out of small businesses but in 1867 the UK's first purpose-built department store, Compton House, was erected in Liverpool.

Bainbridges, Newcastle

The form of these large stores was influenced by social factors as well. In the 19th century a marked increase in wealth led to a remarkable growth in the middle and upper classes. At this time whilst it was considered socially unacceptable for middle class women to work, they were encouraged to have an extensive social life. The number of outfits required during a life of this type of socialising made the needs of this group a major factor in the expansion of shopping in Victorian Britain.

The department stores soon realised that if they were to hold their female customers long enough to extract significant sales from them, then more was needed. So it was that in 1858 the London Crystal Palace Bazaar, in Oxford Street, lit by natural light by day and gas by night, was one of the first stores to have ladies' lavatories and a separate refreshment room for females.

In a very crowded retail market, shop owners keen to give themselves a competitive edge quickly seized upon any new ideas. By the early 1880s Glasgow had become one of the four biggest shopping centres in Britain, and in 1882 its Coliseum department store was one of the first to install electric lighting.

On the east coast of Scotland, the Jenners store in Edinburgh, after suffering a devastating fire in 1892, opened a new ultra-modern building in 1896. This was equipped with lavish electrical lighting, hydraulic lifts and air conditioning. Four hours after the grand opening, 25,000 people had already visited the store.

Alongside these large stores weekly markets still took place on the streets of most towns of any size. As people became wealthier and the middle class became more sophisticated, shopping among the unregulated hustle and bustle of street markets became less attractive. The more so as open air markets were not only subject to the vagaries of the weather but also became to be regarded as unhygenic.

Local authorities started to look around for ways in which regular markets that brought people into the towns looking for low price goods could be maintained without their obvious disadvantages. In 1822 the local authority in Liverpool were the first to throw their hat in the ring by building covered market shopping in the form of St John's Market. This had gas lighting and a plentiful supply of clean water for the traders. Leeds was the next to follow, although this was a private venture providing within the covered Shambles Market spaces for some sixty shops, fifty of which were butchers. As more and more covered markets were built throughout Britain the range and diversity of shops accommodated within them began to increase, to the point where they were described as "the poor man's department store".

Covered markets proved to be very popular not only with the poor but also with the middle classes and by 1866 there were almost 800 covered markets operating south of the border of which over 300 were owned and operated by the local authority.

By the end of Victoria's reign shops at every level had developed a style and approach to retailing that would persist for the better part of the twentieth century.

Jenners , Edinburgh

Dundee

During the Victorian period Dundee moved from being what was still, in many respects, a mediaeval town to being the major retailing centre that we see today. Crucial to this change were the rapid increase in the size of its population, developments in communications, the local authority's efforts to improve the city and to deal with congestion, and changes in the shops themselves.

Population and social factors

As Queen Victoria took the throne in 1837, Dundee's population had already risen to over 40,000, but by 1851 it had nearly doubled again, reaching some 79,000. By the time Victoria died in 1901 Dundee's population had risen to around 140,000. Naturally enough this resulted in a greatly increased demand for food, clothes, and footwear and for the shops in which such goods might be bought. However, it was not only increased demand for the basic staples of life that was important. As the textile, engineering and shipbuilding industries expanded a burgeoning middle class created a growing demand for luxury goods.

Buist's House Furnishers, who had opened their shop at 100 Commercial Street in 1833, was catering for this very market. In the Nethergate could be found a store that sold a wide range of bells with which servants could be summoned by the master or mistress of middle class households.

The rise in the number of shops and those owning and working in them was accompanied by the growing influence of retailers and traders in the governance of the city. This was reflected in the makeup of the Dundee Police Commission whose powers included the watching (policing), lighting and cleansing of streets – all of which directly affected the shopping environment. When the Commission was set up in 1840 shop owners constituted almost 30% of its membership. By the time that its powers were transferred to the Burgh Council in 1851 the proportion had grown to almost 40% and together with traders and craftsmen retailers constituted two thirds of the Commission members. The Burgh Council that took over the Police Commission's powers also reflected the retailers' interests, and in the period from 1875 to 1910 over 40% of City Councillors were the owners of shops or small businesses.

This was not altogether surprising for as early as 1850 Dundee could boast some 435 grocers, 344 wine and beer spirit sellers, 76 shoemakers, and 91 tailors as well as a wide variety of shops dealing in speciality goods such as wigs, photographic equipment, gloves and hats.

Communications and congestion

The number, range and size of shops in Dundee was directly affected by the accessibility of its centre to Angus, Perthshire and Fife. This emphasised the need for good communications.

In the latter part of the period the bringing of public roads under County Road Boards, and later the newly formed County Councils, resulted in systematic improvements to the regional road network. Improvements in the paving of roads in both town and country and the introduction of trams into Dundee – at first drawn by horses, later powered by steam and then electricity, improved the ease and speed of travel. This encouraged more folk from the areas surrounding Dundee to use its commercial centre.

The introduction of steam locomotives on the Dundee & Newtyle railway in 1833 resulted in a significant increase in the number of passengers travelling into Dundee from the Vale of Strathmore. Accessibility was further improved by the opening of the Dundee - Arbroath railway in 1838 and the Dundee - Perth Railway in 1847. These developments brought many more shoppers into the city as did the increased frequency of ferries between Newport on Tay and Dundee.

As a result in 1860 the Peoples Journal of 28 September felt able to describe Dundee as "full of shops". One of these was Ramsay the Jewellers who opened up at 22 Reform Street in that very year, although it would be another seven years before the last feu in Reform Street was taken up.

However welcome the shop owner found the increased numbers of people in Dundee, these had to be accommodated by a street pattern largely unchanged since mediaeval times. Whilst congestion of the city centre had been a cause for concern from the Middle Ages onwards none of the problems encountered in previous times could begin to compare with the situation that confronted Dundee in the late 1860s.

The number of pedestrians on the streets of the burgh had greatly increased as the introduction of trams had helped to facilitate the flow of shoppers into and through the city centre. In addition a rapid growth in the amount of goods arriving and departing from the burgh by sea and rail was leading to significant increases in vehicular traffic. One particular example of the impact that the harbour was having on the city centre was the delivery by coastal shipping of around one thousand tons of coal a day to serve the farms, factories and houses of Dundee and Angus.

In addition the centre was traversed by vast numbers of horse drawn carts carrying raw jute from the

Victorian Harbour

harbour to the works and mills located in Blackness and around Dens Road and the Hilltown, and then taking finished goods back to the ships waiting at the harbour wharves.

The harbour traffic passing through the centre of the town was also augmented by the traffic generated by the shops and commercial premises located there. Further congestion was caused by the weekly markets that took place on the High Street.

In 1840 the Dundee Advertiser commented on the congestion in the narrows of the Murraygate which at that time were then only eighteen feet in width, as follows:- "A great number of fellows with barrows and carts hawking whitefish in the street congregate in front of the shop doors and windows..... gathering into mobs and great numbers of people, not to buy fish, but to hear the sellers bawling out their coarse and vulgar slang in the most awful manner, and that at the top of their voices". The situation was little better in the narrows of the Seagate.

A side issue arising from the number of horse drawn vehicles was the large amounts of manure left upon the city streets creating another cleansing problem. However the city fathers could console themselves with the thought that the manure did have a commercial value – so much so that among the city centre shops could be found two manure merchants.

Narrows of Murraygate

There were other problems associated with the high volume of horse drawn transport. Among these was the enormous noise generated by iron-hooped wheels on the granite setts that now formed the carriageways of the new streets. In the 1840s wooden blocks were introduced as a road surface in order to reduce the noise and to allow horses to travel over greater distances. This was not a success and in the 1850s granite setts were reintroduced. The noise problem was only resolved with the use of asphalt as a road finish in the 1870s.

City improvements

Dundee entrepreneurs were well aware that to take advantage of the city's burgeoning economy there would not only have to be drastic changes in the nature of shopping provision but also in the improvement of its streets.

This left the Town Council, whose members were mostly small tradesmen and property owners in the burgh, in a situation where their natural instinct to keep local taxes at the lowest possible level, was at odds with the obvious need to improve the city to cater for the increased level of population and economic activity.

In 1869 James Cox, who owned the Camperdown Works in Lochee, was elected to the City Council and later, in 1871, became Provost. With Cox at the helm things began to move rapidly. In December 1869, spurred on by Cox, and in spite of their reservations, the Council brought forward a Dundee Police & Improvement Bill giving them powers to carry out improvements to the town centre.

Even before the bill was approved by Parliament the Council took action to ease the congestion of the streets of the town centre and to improve the infrastructure.

The Council's first move was to try to increase the available road space and thereby ease congestion. To this end it was decided to remove the Union Hall at the West end of the High Street. The building was demolished in 1870 and in the following year the long awaited widening of the 'narrows' at the west end of Murraygate was finally put in hand. However, whilst these measures were useful, they still did not deal with lack of a road link from the harbour to the burgeoning industrial areas situated around the Dens Burn and the north of the Hilltown.

Although in 1844 the Council had brought forward the Dundee Water Bill and in the same year the Dundee New Gas Light Company had been set up, progress on installing both services had been

James Cox

unsatisfactory. In 1869 the Dundee Gas and Water companies were taken over by the local authority. Beneath the streets a comprehensive network of sewers was installed and after initiating a series of Water Acts between 1871 and 1874 the Council put in place a proper system to provide piped water supplies to the town centre.

The crucial year for the development of Dundee as a shopping centre was 1871. This was the year when the Dundee Police and Improvement Act came into force. A new post of Burgh Engineer was created and William Mackison was appointed to the job. A Dundee Improvement Trust was set up with Cox as its chairman and with Thomas Thornton – a colleague of Cox – as its legal agent. The Trust's objectives were the improvement of the efficiency, cleanliness, and appearance of the town. As Charles McKean later remarked "Between them, Cox and Thornton transformed Dundee".

At the heart of the 1871 Act were proposals for the creation of a major north south road link between Dock Street and Meadowside. This was to be created by the widening of the existing cul-de-sac that was Commercial Street and its extension north-wards to Albert Square connecting with Seagate, Murraygate and the High Street on the way. The new Commercial Street was to become a major shopping street and was to be fronted by buildings designed in the grand style. These were intended to provide commercial offices, possibly connected to Dundee's overseas trade, on one or two floors, with flats above and shops beneath, each with a basement below.

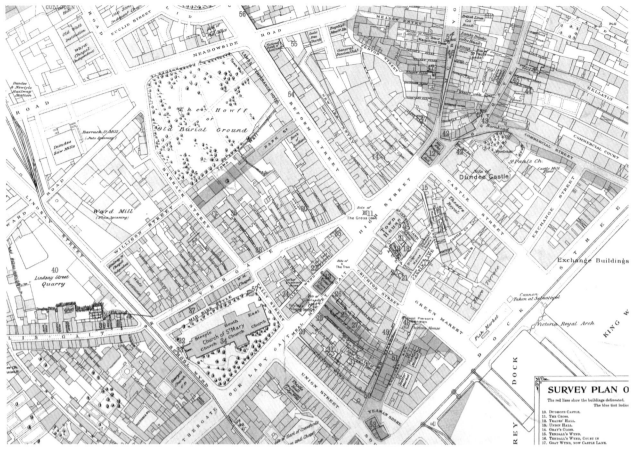

Plan of 1874 Improvements Act Proposals

The Act also contained important provisions for the widening and the improvement of the gradients of the Murraygate, the Seagate, and the Nethergate, the improvement of the High Street, Gellatly Street, Guthrie Street and Victoria Street. In December 1872 the Council decided to remove the Corn Market from the High Street where it had been for the last four centuries.

To ensure that the programme of improvements was properly carried through they were to be overseen by the City Engineer, William Mackison, assisted by a young man, James Thomson, who was later to be extremely influential in steering the way in which the city was to develop.

Mackison consulted with the famous architects John Lessels of Edinburgh on the elevations for the upper half of Commercial Street, the design of which paid homage to Baron Haussman's buildings in Paris. A consistent theme was the use of domes as corner features. The actual buildings were designed by various architects, including Ireland and Maclaren and Robert Keith, all of whom had to conform to the overall scheme of design set down by Mackison. It was also proposed that opposite the City Churches a new and major shopping and commercial area would be created. This was to be done by cutting through the south side of the High Street to form

what is now Whitehall Street and Whitehall Crescent. In the process this swept away the Fish and Butter markets and Butcher Row. All the new works were to be carried out in a style appropriate to the growing city that was Dundee.

In 1883 the Council began to acquire and demolish buildings to enable the formation of Whitehall Street and Whitehall Crescent. Only two years later the land for the road had been purchased and the carriageway laid out.

In March 1885 William Kidd, the printer, commissioned Robert Keith to design the first building in the new Whitehall Street in a style set out by the city's architect. The next to move in were Moon & Langlands (later to become Draffens) who in 1887 had been displaced by a fire from their premises in Albion House on the Nethergate. As the development of Whitehall Crescent went ahead early takers of premises were Lawsons, who established their clothing shop at 10/20 Whitehall Crescent, and Cantrell's Fish Shop.

The growing importance of Dundee as a commercial and industrial centre was recognised in 1892 when the Burgh of Dundee became a County of a City. In the period leading up to the turn of the century the new city continued to prosper.

Changes in the shops

The Victorian era was a period of innovation and technical change in industry and commerce, and the retailing sector was no exception. Indeed, the introduction of railways, the telegraph in 1854, and the existence by the mid 1840s of a major newspaper in the city meant that Dundee became keyed into developments occurring throughout the United Kingdom and Europe.

Given Dundee's aspirations as a growing centre of commerce it was not surprising that the local authority was aware of the successful introduction of covered markets throughout Britain. The Council was also not happy with the congestion caused by the weekly street markets and the image that this gave to the city.

In October 1857 the Dundee Advertiser reported that a "proposal for a series of public markets for Dundee has been very favourably received by the community. The conviction gains ground daily that something should be done to provide all classes with additional facilities for the purchase of articles family consumption, and it is certain that if proper accommodation were provided the amount of business transacted in these articles would increase largely from year to year". However the public pressure was in vain as the proposals were not taken forward.

It was not until the late 1870s that, again urged on by the Dundee Advertiser, which declared that "Almost every town of any pretensions has its market and arcade", that the Dundee authorities finally decided to act. It may have been that the opening of the Waverley Market in Edinburgh in 1876 was the final straw.

In 1877 the Police Committee commissioned a Mr Robertson to produce proposals for an Arcade and Market in the centre of Dundee on a site bounded by Crichton Street, Nethergate, Coutties Wynd and Dock Street. The result was a very impressive scheme incorporating a large covered market, an arcade, shops and offices. At the meeting of the Police Commission of 16 May 1877 a somewhat confused discussion took place on the proposal. It was decided that the Council had no intentions of carrying out the proposal itself but would make the drawings available to private investors in the hope of its construction without the use of public funds.

In the event this scheme was not proceeded with and on 8 June 1877 the Council instead decided to rely upon an alternative proposal put forward by a David Stewart to create a privately funded indoor market, arcade, shops, offices and dwelling houses on a site formerly the grounds of King Street House and bounded by Victoria Road, Idvies Street and King Street.

This was to accommodate a butter market, fish market and stalls for fruit and vegetable traders. The new building was composed of an arcade entered from King Street with 10 shops, and a main arcade 100 feet long with 31 shops on the ground floor and another 36 shops in a first floor gallery. A line of stalls ran up the centre of the ground floor arcade and around the first floor gallery.

There were also many changes in both the external and internal design of shops. After the excise duty on glass was abolished in 1845 shopkeepers were among the first to take advantage of cheaper sheet glass to create large windows with the view unbroken by glazing bars. It was thus a sign of the

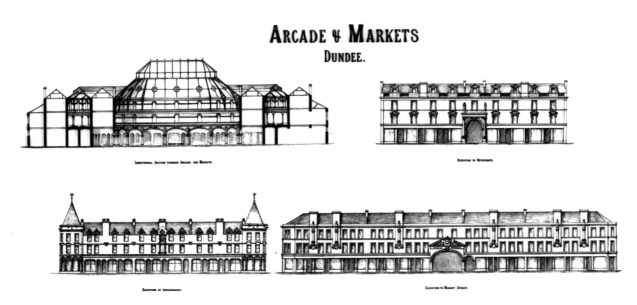

ARCADE & MARKETS
DUNDEE.

1881 Proposals for an Arcade and Market between Whitehall Street and Crichton Street

times that when, in 1850, it was decided that shops lying beneath the Trades Hall were "insignificant" for the increasing levels of trade being experienced, it was resolved that they should be altered and modernised.

As part of the modernisation the old fashioned windows were removed and sheets of plate glass installed. The new large windows greatly facilitated window-shopping, and many stores began to install canvas blinds or canopies on their frontages to encourage this outside their own premises.

At the start of the period shops relied on candles and oil lamps for lighting, and on coal fires for such heating as was provided. This tended to restrict the size of shops and in some cases their hours of operation. The introduction of gas supplies in 1826 by the Dundee Gas Company offered a way to overcome both these problems. However, the installation of gas mains was rather slow and it was only in the 1860s that the gas lighting began to be used inside shops. In the later part of the period gas lighting became the norm for the lighting of shops and this led to an extension of opening hours during the winter.

This only became really effective due to improvements in the lighting of streets. In 1850 a consignment of oil street lamps had been purchased from London and the number of lights was systematically increased. After the establishment of the Dundee Gas Company in 1826 gas lighting was introduced, slowly but progressively, from the east end of the town. By 1848 this had extended to the High Street making shopping safer on winter evenings.

The last decade of the 19th century was marked by the introduction of electricity in the city. In 1890 the City Council had taken over the responsibility for providing electrical power supplies to the city. In 1891 a public electricity supply was inaugurated in Dundee and in 1893 the city's first electrical power station came into operation.

The new and clean source of power was rapidly taken up by Dundee store owners. A sign of this was the effects of the first electric power failure in Dundee which was experienced on 21 January 1896. The Courier reported that:-

"Since the introduction of electricity many shopkeepers have had gas lighting removed. A tour of the shops showed how serious was the interruption of business. William Hunter, who fortunately were stocktaking, had candles to hand. But G. L. Wilsons had to close as did Smith Brothers".

However such were the advantages of electricity that the frequent incidence of power cuts in the growing electrical network did nothing to slow its rapid adoption. In May 1897 the drapers, J. P. Smith, were the first store in Dundee to remove all gas appliances and to install electrical lighting throughout the shop.

In an age when the quality of personal service was seen as crucial in offering a competitive edge staffing was an important issue for shop owners. But hours of work were long and the work could

Blinds and canopies on the High Street and Union Street

be tiring. Shop staff worked longer hours than mill workers, and in licensed grocers sometimes up to 90 hours per week. Male assistants in large shops were not allowed to sit and were told that they must be constantly active.

In 1876 the Council decided that shop opening hours were to be limited by closing at 7.30pm on weekdays and 9 o'clock on Saturdays. This measure was fiercely opposed by the Dundee shop owners but their efforts were in vain.

Nevertheless shop working hours were still very long. A sign of the changed times was that in April 1890 a large meeting of store owners themselves opted for half day closing on Wednesday afternoon. That was not the end to disputes as the shop workers were well aware that skilled workers were in demand. In 1894 there was a dispute between the Tailors Union and their employers that led to the setting up of the Dundee City Drapers Association.

Shopping in Victorian Dundee

When one went shopping in Dundee at the end of the 19th century the first impression would have been of the sheer busyness of the city centre. Throngs of people filled the streets, some brought into town by the trams, now powered by electricity. From further afield others arrived on the railways that connected Dundee not only to the nation, but also to the suburban stations in its hinterland in Angus, Perthshire and Fife. Shoppers also came into Dundee on the ferries from Newport and Woodhaven

Shops were now to be found in profusion with grocers and wine merchants on almost every street. Although Dundee remained a compact city largely confined to the area between the Law and the shore of the Tay, retail premises could now be found not only in the city centre but also extending outwards along the Wellgate and the Hilltown to the north, along Victoria Road and Princes Street to the east, and through the Overgate to Hawkhill and the Nethergate to the west. But not only were there greater numbers of shops, the shops themselves were growing in size and in contrast to the Georgian period, street lighting was now the norm.

The early 1880s saw the establishment of a number of retailers who were to be present in Dundee right through to the 1960s. Examples included Adams & Cushnie (later to become Cooper and Mackenzie) who in 1874 established themselves in Reform Street, and Smith Brothers who set up in 1884 in the Murraygate as Furriers & Furnishers.

By the end of the nineteenth century many other shops that were to become long established in the city had arrived in the central streets of the town. Greenhills the chemist was to be found in the Overgate alongside two branches of Franchis - the confectioners - who had another establishment on the Esplanade, while Gows the gunmakers could be found at 12 Union Street. Wallace's Land O' Cakes was established in Crichton Street in 1898.

However the biggest number of retailers who were to survive in the long term were to be found on the High Street. Here, by the turn of the century, one could saunter past Braithwaites, the tea and coffee merchants, and the goldsmith and jewellers Ramsay's and Robertsons and Watt. William Chalmers' shoe shop, Keith Scott's hatters and Laird & Sinclair's, the seedsmen were also operating from the High Street at this time.

Elsewhere, the locally based Frain's China Shop, Winters the Printers, and Buist's cabinet making department could all be found in Castle Street. In Murraygate another long term survivor in the shape of Stead & Simpson's shoe shop could be found, although this was a branch of the Leicester based shoemakers. Unfortunately Its near neighbour – the Ting Tong Tea Shop – was not to last.

The relatively new Commercial Street had turned out to be just that, with its ground floor premises largely occupied by commercial offices. However, there were a number of shops grouped around the junction of Commercial Street and the Murraygate, including the Dundee Supply Company at 80 Commercial Street, and Buist's the Furniture and upholstery business that was located at No.102. In upper Commercial Street the Dundee Fur Company could now be found at No 63, next door to Croll's the seedsmen.

Nearly all of the shops in the centre had originated locally, particularly the large department stores, such as Draffen and Jarvie in Whitehall Street, D. M. Brown in the High Street and G. L. Wilson and Smith Brothers on the corner of Murraygate and Commercial Street, all of whom were now well established. However, chain stores could now be seen in Dundee. Examples of these were the London and Newcastle Tea Company in the Overgate, the Home and Colonial Company in the Overgate, and Hepworths the tailors in the Murraygate.

Specialised shops were now to be found scattered throughout the centre and included, for example, James Ross who sold "Every modern appliance for Fire Extinguishing purposes". For followers of hair fashion Farrell's wig shop in Castle Street and Allens in Reform Street selling "Ornamental Hair" were there to satisfy their needs. Those interested in music could visit Methven Simpson whose Nethergate shop sold pianos and pianolas along with instruments and musical scores.

At a more mundane level the almost universal use of coal for domestic heating meant that there were many coal merchants in the city centre, such as Smith & Hood in Union Street and Ireland Bruce in the Nethergate.

The Greenmarket continued to flourish at the foot of Crichton Street but now was overlooked by the partly constructed Mathers Hotel. However, as greengrocers shops developed the Greenmarket began to change its character, moving towards the concept of a flea market. In 1873 it was described by W. J. Smith as being "greatly frequented on Saturday evenings, the attractions being of an extremely varied and diverse nature. With galvanic batteries, beef and sweets all being sold in close juxtaposition".

In the period up until 1900 the Lady Mary Fair, which was still held annually in the High Street, gradually declined as a place to buy goods and became more of a place to find entertainment that featured waxworks, menageries, peepshows and boxing booths.

There were also new kinds of shops appearing in Dundee. By 1901 the Dundee Eastern Co-operative Society which had been founded in 1873 had become a flourishing business with seventeen branches located throughout the city. Photography shops had begun to appear, including Valentines in the High Street and Peter Feathers' shop in Castle Street. In the Nethergate could be found Rossleigh Motor Sales and the Dundee Motor & Cycle Company.

Whilst motor vehicles had begun to appear, horses still provided most of the motive power available and thronged the streets of the city centre. The Eagle Inn at 108 Murraygate had a Posting, Hiring and Livery stable and also hired out closed and open carriages, wagonettes, dog carts and gigs. The Dundee Tramway and Carriage Co were hiring carriage brakes, private buses for evening parties and concerts, and undertook contracts for the horsing of vans and lorries.

Dundee's prosperous and expanding city centre now had a strong grip on its catchment area and could look forward to the new century with a feeling of optimism.

Greenmarket in the Victorian times

5 THE EARLY 20th CENTURY

The first half of the twentieth century was a turbulent period encompassing two world wars and a major international depression. It was a period of great change when department stores firmly established their position at the top of the retail tree. It was also the time that chains of stores, or multiples, began to appear.

In Chesterfield in 1903, Montague Burton, a Lithuanian refugee opened his first tailoring store which was to be the start of a chain of shops that was to become the largest men's clothing retailer in the world.

In 1909 the Americans began to arrive in Britain. In Liverpool, F W Woolworth opened the first UK Woolworths store, with the slogan "Nothing over 6d". At the opposite end of the market the American, Harry Gordon Selfridge, opened his department store on Oxford Street. The company's innovative marketing promoted the idea of shopping for pleasure rather than necessity.

Selfridges, London

The onset of the First World War affected different parts of the UK retail industry in different ways. Attempts by the public to stockpile food and the shortages of some goods such as sugar and meat caused particular difficulties for food and provision shops. Inflation was rampant and some grocery stores did quite well during the war. This situation did not improve with the introduction of rationing of certain goods in 1917 which was not to end until 1920.

In all sectors the loss of male staff, some of whom volunteered for service at the outbreak of war and many more who were later conscripted into the forces, did cause problems, particularly for larger stores. A side effect of this was to significantly increase not only the number of women working as shop assistants but also in more senior posts. There was also a decrease in the sale of luxury goods, which were in any case in short supply, and this caused particular problems for the large department stores.

At a minor level middle class children might have noticed the lack of the popular mechanical tin toys that had previously been imported from Germany, but this was offset by the huge increase in the number of UK produced lead soldiers for sale. Across the Atlantic business went on as usual and in 1916, Clarence Saunders opened his first Piggly Wiggly grocery store. Although this sold only dry goods, the fact that it was the first self-service store was a sign of things to come.

The inter war period was, up until the stock market crash of 1929, a prosperous time for many parts of the United Kingdom. One side effect of the war was the opening of numbers of small shops specialising in the sale of fashion goods, hosiery, and lingerie. Many of the owners were women who had been widowed during the war or who had been displaced from their jobs by men returning from war service. In 1919 Jack Cohen started selling groceries at markets in the East End and in 1924, established the first of his chain of Tesco shops. (The name Tesco originated as a combination of T E Stephenson and Cohen - the former being the tea buyer for the company). Although London continued to prosper as a shopping centre after 1929 the effects of the economic downturn that followed the stock market crash were felt quite strongly in Britain's provincial cities.

It is a truism that bad times for the economy often lead to the merger of many retail companies. So it was in the post 1929 retail industry. Some of these mergers created large retail businesses owning many shops that became known as chain stores. Perhaps the biggest of these in Britain was the merger in 1929 of the Lipton Tea Company with Home and Colonial to form a multiple grocery group with more than 3,000 stores. The business traded as Home & Colonial until 1961, when it became Allied Stores, owned by Unilever.

In the 1930s the introduction of the Art Deco style, with its large windows and chromium mouldings

Home & Colonial Store, London

seemed made for giving shops a smart and modern appearance. Like the new cheap neon lighting, Art Deco was readily adopted as a house style by many of the chain store companies such as Marks and Spencer and Woolworth who were opening stores throughout the UK.

A recovery in retailing slowly began to take place in the 1930s but this was stopped in its tracks by the onset of World War Two. The impact of the war was felt almost immediately with the introduction in April 1939 of conscription and, only six months later, the rationing of first petrol and then food.

For provision shops, just as in the First World War, there were problems caused by people attempting to stockpile food. However all kinds of goods were much scarcer throughout the war. This caused big problems for the department stores particularly when the Government introduced the rationing of furnishing fabrics, carpets and clothes upon which so much of their sales depended.

Clothes rationing presented particular problems as this was done on a points system but when it was first introduced, no clothing coupons had been issued, and at first the unused margarine coupons in ration books were valid for buying clothing. Initially the allowance was for approximately one complete new outfit per year, but as the war progressed the points were reduced until buying a coat used almost a year's clothing coupons. A measure of the extent of restrictions was that even the number of buttons was restricted and that lace and frills were not allowed on ladies knickers!

Not surprisingly the war years saw a significant growth in the sales of paper patterns for making clothes, second hand clothes shops, and shops specialising in the repair and mending of clothes and other consumer goods.

Staff shortages caused by male conscription were a big problem for all kinds of shops. As in the First World War shop owners responded by employing more women. However, as conscription was soon extended to single women and many women also went to work in industry where wages were higher, staffing shortages, particularly of experienced staff, remained a problem for shop owners throughout the war years.

During the war investment in retailing virtually ceased, although a notable innovation was made in 1942 by the London Co-operative Society (LCS), who, because of labour shortages, introduced the first self service store in Britain. This was quite small having only 176 square feet of floorspace and being furnished with used war damaged shop equipment.

London Co-operative Society self service store 1942

The declaration of peace in 1945 resulted in the end of hostilities but not the re-strictions and rationing that had been introduced during the war. The fact was that the United Kingdom was bankrupt and the economy of Europe was in ruins. The country's infrastructure had been badly damaged and having had no significant investment, for over six years, required massive expenditure.

Nevertheless, the public were determined that after two world wars and a depression, things just had to be better in the future. It was because of this urge to look forward rather than back that the words 'modern' and 'contemporary' appeared in so many adverts of the time.

Modernisation was required everywhere, and the Government, in spite of the desperate economic straights in which it found itself, was determined not only to create a Welfare State but also to bring the major infrastructure services of rail, electricity, and coal mining into state ownership.

In these circumstances, it was not altogether a surprise that throughout the late 1940s the production of consumer goods was focussed on export markets, and that the upgrading of shops was just not on the list of the country's priorities. Indeed the retail industry was still subject to the rationing of both food and clothing and the only new furniture available was the ranges of "Utility" furniture which had been introduced during the war because of shortages of timber. Things became a little better with the ending of some clothes rationing in February 1949, but as the shortage of goods still persisted, this had less effect than might have been expected.

As the period came to a close, two innovations in retailing occurred that would result in major changes in the way people shopped. Firstly in 1948 the London Co-operative Society opened in Upton Park the first purpose built self-service store in the UK. Then, in 1950, the first fully self-service supermarket was opened in Streatham Hill by Express Dairies. This was 2,250 square feet in area and unlike the Co-op store had checkout lanes.

Streatham Hill self service supermarket

Dundee

The history of retailing in Dundee in the first half of the 20th century was broadly similar to that of the northern part of the UK and things started off well.

At the start of the century the population of the city had risen to 161,000 and the Dundee Guide for 1900 loudly trumpeted that 'the jute trade is thriving, shipbuilding yards are infused with new life and the city continues to extend on all sides'. However, promising this appeared it was not, unfortunately, to last.

In the next few years the growth of the jute industry in Asia put pressure on textile sales both abroad, and in the UK, and drove down wage levels in the city. Exports were also affected by the 1907 stock market crash in the USA. The low wages resulting from this were to some extent offset by the fact that Dundee had become a pioneer of the dual income household, where both wives and husbands worked. Nevertheless, for many Dundonians the money available for spending in shops sharply diminished.

However, for those who were well off, the years between 1901 and 1914 were a time of prosperity. The electrification of the trams, which in 1902 were carrying 9 million passengers per year, made it easier for Dundonians to get to the city centre and to carry their purchases home.

The city had by now firmly established itself as the regional shopping centre and in 1907 there was an expansion of the city boundaries to take in the growing suburb of Downfield. In 1913 the city boundary was again extended – this time to take in Broughty Ferry. This meant that another 11,000 were added to the city population which was to steadily increase throughout the first half of the 20th century.

In these circumstances, it was a good time for the major department stores in Dundee. Smith Brothers, G. L. Wilson and D. M. Browns all expanded their operations, and Draffens strengthened their position as the top retailer in the City. The number of tailors greatly expanded and Reform Street had become a centre for these, with some 12 or more outfitters present in the street.

Small shops were also doing well. Braithwaites the tea merchants, Laird & Sinclair's seedsmen's business, William Chalmer's bootmakers shop, and Robertson and Watt the jewellers were all thriving in the High Street. Phin's ironmongers business was established at 29 Nethergate in 1902 and the Toyshop, which was to become a Dundee landmark for many children in years to come, set up business in 1906 in the newly completed Whitehall Crescent. Dundee Eastern Coop was in good shape possessing some 17 stores and looking to open more.

A sign that Dundee was seen outwith Scotland as a good place for national retailers to locate was the arrival in 1909 of Samuels the Jewellers, a chain head-quartered in Birmingham, on a prominent site at the corner of Reform Street and the High Street.

Council enterprise

It was clear from the very start of the new century that the City Council was determined to do what it could to improve Dundee city centre as a commercial and retailing hub for the region.

It started by creating a new Fish Market and Dock at Carolina Port in 1902. In 1904 it followed this by deciding to convert the old Fish Market located at Craig Pier Tram terminus into a Fruit and Flower Market. This was open every Tuesday, Friday and Saturday and by 1912 was described as "largely utilised as a popular sales bazaar".

Although the Council had taken effective action to provide for the specialised markets the question of the future of the First, or Lady Mary Fair remained. This was still being held in the High Street and since the turn of the century had begun to attract increasing numbers of itinerant traders. Local shipowners saw these traders as competitors who did not pay local taxes and yet caused considerable congestion. Their resentment increased with the growth of the fair and in 1906 they were driven, to take direct action. They decided that they would outbid the travellers for the spaces allocated for the fair, but then not use them. The itinerant traders just ignored this and used the vacant sites to sell their goods in the High Street. This led to a minor riot, aggravated by crowds of Dundonians who turned out to support the travelling traders. Eventually the police had to be called in to restore order.

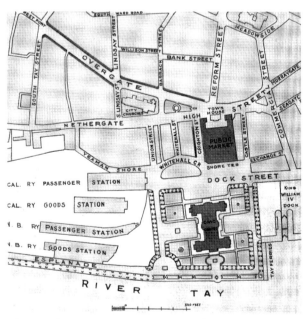

Thomson's 1910 City Improvement Scheme

As a result of this disorder the City Council decided to remove the Lady Mary Fair from the High Street and to relocate it to the Greenmarket in Dock Street. The Fair was held at this location from 1907 until in 1930 it was removed to accommodate a new central bus stance. The Fair was relocated to a site at Craig Street where it operated until 10 April 1934 when the Lady Mary Fair was finally abolished.

In 1904 the City Council made what turned out to be a crucial decision. Upon the death of William Mackison, the City Engineer who had overseen the 1871 city improvements, the Council appointed as his successor James Thomson. Thomson was an active and ambitious professional and in 1910 brought forward his first City Improvement Scheme. This involved, among other things, a plan for the widening and improvement of the Overgate, proposals for the widening of Crichton Street and the Greenmarket and, interestingly, the creation of an indoor market.

Crichton Street with proposed planned shops and market on left

Although at a national level the popularity of covered markets had begun to fade towards the close of the 19th century, Dundee's enthusiasm had not. Thus James Thomson's plan for a new civic centre incorporated a proposal for a large covered market. This was to be sited on the area lying between the old Town House and Dock Street (the site currently occupied by the City Square and Caird Hall) and to be surrounded on the Crichton Street and Castle Street frontages by high class shops. The interior of the proposed Indoor Market would be some 200 feet in length and around 220 feet in width "giving space to accommodate approximately 10,000 persons." It was also envisaged that it could be used for carnivals and the whole block would be surmounted by a roof garden.

Whilst this proposal did not come to pass the idea of a new City Square at the centre of Dundee's shopping centre was taken forward. This was greatly assisted by the offer in 1914, by Sir James Caird, a Dundee textile magnate, to provide £100,000 for the construction of a new City Hall.

Although, with the outbreak of hostilities in 1914, plans for the improvement of the city centre were put on hold, the City Council proceeded, in the face of opposition by the Chancellor of the Exchequer, to acquire property to enable the construction of the new City Hall and the creation of a new City Square behind the old Town House.

For retailers in Dundee the jute boom generated by the war, and which was to go on to 1921, meant that there was much more disposable income to be spent in shops. However, whilst during the war the major retailers went about their business more or less as usual despite coping with a shortage of goods and staff, they did cut back drastically on investment in their stores. The only major exception was Caird's who, in 1915, moved from Union Street to Reform Street where they opened a much larger store.

The Inter War period

In 1919 the city was in the grip of a post war boom. The retail scene was very lively. New kinds of shops were appearing and in 1919 J. D. Brown opened their photographic equipment shop at 28 Castle Street. By the 1920s the drapery stores had become a sizeable part of the retail economy of the city. Training courses for assistant drapers were held at the Harris Academy and regular well-attended events, such as dances and picnics, were organised by the Dundee Drapers Society.

National events such as the opening of the Empire Exhibition at Wembley in 1924 resulted in Empire Week displays in Dundee shops. In 1934, to coincide with Empire Week, fashion parades took place at the Caird Hall on two nights at which four model dresses supplied by G. L. Wilson, Henderson & McKay, Draffen & Jarvies, and D. M. Browns were given away.

During the 1920s the construction of the Caird Hall complex began to take place behind the south side of the High Street. This brought about many changes, including the cessation of the centuries old Lady Mary Fair which after its removal from the High Street, had been relocated to the Greenmarket.

It was probably these signs that Dundee was determined to upgrade its city centre that led in 1926 to the takeover of D. M. Brown's department store by the Scottish Drapery Corporation, and to Boots, a Manchester based multiple, deciding in 1929 to invest in a new store on the corner of the Overgate and Reform Street.

Unfortunately, 1929 was not exactly the best time to open new shops as the Stock Exchange

Empire Week Parade

collapse in America had drastic repercussions all around the world and this was particularly so in Dundee, dependent as its economy was on jute and shipbuilding. Unemployment in Dundee reached levels of 35% which were unparalleled in any other part of the UK. Even the eternally optimistic preamble to the Dundee Guide in 1931 recorded "The general position leaves much to be desired".

In these circumstances the determination of the City Council to press ahead with its restructuring of the city centre by creating one of the most advanced urban complexes of its time is quite amazing. When completed in 1932 it incorporated the new City Square, the Caird halls, new municipal offices, an underground garage, new shops in the square and on the east side of the widened Crichton Street, and beneath the Caird Hall, a covered shopping arcade.

Boots Store Reform Street/High Street   D C Thomson

The first firm to take up premises in the new City Square was a branch of Montague Burton. They were soon joined by local drapers in the shape of Sparks and Barnets, Laird and Sinclair the nurserymen and on the first floor level by the Café Val D'Or.

The City Arcade which was opened in 1929, was located located beneath the newly built Caird Hall. and was entered from Shore Terrace. It was popular

City Square   *D C Thomson*

from its inception but its success was assured in 1933 when the Council decided to locate its central bus station on Shore Terrace. The Arcade had many long term tenants who included Packel's fancy goods, Mrs Agnes Hynd's Amusement Arcade, Imries fruit and Vegetable store, Douglas Craig's Radiant Health Centre, Sam MacLeish the fishmonger, Mitchells of Letham's poultry shop, John Ray the fruiterers, David Forbes' gift shop, Campbell's Choc Box and later Cathie McCabe's record and fancy goods store.

Other tenants included Frank Russell's second hand book shop, Cantrell's fishmongers, Miller's Lino store, and Redwood's plant and seed store.

Although unemployment in Dundee remained at stubbornly high levels things gradually began to get better. In 1934 the preamble to the Dundee

City Arcade Interior

guide remarked that " a revival of trade has been noticeable and we are able to record a general increase in employment". Retailing played its part as public expenditure on the city centre was reinforced by private expenditure. In 1934 Draffens made a major investment in their new Menswear Store in the Nethergate and D. M. Browns and Smith Brothers also invested heavily in the improvement of their stores in an attempt to keep up with Draffens. The competition between stores was not just limited to their premises and May 31 1932 saw a football match take place between the staffs of Draffens

and Justices - won by Draffens on this occasion. In November 1937 the Dundee drapery stores held a charity concert attended by employees of all the major stores in the city.

As the international political situation worsened in the late 1930s the City Council was still looking forward to the future with the preparation of another plan for the redevelopment of the Overgate, developing the Kingsway industrial estate and debating the line for a road bridge across the Tay. But by this time it was clear that war was likely to break out in the near future.

World War Two

The start of the Second World War had almost immediate effects upon the shopping scene in Dundee with the introduction in 1939 of conscription and rationing of fuel and food. Although it was the rationing of clothes in 1941 that had the greatest effect upon the larger stores, the rationing of food affected everybody, as it was not sufficient just to have a ration book - for some goods one also needed to be registered with particular shops.

Wartime conditions even affected the way in which shops were operated. At the out-break of war shops were still open until 7pm in the evening but this simply could not be maintained in wartime conditions and closing by 6.00 pm soon became the rule. Older staff were kept on to replace younger men who had been called up for military service.

The way in which food was served was also affected. Although throughout the first part of the century the packaging of goods had developed at a steady rate, the onset of the Second World War brought a halt to this trend. This was particularly the case in respect of grocers and greengrocers. Packaging of goods was severely cut back to save paper and grocers had to revert to weighing out potatoes, sugar and dried fruit from large containers in the shops. Butter was a particular example, being delivered in barrels from which the shop assistant would use a pair of wooden paddles to prepare a block of butter of the exact weight required. Pickles and other preserves were also kept in barrels in the shops.

But the biggest problem for Dundee retailers was that supplies of virtually everything were extremely limited. This created the ironic situation that although the wartime boom had put more money into people's pockets, there were actually less goods to buy.

The Post War Period

In 1945 Britain was bankrupt and the first priorities were seen to be producing goods for export and providing homes for returning servicemen. Some additional rationing was even introduced after the war ended and clothing rationing did not cease until May 1949. Even when rationing ended in the 1950s there were still serious shortages of goods available for sale. As ever, people tried to ring the changes with what they had. Woollen garments were recycled and many women made or altered their own clothes. One device used by Dundonians was to wear a cardigan back to front under a jacket thus giving the impression of a sweater. In the Overgate those shops selling second hand clothes and mending and altering clothes were prospering in the period of post war austerity.

The effects of national and local government action to improve housing and to decentralise population began, subtly at first, to affect the city centre shops. As early as 1944 the city had begun work on the development of a housing estate at Kirkton and it had also let contracts for the construction of prefabricated houses around the fringe of the city. This programme of decentralisation of the population was continued in 1949 with the commencement of housing estates at Douglas and Fintry where shops began to be established, particularly by Dundee Eastern Co-operative Society.

By the end of the 1940s things were beginning to get better and the creation of Dundee as a Special Development Area by the government was starting

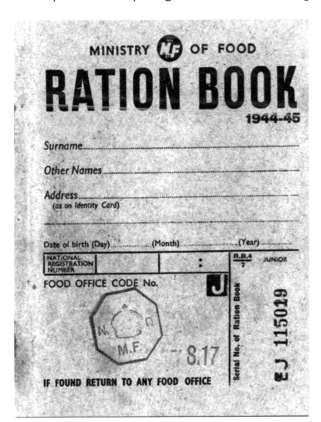

Wartime Ration Book

to affect the city. The arrival from America of, among others, the Timex, Veeder Root and the National Cash Register factories in the late 1940s provided a big boost. This, together with the general improvement in the post war economy meant that people had money to spend and that unemployment was very low. Car ownership was slowly increasing and this was underlined by the Council's decision in 1950 to improve parking around the Tay Ferry terminal.

Dundee was now ready to embark upon a period of sustained economic growth that was to see the city centre in its prime as a regional shopping centre .

Shopping in the 1950s
In the 1950s Dundee was, in many ways, in its prime as a shopping centre. Dundee's population was increasing and by 1951 had reached 177,340. There had been a post war baby boom and Dundee had a much younger age profile than it was to have in the later decades of the 20th century.

The end of the War and the additional employment from new companies such as Timex led to a feeling in the the Dundee of the 1950s that things were improving. The progressive removal of the rationing of goods helped, although the practice of closing on Wednesday afternoons and all day on Sundays indicated that frenetic conspicuous consumption was still not the order of the day.

Most Dundonians of all classes still shopped in the city. With no Forth or Tay Road bridges or long distance buses, and no dual carriages in Tayside beyond the Kingsway, shopping trips to Edinburgh or Glasgow were rare for any but the well-off.

Not surprisingly many people from Angus, Eastern Perthshire and Fife naturally came into the town on shopping trips. Indeed it was easier for many Fifers to get to Dundee than to travel to Edinburgh. Hamish Ramsay recalls travelling from Windygates in the south of Fife to go shopping in Dundee. "it was a great day out, first a bus to Newport on Tay and then the ferry across the river to Dundee".

As large numbers of houses began to be built on the periphery of the town more and more shoppers came in by bus. There were of course well established local centres in the Hilltown, Lochee, Albert Street and Broughty Ferry, but most Dundonians still came into the city centre not only to make larger purchases but also to buy their day to day supplies. It was not therefore surprising that in the 1950s the city centre was thriving and shop vacancies were few and far between.

Although the parking of private cars had begun to cause problems in the city centre, car ownership was still quite low. As a consequence, most people still tended to make their shopping trips into the centre on foot, or by bus or tram. Significant numbers going to the town centre still walked down through the Hilltown or Victoria Road or along the Hawkhill.

At weekends the city centre was extremely busy with trams and buses thronging the streets of

Samuel's Corner   *D C Thomson*

the city centre. The pavements were crowded, particularly under the Samuel's clock at the bottom of Reform Street that was a popular meeting place for Dundonians. One of those was Joyce Smart who recalls, "My friend Vera and I always met up under Samuel's clock before going window shopping". Others met in the queue that could be found outside Wallace's Pie shop on Saturday mornings. In many ways going down town to shop was a social experience when Dundonians could count on meeting friends and workmates. As many still worked on Saturday mornings, a Saturday afternoon trip to the shops, followed by a high tea in the Café Val D'Or might well be undertaken as a preliminary to a visit to the cinema or a walk up to a football match in the afternoon.

Local, rather than corporate values, still dominated the retail scene. Although there were some chain stores in the city, by far the majority of the shops,

were locally owned, and the values that were prevalent were those of the local businessmen who owned these retail businesses. The proprietors of the shops could often be seen working in their establishments, and even when they were not visible they were not far away. Jobs in retailing were abundant and relatively secure. Most shops had at least one 'character' on their staff that had been around long enough to be well known by local shoppers.

The largest of the locally owned shops were the department stores. Draffens were at the top of this hierarchy, closely followed by Cairds, G. L. Wilsons, D. M. Browns and Smith Brothers.

These stores sourced their wares from throughout the whole of the UK and prided themselves in having the latest fashion goods for sale. Twice a year their buyers made trips to London by train to visit wholesale warehouses. Although many goods were purchased in Glasgow others were were still made locally. Specialist items were often purchased from further afield. Blankets, for example, were bought directly from Witney in Oxfordshire while much of the bedding was acquired from wholesalers located in London and the southeast of England.

It was still a time when clothes were made to last. After the hard times of the thirties and the privations of the war, mending of clothes was in the blood. Socks were darned at home and invisible mending was advertised at a number of shops. People were still making and mending their own clothes and paper patterns could be obtained from shops such as Smith and Horner's and Hunters. D. M. Browns and all the department stores had extensive haberdashery departments where materials and patterns for dressmaking were sold.

Visitors from today would have been surprised at the range of headgear on sale in milliners and in men's outfitters. For men, clothes fashions had not altered materially since the inter war period, and hats and made to measure suits were the norm.

Older women nearly always wore hats and gloves, but for younger women it was quite a different matter, as local stores picked up on the New Look created by Christian Dior in 1947. They would be seeking clothes that gave them the nipped waist and full skirt look, while gloves and parasols were also sought after as fashion accessories.

Although in Dundee shops selling clothes and durable goods were concentrated in the city centre, grocery shops such as William Low and McCabe's were also commonplace in city centre locations, as were fruiterers and butchers, spirit merchants and confectioners. There were also very large numbers of local bakers to choose from, each with their own slant on everything from pastries to pies. It was even possible to buy 'Energy Rolls' in Kidd's the bakers' shop in Peter Street.

Personal service was still the order of the day. In the larger stores, regular customers would be allowed to take away goods on approval. In provision shops, customers stood on one side of the

Christian Dior - New Look

counter and were served by shop assistants on the other. In food shops bacon, spam, corned beef and other cold meats were cut by shop assistants with slicing machines to the exact thickness required by each individual customer. In the smaller shops, goods such as biscuits were still taken from large tins and were put into brown paper bags for the customer. In fruiterers the goods sold still reflected the seasonality of the year with shoppers eagerly looking forward to the time when apples, pears and plums, strawberries and raspberries came into season.

As most people still heated their houses with coal, a number of coal merchants were to be found in prominent locations where fuel could be ordered and fire grates and pokers purchased. Ironmongers, and seedsmen's shops were also prominent in the city centre.

Plastic bags were unknown and throughout this period going shopping for most goods meant taking your own shopping bag, although the large department stores had their own bags and boxes, often with a picture of the store prominently displayed upon them.

The local papers, which still remained the providers of almost all advertising, featured a constant flow of advertisements extolling the virtues of washing machines, vacuum cleaners, refrigerators, immersion heaters, electric radiators and room heaters, electric shavers and toasters together with radiograms and television sets. In the immediate post war years many shops selling washing machines, and vacuum cleaners laid on demonstrations of how to use them. But although there were many more goods available, it was still a time when households were satisfied with only one of any article, from radios to washing machines and from vacuum cleaners to cars.

Surprisingly there was far more recycling of goods going on than one might expect. This was primarily through the agencies of dealers in second hand goods, primarily outwith the town centre, but with significant numbers to be found in the Overgate and the Greenmarket.

Some hint of change was in the air - discussions were taking place as to whether trams should go and be replaced by motor busses. In April 1955, the first complete butcher supermarket was opened at 24 Union Street by two Angus farmers. Some shop owners were beginning to voice disquiet about the extent of the relocation of people to the new peripheral housing development. Shoe shops were unhappy about the 'unfair' competition from stalls selling shoes at the Saturday Market in Long Wynd. Nevertheless despite all this and the fact that the City Council was contemplating significant changes to the street pattern in Dundee there was still an air of stability about the city centre.

Perhaps because of this many Dundonians still look back on this time with a sense of nostalgia and have fond memories of the 1950s.

6 TOWARDS THE MILLENNIUM 1951 - 2000

This period was one of radical social changes and technological advances that fuelled growth and stimulated innovation at all levels from the global to the local. It was also a time when population growth and a determination to move into a world that was different from the wars and depression that had characterised the first half of the century, combined to give a desire for change. At first the rate of change in retailing was slow but the pace rapidly accelerated as the world moved towards the millennium.

A significant factor in bringing about change was the land use planning system that had been introduced by the Government in 1947. At first there was little sign of its influence but, as the UK moved into the 1950s, the need for all local authorities to produce plans that looked twenty years ahead began to be a powerful agent for change. This was doubly so because it was also a time when money followed the plans rather than, as so often now, the other way about.

Most of the plans that were prepared by planning authorities allocated large areas for housing on the periphery of the existing urban areas. This led to the rapid decentralisation of people, firstly due to the mass social housing programmes that were undertaken by local councils and latterly by the move to home ownership that gathered pace throughout the second half of the 20th century. Naturally enough the new homes generated a great demand for household goods and furnishings.

The increasing availability of household devices such as vacuum cleaners, washing machines, dishwashers, refrigerators and freezers led to the growth of shops selling electrical goods and to less time being spent on housework. This created a market for goods for home entertainment such as radios, gramophone records, record players and of course, television sets, the sale of which was stimulated by the televising of the Queen's Coronation in 1953. But for larger retailers and particularly for multiples, the big change brought about by television was the start of commercial television in 1955. This brought the selling of branded goods into people's living rooms and publicised shops that were not even situated in the town where the viewer lived.

But it was not just the sale of household and leisure goods that was increasing – more and more people were buying cars. Between 1955 and 1965 car ownership doubled to around 10,000,000 and this naturally spurred central government to improve the national and regional road networks. This made it easier for the growing numbers of car owners to travel to the larger shopping centres.

In the late 1950s as people moved out into the peripheral housing estates and new suburbs, efforts were increasingly made to improve city centres by comprehensively redeveloping major parts of them. The focus of most schemes was the removal of what was seen as out-dated and substandard housing, and catering for the increasing amount of road traffic, commonly by the creation of inner ring roads carved through the urban fabric. These redevelopments often swept away parts of the traditional shopping areas and the opportunity was taken to introduce pedestrianised shopping centres.

The 1960s were characterised by the redevelopment of existing shopping areas in the middle of the larger towns and cities of the UK. The resultant new shopping centres were generally anchored by a major branch of a national chain store and initially were surrounded by a mixture of established local stores and chain stores although, as the period went on, the latter gradually supplanted the former.

The archetypal example of these was the UK's first purpose-built indoor city shopping complex, the Bull Ring Centre, opened in Birmingham in 1964. It cost £8 million and covered 8 acres. It was part of a redevelopment scheme that covered some 23 acres and comprised a mix of outdoor market, indoor market (1,250 stalls), and an indoor centre with 140 stores. This became a model for many local authorities contemplating the renewal of their town centres. But one of the side effects, less celebrated by local communities, was the displacement of the locally owned shops, both small and large, that had previously dominated the central areas of Britain's cities.

Bull Ring Centre, Birmingham

Outwith such shopping centres chain stores were increasingly supplanting the local stores that occupied the major shopping streets of town centres. In passing it should be noted that one side effect of this trend was the depopulation of city centres, as most of the chain stores disliked the residential occupancy of premises above their shops.

These developments all disadvantaged the small shops located in the city centres, but even large well-established shops were affected by two government measures introduced in the mid 60s. The first of these was the abolition of resale price maintenance in 1964. This stimulated the growth of cost cutting stores by giving an advantage to larger retailing chains that could buy in bulk. The second was the introduction in 1965 of Selective Employment Tax (SET) a payroll tax levied on all industries but also including retailing among other service industries. Although SET was dropped in 1976 with the introduction of Value Added Tax, the damage had been done. Many locally based department stores found that the larger numbers of staff they employed to give a personal service could not be maintained, and many closures of such stores resulted throughout Britain.

In 1967 public transmissions of colour television began in Europe, greatly increasing the attractiveness of adverts for branded goods and in the same year the first bank cash machine (ATM) was opened in Barclays Bank in London.

The first ATM Machine

But behind the scenes in the 1960s there were a number of other technological developments taking place that were to strongly influence the way that shops would develop. Among these were the first laser, the first home video recorder, the introduction of the first compact cassette, and the launch of the first communications satellite.

There were also retailing developments under way abroad that were about to change the way that

people shopped. In Belgium following the abolition in 1961 of a law restricting the size of department stores, a retailer called Grand Bazar opened 3 hypermarkets (in effect a grocery superstore combined with a department store).

In Britain in 1964, the same year that the Bullring centre opened in Birmingham, GEM, an American retailer opened the first superstore in a suburb of Nottingham. Two years later this was purchased by a group of farmers trading as Associated dairies – later to become ASDA.

By the end of the 1960s grocery chains began to increase in size and number as it became easier to

GEM Store Nottingham

supply a wide network of branches across the UK from centrally located depots – a benefit of the improvement of the national and regional road networks. At the personal level the availability of larger refrigerators, and the use of the car boot for shopping trips, were encouraging families to shop for food once a week. This trend was further encouraged by the on-going decentralisation of population occasioned by the rapid growth of peripheral housing estates, most of which had little in the way of shopping provision.

In the 1970s the move out from the city centre that had been pioneered by the supermarkets was rapidly followed by the chain stores selling durable goods. This development was started in 1971 when the Bretton Centre, the first out of town shopping complex and with a sales area of 54,000 square feet, was opened near Peterborough. It was to be the first of many.

The large grocery chains now began to seek opportunities throughout the UK to establish out of centre superstores alongside large amounts of free parking, something that was not available in town centres. This inevitably brought them into conflict with planning authorities that were trying to protect their existing town centres.

Technological advances meant that new kinds of goods appeared, such as pocket calculators, personal computers, the Sony Walkman, microwave ovens, VCRs and car phones. Most significant though was probably the launch by Apple Computer Company in 1977 of the first mass produced personal computer targeted at home users. This was to be the essential first step towards on-line buying. After the mid 1970s many goods began to have bar codes on them, facilitating the central control of the stocking of goods, a vital factor for large stores and chains.

In 1979 the English entrepreneur Michael Aldrich invented the first online shopping system, but its widespread use did not occur until much later with the development of the world wide web in 1991. By the end of the 1970s credit cards, began to transform shopping. In the UK the introduction of the Barclaycard in 1966 marked a major step forward and by 1980 credit cards were accepted by most supermarket operators in the UK without a commission fee being payable by the customers. A side effect of this was that there were fewer visits to banks and the ground was being prepared for a great reduction in the number of bank branches to be found in city centre streets.

The effects of these developments upon city centres were at first masked by the generally increasing

Barclay Card

prosperity that was experienced in the period up until the oil crisis of the 1979 and a rapid increase in home ownership which meant that building societies, lawyers and estate agents were now all vying for space in city centre streets. But as the area of shopping floor space increased exponentially the smaller and less prosperous towns, particularly in areas outwith south-east England, found their recently built post war shopping centres declining.

In the late 1980s the hypermarket began to appear. This was a store combining a supermarket and a department store and extending to between 14,000 and 20,000 square metres of floor space

The period from the 1970s to the 1990s was later to be dubbed "the time of the big box store" as all kinds of large shops began to locate on out of centre sites, sometimes individually, but increasingly as part of retail parks. Although such moves often conflicted with the planning policies of local authorities, developers successfully argued that the type and size of goods now being sold had been significantly increased, particularly of electrical goods now not only manufactured in the UK but also being imported from Germany, Italy and France. To properly exhibit them required much greater areas of floor space. More choice meant bigger shops, and bigger shops needed less labour for each pound of turnover. This created significant disadvantages for those stores still operating in the city centres.

Some of the new out of town retail centre were very large to the point where they contained more shopping floor space than any of the town centres in their region. In 1986 the Metro Centre, then Europe's largest shopping centre, opened in Gateshead. It now has 342 shops and covers over 2 million square feet of retail floor space attracting shoppers from as far away as Dundee.

In the 1990s more and more of people's disposable income began to be spent on leisure. Much of this money went on new electronic gadgets such as satellite dishes, MP3 players, digital cameras. DVDs, and particularly the introduction of hand held mobile phones. This was to radically change the kind of shops to be found on high streets throughout the country.

Metro Centre, Gateshead

More indirectly, but no less surely, the development of the internet, the world wide web and email systems together with rapid increases in computer power enabled the growth of buying online and thus the creation of firms such as Amazon in 1995, who initially only sold books.

A clear indication of the way things were developing was that in 2000 Asos.com was launched, probably the definitive online specialist retailer of fashion (particularly aimed at the young) with 50,000 branded and own label product lines across women's wear, menswear, footwear, accessories, jewellery and beauty. Asos eventually had websites targeting the UK, USA, France, Germany, Spain, Italy and Australia generating annual revenues of over £1 billion.

Size was now everything and consolidation and takeovers among grocery retailers meant that by the year 2,000 almost 75% of the UK's grocery trade was controlled by the four biggest supermarket chains. More importantly their stores were mainly out of centre.

Dundee

In the period between 1950 and the year 2000 the pattern of shopping in Dundee and the shape of the central area were to change significantly.

A large part of the change was due to the effects of the post war planning acts that required local authorities to prepare land use plans covering a period of twenty years.

To help with the preparation of a plan for Dundee the City Council appointed planning consultants, in the shape of Dobson Chapman, to prepare an advisory plan for the city's future. The plan was duly delivered in 1952 and contained a comprehensive series of proposals for the future development of Dundee. Among these were plans for the creation of an Inner Ring Road around the city centre, part of which was to be in the form of shop lined boulevards, the redevelopment of the Overgate, the creation of a large covered market to the south of Seagate and the recasting of district shopping centres. Although the Dobson Chapman plan was never formally adopted by the City Council, and despite the uproar the plan created in the local press, its measures did form a basis for many decisions subsequently taken by the local authority.

Whilst the proposed physical changes were plainly set out in the plan, much less obvious were the assumptions underlying the actions of national and local planners and of commercial developers who implemented change throughout the succeeding years. In the first part of the period a major assumption was that the population, both nationally and locally, would continue to increase. In the second part of the period it was assumed that disposable incomes would inexorably continue to rise. Added to this was the assumption that throughout the foreseeable future people would satisfy all their retail needs through the medium of shops. As it turned out for the Dundee catchment area none of these assumptions would hold good.

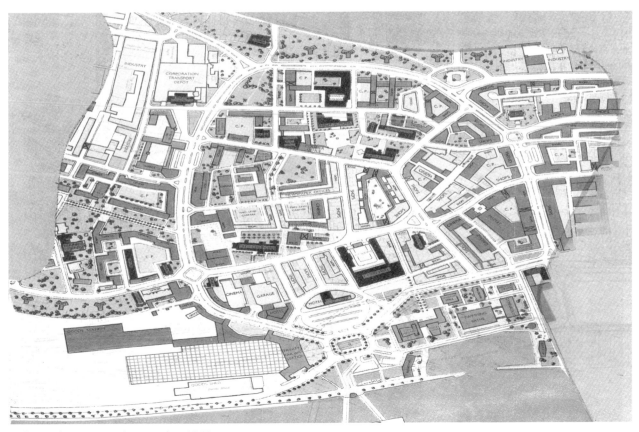

Dobson Chapman - Advisory Plan 1952

At first this was not at all clear, for in the 1950s the population did increase dramatically. Not surprisingly in these circumstances the main focus of the City Council was on the expansion and upgrading of its housing stock, particularly since Dundee had some the worst housing in the United Kingdom.

The quickest way to build additional housing was – as it always had been - to build on the fringes of the existing urban area, and this was done with great vigour, on one occasion achieving an annual build of 3,000 dwellings. Although this resulted in a great dispersal of the inner city population, only gestures were made to provide new shops to serve the newly developed areas. The city centre remained the focus for Dundee's shoppers and in 1960 was still taking over half the city's retail turnover despite having only a fifth of its shops.

Despite relatively low car ownership in the city as a whole, within the city centre lack of car parking was becoming a problem and the City Council was concerned that this could harm the city centre's role as a regional shopping centre. As early as December 1952 the Chief Constable reported that that although there was already an average demand for 765 off street public car parking places, the actual provision stood at only 110 spaces. He recommended that to cater for future demand around 1,100 spaces would be required. However, as the decade went on the plentiful supply of temporary car parks on sites made available during redevelopment of different parts of the central area and the Waterfront would mean that it would be some time before a permanent solution to this problem was achieved.

The 1960s
This was to turn out to be the decade that threw out its feelings for the past and embraced the new in everything from fashion and furniture and housing to hospitals. As Andrew Marr said "if the 1950s was a black and white decade the 1960s was in Technicolor."

At the start of the 1960s the population of the city was about to reach its peak and the children of the post war baby boom were growing into teenagers.

Car ownership was low and there was still only one off street public car park in the city centre. Even as late as 1967 over half the city centre shoppers arrived by bus and only a quarter by car.

Prosperity was growing and changes were now being seen at all levels of shopping provision. In April 1961 Draffens took over Henderson and McKay, only months before being taken over themselves by

Blythes of Edinburgh who initially kept the business trading under the Draffen name.

Chain stores began to take over local shops. Examples of this were the purchase by Richards Shops of 65/71 Murraygate in June 1960, and the sale in the same month of William Miller's grocery shop in the High Street to the British Shoe Corporation. Long standing local shops such as I. J. Collins, a clothing shop that had been in the Whitehall Crescent since 1905, and Millar's delicatessen in Commercial Street closed in the 1960s. The net result of changes like this was that by the mid 1960s the number of shops in Dundee had declined to around 2,700 – a thousand less than the total of 3,700 present in the city in the mid 1950s. The biggest fall was in the number of drapers and clothing shops but there were also significant drops in the number of shoe shops and grocery stores.

Outwith the city centre small groups of shops were being built to serve the new housing estates. The most prominent of these was probably the MacAlpine Road shopping parade developed by Murrayfield Estates and Co-op stores. However these shops only served local needs and had no real effect upon the shops in the city centre.

In the city centre the most important instigator of change was the City Council, who, as the city moved into the 1960s began dealing with what was

MacAlpine Road Shops

regarded as substandard and slum housing in the inner areas of the city. The close textured mixture of ownerships and uses was obviously going to make this a slow business and the Council decided to create a number of Comprehensive Development Areas (CDAs). Within these areas compulsory powers of acquisition would be used to enable complete clearance and redevelopment.

The Overgate
The condition of the housing in and around the Overgate had been a matter of concern even before

World War Two, and so it was no surprise that the City Council's programme of redevelopment started there. As early as the beginning of the 1950s the City Council had started to acquire properties in the Overgate area on a voluntary basis. When in June 1957 the City Council submitted its proposals for the Overgate CDA to the Secretary of State the plans not only affected large numbers of sub standard dwellings but also some 162 existing shops and businesses.

After some consideration the City Council selected Murrayfield Real Estate as the developers for the new Overgate. The scheme produced by Murrayfield did not include any new housing but was for a shopping development on two levels comprising a hotel, 4 department stores and 93 shops. This was to be the first central area shopping redevelopment in post-war Scotland.

First Overgate Development   *D C Thomson*

Demolition of the Overgate

Construction started on a phased basis in October 1961 with the building of the hotel at the western end of the site. The first phase also included a number of shops and the first shop tenant was a branch of the Civil Service Stores chain. The new Overgate was at first occupied by a mix of large local firms and chain stores, but of the small, quirky, local shops that had occupied the former Overgate there were none. The last phase at the eastern end was completed in 1968 and incorporated stores for C & A and Littlewoods.

One of the unintended effects of the building of the Overgate was to cut the pedestrian flows that had previously entered the City centre from the

Hawkhill. The simultaneous construction of the western leg of the Inner Ring Road further reduced the flow of shoppers and it was later to be totally eliminated by the demolition, as part of the creation of the University precinct, of the housing that lay around the Hawkhill.

There were some other unintended changes brought about at this time by local authority decisions that impacted upon shopping patterns in the city centre. The opening of the Tay Road Bridge in 1966 brought about the cessation of the Tay Ferries and removed the flow of shoppers coming into the town via Union Street. Castle Street and Crichton Street were similarly affected by the closure of the Shore Terrace Bus station and the Dundee East Railway Station.

The 1970s

At the start of the decade the Government published the Tayside Study. The preparation of the study had been prompted by the continuing growth of population experienced in the 1960s, and was designed to explore how a significant increase in the regional population might be accommodated.

In fact, during the 1970s the number of people residing within the City's boundaries started to decline, but as much of the reduction was due to people moving to areas around the city in North Fife, Angus and the Carse of Gowrie the numbers within the city's shopping catchment remained much the same. The bulk of the private housing that was erected during the 60s and 70s lay in Balgillo at the east end of the city and for many of these their main shopping centre now became Broughty Ferry.

By the start of the 1970s the large department stores that had dominated Dundee's shopping scene in the past began to decline. In 1970 Smith Brothers merged with Draffens and closed their store in the Murraygate. In December 1971 Garnet Wilson closed the doors of the G. L. Wilson department store for the last time., When the former D. M. Brown store was renamed as Arnotts by its Glasgow based owner, Frasers, it was clear that the concept of local loyalties was beginning to die.

At a smaller scale consolidation of Dundee shops into chains was taking place. In 1970 Birrells – a Glasgow based firm who had long had a number of branches in Dundee - acquired the Val D'Or Café and nine Dundee shops from R. S. McColl. The Dundee Eastern Co-operative Society that had been suffering a loss in sales to the newer and larger supermarkets now beginning to appear around the city, merged with the Glasgow based Scottish Co-operative Society in November of the same year.

In contrast one locally based chain that was growing was William Low's group of grocery stores. They had decided that large supermarkets were the way forward and had adopted a vigorous programme of expansion. In 1971 alone they not only opened another store in the new Overgate but also stores in Albert Street and in MacAlpine Road. But William Low was an exception and smaller shops continued to close.

The redevelopment of the Overgate also brought about changes to the open air markets that had operated in Dundee in one form or another since medieval times.

To accommodate the construction of the Overgate CDA, it was decided to move the 50 stalls that were sited at the open air market in Long Wynd to a

Buster Stall

temporary location in Hawkhill. This meant the end of the stalls selling "Busters" (chips and mushy peas) so beloved by Dundonians, along with the small traders dealing in second hand clothes and bric a brac.

The market did not survive for very long in its new location and in 1969 to provide a substitute David Soutar set up Dens Road Indoor Market. This was located at the junction of Arklay Street and Dens Road in the former Rashiewell Works. Containing some 80 stalls it was immediately popular but after a heyday, in the 1970s and 1980s the market entered a slow, lingering decline. It was eventually to close in October 2013.

Among all of this change there began to be heard sounds of popular disquiet. In 1971, under the banner of "Lets keep the corner shop," a meeting was held in Dundee at which objections were voiced to "the squeezing out of the small trader by large shopping developments." The meeting had probably been triggered by the approval in January 1971 of compulsory purchase orders for another area full of small local shops – the Wellgate.

Wellgate Shopping Centre 1980

The Wellgate

During the 1960s, whilst the City Council had been busy with Overgate, it had also made moves to redevelop another shopping area in the city, namely the Wellgate. This was in two parts, a commercial CDA and a residential CDA. Whilst the first of these directly affected the steep shopping streets that linked the Hilltown to city centre, the second removed a large number of shops on the south side of Victoria Road.

After a lengthy process of land acquisition and construction the new Wellgate mall was completed in 1978. The resultant covered shopping mall was a multi level development with three floors of shopping used to take up the considerable fall in ground levels from the north to the south of the

Wellgate. It incorporated a multi storey car park and had the advantage of straddling the main pedestrian route into the City centre from the north and more particularly from the Hilltown district. The development also had the advantage of housing the City's main library, and, for a time, a market stall area on the top floor – all in an environment free from the vicissitudes of Scottish weather.

When opened the new Wellgate Centre rapidly filled with traders. Some came from the rather exposed walkways of the Overgate centre. But not only from there - the attractions of the covered mall of the Wellgate were such that even Woolworths would eventually decide to relocate there from a prime location in the Murraygate. Unlike the Overgate where larger local stores took up some of the shop units, none of the retailers that leased space in the Wellgate were locally owned.

But the Wellgate was not the only investment being made in the city centre. In January 1975 a shopping mall connecting the Nethergate to Yeaman Shore was opened.as part of a major office development. However this was not a success in either the short, or the long, term.

At the end of 1975 plans were unveiled for the creation of a shopping court on the site of the former Keiller marmalade factory. This proposed a development of around 200,000 square feet consisting of 7 shops and 25 market stalls. Eventually the scheme was approved but did not actually open until four years later, although when it did it was totally occupied by small local traders.

By now the Inner Ring Road was more or less complete and in 1975 the Murraygate was pedestrianized on an experimental basis. It was declared a success and was made permanent in 1979.

As the decade progressed the effects of removal by the Council of housing from the city centre began to

Murraygate   *D C Thomson*

have its effects. The number of food and convenience shops in the city centre began to diminish and a common question to the city planners was "why can we not have more small shops in the centre". In December 1980 when Cantrell's, a shop the that had thrived in Whitehall Crescent for over 60 years closed its doors, the owner Angus McDonald blamed "the shift in shopping population. There is no passing trade now".

Concern about the number of shops and its consequences for the city centre grew and in 1975 the Evening Telegraph ran an article headed "Does Dundee have too many shops?"

Nevertheless in November 1975 plans were tabled for a superstore on a site at Arbroath Road/Baldovie Road. This was refused by the District Council but in February 1976 a proposal for a superstore north of the Kingsway, on a site at Derwent Avenue in Kirkton was approved. This was despite the application being strongly opposed by Dundee Chamber of Commerce on the grounds that "there were too many shops in Dundee".

While all of this had been happening in the city centre, things were beginning to happen elsewhere that would affect the city centre. At a national level the Forth Road Bridge opened in 1964 and work was in hand to improve the main roads between Aberdeen, Dundee, Perth and Edinburgh. In time this would allow day trips to be made to shop in Edinburgh or Aberdeen.

The 1980s.

This was a decade when decisions were made that would result in significant and irreversible changes to the pattern of shopping in Dundee.

The effects of the opening of the Wellgate shopping mall were still being felt throughout the city centre. Bercotts jewellery business decided in May 1980, to relocate to the Wellgate from its premises in Reform Street. More of the Overgate's tenants began to move out or close down. In November 1981 the House of Clydesdale relocated from the Overgate to the Wellgate and Carrick's Furniture store attributed the closure of its premises in the Overgate in the same year to the effects of the Wellgate development.

The landlords of the Overgate centre, the Land Security Trust, responded by announcing in February 1981 that they would be embarking on a programme of systematic improvements the centre. However, in spite of regular statements about improvements to come, nothing significant was done, and in 1989 the centre was sold to Molyneux Estates.

For the SCWS the 80s was a decade of decline. It made attempts to respond to changes both organisational and operational that were taking place in the wider world of retailing – for example by converting, in March 1980, its flagship city centre store in the Seagate into a self service store, This was unsuccessful and within the space of 12 months the store had closed. In March 1984 the Scottish Co-operative Society closed a further three of its Dundee stores in Camperdown Road, Albert Street and Hilltown. In April 1985 it closed its store in the Cowgate and the decline in its business in Dundee was marked by the closure and demolition 1988 of its warehouse in the Seagate.

The decline in the number of retailers in the existing city centre streets was at first masked by a radical increase in the number of building society offices at street level and a move of solicitors to establish property offices in the premises formerly occupied by shops. This was in spite of efforts made by the city planners to avert this, an example being in the refusal of an application by the Gateway Building Society to establish an office in Reform Street.

Even so the number of vacant shop premises were beginning to increase in the city centre and the District Council found this both undesirable and alarming. A report prepared by the Chief Planning Officer of Dundee District Council in June 1981 indicated that there were some 100,000 square feet of retail floor space lying vacant in the city. Signs of this could be seen even in Reform Street where, in June 1981, Cairds had sold off half of their frontage. The District Council decided that in view of this it would adopt a policy of restricting major retail developments outwith the city centre. Somewhat at odds with this approach, in 1982 the District decided to close the City Arcade at Shore Terrace that was full of small shops.

Nevertheless applications for major stores outwith the city centre continued to be made and January 1982 the Council gave permission for William Low to build a 30,000 square foot grocery store and 200 car spaces at Pitkerro Road, north of the Kingsway. In 1982 the District Council also gave permission for B & Q to open what was at that time a large retail warehouse on South Road. This opened in March 1983 and proved very popular. In 1984 the Council, having considered the likely demand, decided that there was scope for the development of a large store in the eastern part of Dundee. Not surprisingly this led to a several applications for such stores.

By the middle of the decade planning applications for large retail developments outwith town centres

B&Q DIY Store, South Road, Lochee 1980's

were being received right across Tayside. Tayside Regional Council decided to call these in, and in 1984 appointed Hillier Parker as consultants to advise on existing and future shopping provision across the whole of Tayside Region. The consultants made a number of very specific recommendations about future shopping provision in Tayside in general and in Dundee in particular.

In respect of the town centre they came to the view that "Dundee had failed to achieve its full retail potential as the centre has a restricted range of multiple retailers, due to a shortage of suitable accommodation in prime areas and difficulties with the Overgate and Wellgate centres".

To overcome these problems Hillier Parker proposed the redevelopment of the area lying to the south of Murraygate and bounded by Seagate, Cowgate, St Andrews Street, Allan Street and East Dock Street. This should be designed to link into the existing prime shopping areas and would incorporate 1800 car spaces and a bus facility. The scheme would be a covered shopping mall that would consist of a department store, a variety store, an extension to Marks & Spencers, a food court and up to 55 shop units, amounting in all to 286,000 square feet of shopping space.

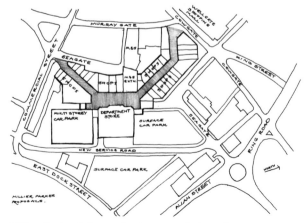
Hillier Parker Scheme for increased shopping

Hillier Parker's recommendations to the Regional Council in respect of decentralised shopping turned out to be very influential in changing the pattern of shopping in Dundee. They were of the view that "in principle the current demands for decentralised non food retail would pose no significant threat to the city centre" and suggested that two retail parks should be created, one at Milton of Craigie on Kingsway East and the other at a location adjacent to Kingsway West.

These recommendations stimulated a large number of applications on a wide range of sites throughout Tayside. As the Regional Council gathered and considered these applications the Scottish Office issued a National Planning Guideline on The Location of Major Shopping developments that stated that "planning authorities should give adequate consideration to opportunities and likely demand for investment in new forms of retail shopping in off-centre locations". As if in response, in March 1987 the District Council approved a major retail development of a food store on the site of Bowbridge Works near the top of the Hiltown.

The Regional Council's subsequent decisions followed up the consultant's recommendations. In July 1987 approval was given for a large non food retail development at Kingsway West and another at Milton of Craigie for 142,000 square feet of retail floor space which included a major store for Asda, together with parking for 1,240 cars. The Regional Council did impose conditions restricting the range of goods that could be sold in the retail warehouses developed on these sites. This was intended to minimise any damage to shopping in the town centre of Dundee.

The retailers and property owners in the city centre realised that they too would have to take action to fight off competition from the proposed retail parks. As the 1980s came to an end the new owners of the Overgate publically committed themselves to upgrading the centre, Marks & Spencer completed a £500,000 improvement of their store in the Murraygate and the Keillor Centre carried out a programme of improvements, after which it was renamed The Forum Centre.

The 1990s
By the opening of the new decade car ownership had increased to 43% and it was estimated that 84% of shopping trips were now being made by car. More worryingly, a fall in the population of Dundee was, for the first time accompanied by a drop in the population of the city's retail catchment area.

The year 1990 proved to be one of considerable change. It opened with investments in both the town centre and on the Kingsway. In January Next opened their rebuilt store in the Murraygate and Joanna Lumley opened a new 50,000 square feet ASDA store at Kingsway East Retail Park

The District Council was still considering the Hillier Parker proposals for additional shopping space in the city centre and November 1990 decided to incorporate a 250,000 square feet extension to the prime shopping area of the city centre into its City Centre Local Plan.

Meanwhile Hillier Parker was reporting to Tayside Regional Council that the proposals for shopping on the Enterprise Zone at Riverside constituted a "real danger" for the future of the Wellgate centre. Nevertheless, in that very same month Tesco, moved out of the Wellgate centre and into a 65,000 square feet store on the Enterprise Zone at Riverside. Alongside Tesco a 30,000 square feet store was constructed and occupied by Texas Homecare.

In March a proposal for a Leisure Park was made by on the site of the former Camperdown Works in Lochee. This was subsequently approved and included a major Willliam Low store. During the late 1980s and the early 1990s William Low had been going from strength to strength and in June 1990 had had its proposal for a 40,000 square feet store on the site of the former Ice Rink at Kingsway West approved by the District Council.

However William Low's success had attracted a takeover attempt by Tesco. When this was rejected Sainsbury made an offer but they too were rejected. Subsequently an improved bid made by Tesco in 1994 was successful.

In 1991 the Northern Co-operative Society finally opened a 50,000 square feet superstore on the site of the former Bowbridge works. However it was not a success and closed in 1993.

The Regional and District Councils and Scottish Development Agency were determined to upgrade the city centre of Dundee and in July 1990 their attention turned to a major programme of city centre environmental improvements which included a major upgrading of the Murraygate and a pedestrianisation scheme that linked the High Street with Reform Street and the Murraygate.

Perhaps stimulated by this, in 1992 a start was finally made on the upgrading of the Overgate centre but the improvements were minor and ineffective.The Wellgate too was feeling the competitive effects of the Kngsway retail parks and in 1993 its owners embarked upon a comprehensive upgrading of their shopping mall.

In 1994 in the aftermath of Tesco's departure from the Wellgate, Woolworths relocated from the Murraygate into the Welllgate premises formerly occupied by Tesco. In turn Menzies moved into the Murraygate store vacated by Woolworths only to be taken over in 1998 by W. H. Smith.

In the late 1990s significant investment in retailing was still taking place in the city centre. A major investment was made in 1996 in the total internal reconstruction of the premises at the junction of Commercial Street and Murraygate that were formerly owned by G. L. Wilson. The resultant one level shops were occupied by a Disney shop and a Monsoon ladies fashion store.

The Overgate was sold to Land Lease, an Australian based concern that in 1998 commenced the total demolition and redevelopment of the centre. While the rebuilding of the Overgate was underway the Wellgate was almost fully occupied.

The following year the City Council embarked upon a £620,000 programme of environmental improvements for Castle Street, Commercial Street and Shore Terrace that was attempting to encourage the growth in the area of what was called "speciality shopping".

Investment in retailing was also taking place outwith the city centre. In 1999 Sainsbury were finally given permission for a store at the junction of Arbroath Road and Baldovie Road. ASDA were trying to find a site at Myrekirk Road for a new superstore although their efforts were being thwarted by the presence of ancient standing stones on their preferred site and Matalan, an English based chain of clothing stores, announced that it was looking for a 30,000 square feet store in Dundee. In December 1999 Tesco upped the stakes by proposing a 100,000 square foot store on Kingsway West Retail Park.

In 2000 the new enclosed Overgate shopping mall opened in in March with Debenhams moving in as the anchor store. This resulted in the closure of their previous premises in Whitehall Street. These were to remain vacant for some considerable time.

At the east end of the Overgate, Littlewoods and Samuels were upgrading their stores to fit in better with the new shopping mall, whilst the City Council were upgrading the pavements around the City Churches. Plans were also unveiled for a 30,000 square feet ft. development of factory outlet shops at Victoria Dock that was predicted to create some 500 jobs.

Second Overgate Redevelopment

Not everything in Dundee garden was coming up roses and in early 2000 the closure of the C & A store that had been in the Overgate since 1968 reopened worries about the health of the city centre. These concerns were reinforced by the consolidation and takeovers among the grocery retailers which meant that by the year 2000 almost 75% of the UK's grocery trade was controlled by the four biggest UK supermarket chains, three of which now had out of centre stores in the city.

Consolidation was also taking place among retailers of comparison goods and in April further worries were raised when Arcadia Stores closed their Wallis, Miss Selfridge and Principles stores in the Murraygate.

At the Millennium, despite competition from out of centre shopping developments the city centre was generally doing well, but what the future would bring was still uncertain. The year saw two events that pointed in quite different directions. On one hand new population projections were published that envisaged a drop in the city population from its current figure of 142,000 to 120,000 by 2016. On the other hand, the City Council in February 2000 received a long term plan prepared by EDAW consultants for the future development of the Central Waterfront that envisaged thousands of jobs and millions of pounds of investment being attracted to the city. Although the two pictures of the future were quite different, the one thing that was certain was that significant changes were on the way.

Going Shopping in 2000

Going shopping in Dundee in 2000 was a very different thing from going shopping in the 1950s. For a start shopping was now a seven day a week business with shops now opening on Sundays but, it should be noted, closing earlier in the City centre than was the case in the 1950s. The biggest changes were that most people would now be going shopping by car, and that where one went shopping very much depended upon what was required.

For food or groceries of any kind the majority of Dundonians would head once a week for one of the large supermarkets, located outwith the town centre, probably on Riverside or adjacent to the Kingsway. The same applied if one was looking for materials for Do It Yourself or gardening supplies. It was increasingly the case that one would also buy large electrical household goods and television sets on one of the out of centre retail parks. For them the car boot had now replaced the shopping basket.

If, on the other hand, one was looking for clothes, shoes, fashion accessories, music or a record player, and particularly if searching for a mobile phone or a computer, then it would be a store located in the city centre.

If you were travelling by car to the centre then one would be using the off street cars parks at the Wellgate, Overgate, Gellatly Street or the wide open spaces alongside the Olympia swimming pool, for it was no longer possible to park outside shops on the main shopping spine as most of it had now been pedestrianized.

Even for those using public transport things were different. For a start there were no trams and there was no longer any central bus station. For shoppers coming from further afar there were no longer ferries arriving at Dundee harbour from Fife. In addition the loss of the suburban railways to Newport, Tayport and further afield together with the closure of the Dundee East railway station meant that few now travelled by train into Dundee for shopping trips.

When one arrived at the City centre much had changed. The old Overgate and Wellgate areas had gone and in their stead were covered shopping malls

Of the grand department stores that once were to be found in the City centre all had gone except Debenhams, which had only recently relocated from Whitehall Street to the newly opened Overgate Centre.

Because of this Whitehall Street had temporarily become a one sided street, as the premises along the west side that had formerly been occupied by Debenhams now lay vacant. Buses there were in plenty in Whitehall Street and this thoroughfare was in many ways the nearest thing there was to a central bus station in Dundee.

Shoppers were now concentrated much more on the main shopping spine comprised of the Overgate, the Murraygate and the Wellgate. The side streets such as Castle Street, Crichton Street, Union Street, and Reform Street were less busy with shoppers. Reform Street, in particular, was much changed as most of its fashion shops had now been replaced by building society offices.

By the Millennium the City Centre had become a different and much less varied kind of place. Food stores were far fewer and the tradesmen's shops where everything had once been available, from fireguards to electrical fuses and from drain cleaners to candles, had either closed or relocated to premises on the industrial estates.

The small independent traders that had once been located in the city centre had largely vanished. Of the few that remained most were to be found within the Forum Centre that now occupied the site of the once thriving Keillers factory.

Pubs there were in plenty - many of them increasingly patronised by the large number of students that were now studying in Dundee and Abertay Universities. New kinds of shops had appeared - in particular charity shops and phone shops. There were more coffee shops and building society offices but all of the commercial cinemas had now closed.

The shopping environment, from the paving of the pedestrian areas to the artworks now to be found on the city centre streets, was much improved. However, the street markets with their local traders had gone and been replaced by special markets organised by the City Council some of which were exclusively manned by businesses from the continent. Hygienic though they were, somehow there seemed to be less bustle and variety about them.

At the start of the new millennium the task for the City Council was keeping the city centre alive in an age of out of town and on line shopping.

7 THE STORES

Allardyce

In 1890 Charles Allardyce, a master saddler, and William Pettie, a cutlery maker, together with a Dundee entrepreneur called Whitelaw, set up in business making artificial limbs in Commercial Street. Quite soon after the establishment of the business Whitelaw left the partnership. This was not the end of their difficulties for in 1901 Allardyce and Pettie fell out and set up in competition with one another on opposite sides of the Overgate.

Over the next decade Allardyce prospered in this location, but the firm really took off after 1914. Sadly this was due to the desperate need that arose during and after the First World War for artificial limbs and prosthetic devices, an area in which the firm came to specialise.

In the inter war period the company continued to develop its business, only interrupted by the death of Charles Allardyce in 1921 when his son Edward took over the business.

Just as in the First World War war, the 1939-45 war generated a large demand for artificial limbs and prosthetic devices. This persisted into the late 1940s when demand was augmented by the needs of the newly created National Health Service.

To cope with these demands Allardyces took on a number of Polish ex-soldiers and opened an orthopaedic workshop. One of their new Polish recruits, Stanislaw Kochaniuk, turned out to be a brilliant craftsman and an innovator. Together, Stanislaw and Edward's son John, produced a range of innovative designs for callipers and braces. With these devices in their range the business became so successful that Allardyces were asked to carry out clinics for Glasgow surgeons. However, the cash provided by the National Health Service at that time was not sufficient to pay for the effective and sophisticated prosthetic devices produced by the firm.

John's twin brother Charles, a pharmacist, joined the business and in June 1966 they moved to larger premises in the new Overgate centre where they opened a surgical shop and pharmacy. Edward eventually retired after which John and Charles jointly ran the business. They decided to build up the hospital and chemist wholesale side of the business, locating this in a property in Tay Street Lane. Due to an expansion in orders this side of the business eventually moved to Blinshall Street and then to Bellfield Street. By this time Charles's daughter Karen had joined the business along with John's son Stephen and later his son Richard. The company also had a retail shop in Perth.

But renting premises in the Overgate was an expensive matter and regular rent reviews made it difficult to plan ahead. The company therefore relocated the Pharmacy to Castle Street and the rest of the business to Bellfield Street. John retired due to ill health and when Charles also retired, the pharmacy part of the business was sold.

The company continued to grow and in 2007 moved to larger premises at Tom Johnson Road, West Pitkerro Industrial Estate where it continues to operate over 125 years after it was first established. Stephen, the only family member now in the business, runs the firm along with his fellow directors. Steven Sidowra and Mike Skinner.

Braithwaites

The great thing about Braithwaites is that even if one was blindfolded, one could still find the shop by following the smell of freshly ground coffee. It has been that way for quite a time as the business was established in 1868, by James Steele - a relative of the Braithwaite family. It was first located in a shop behind the Pillars that fronted the old Town House in the High Street.

The tea business was naturally attractive to James Steele, who was a Quaker, for tea was a socially acceptable non-alcoholic drink that could safely be sold to Dundee folk. He later went into partnership with his nephew, James Allan Braithwaite. While Braithwaite concentrated on the retail side Steele traded mainly in wholesale tea from a store in the Hawkhill. Eventually the partnership was dissolved and Braithwaite started importing coffee but tea remained the focus of the business until after World War Two, when the coffee part of the business grew in importance.

The 1930s were a time of change for the firm. This was because the City Council, contemplating a new City Square, decided to demolish the old Town House thereby forcing the firm to move. In the event they moved to the premises in Castle Street that they occupy today. However when the owners moved they did not move alone, for they took all of the fixtures and fittings from the High Street shop,

including the door to the street and installed them in their Castle Street premises. It is these that one can still see in their shop today.

In 1919 James Allan Braithwaite had three sons – James, Thomas, and George Holden Braithwaite. James went straight into the business as did Thomas, but George did not. Initially he took up an apprenticeship with Liptons, the grocers, until the outbreak of war in 1939.

World War Two brought about many changes and Braithwaites found that if they were to survive under wartime conditions that it would be necessary for them to sell some kind of food. Surprisingly they decided to sell butter and this they did for the duration of the war. The war also brought about other changes for the family. Thomas became a naval wireless operator and died during the war. As a Quaker George was a conscientious objector and ended up working with difficult boys.

In 1944 while he was working in England he became involved with bees, becoming a professional beekeeper. During this time he met his wife June. George and June married in 1950 and had three sons, Allan, Ian and Christopher. The couple continued working as professional beekeepers until a run of bad years led George to go into the family firm.

At that time this was being run by his brother James, and at first George's involvement was on a part time basis. He eventually took on a full time role in the business and took over the firm when his brother James retired in 1969. George's son Allan was working in the firm, and George gradually handed over the running of the business to him, eventually retiring on the grounds of ill health. He died in November 1999 having been an active Quaker throughout his life. The business is now run by his son Allan.

D. M. Brown

D. M. Brown's department store was a landmark for many generations of Dundee's citizens. David Miller Brown, the founder of the company, was the son of a coal merchant, and was born in Lochee on 17 July 1864. He completed an apprenticeship as a draper with Stewart & Sons of Lochee before joining James Spence as a junior salesman. His energy and talent were soon noted and he was quickly promoted to become the small-ware manager for the company.

In 1888 he secured a shop in 80 High Street, which also had a window onto Rankine's Court, and went into business for himself with a staff of only three employees. The counter occupied most of the floor space of the little shop and a small spiral staircase led to a narrow balcony where spare stock was kept.

Such was the success of the business that only twelve months later the two rooms above No. 80 had been leased and incorporated into his shop. Within another year he managed to acquire two more rooms and very soon was the owner of the whole building from basement to attic.

In 1893 David Miller Brown married Annie Kerr – the daughter of an upholsterer- and they set up house at Tortola in Scotswood Terrace, Dundee. Although they had a son and two daughters, none of the children took an active part in the business.

Brown's next move was to acquire the shop at No. 81 and to make extensive alterations to extend his shop once again. In 1894, the shops at No. 83 and No. 84 High Street,were taken over and in 1896 the second and third floors and the attics above them were all incorporated into the business.

To get a picture of what the shop looked like at the time we can turn to the Courier of 28 June 1895 in which it was described as follows:-

"The outside is painted white and decorated with gilt lines. On either side of the entrance are elaborately carved columns, touched up with gilt. There are nine large windows, decorated in the London style, and as Mr Brown has on his staff a young lady, an expert, who does nothing else but window dressing, the changes are very frequent and always tasteful. On either of the door pillars there are large glass cases filled with gay flowers. Entering we find ourselves in the midst of pretty things of all sorts. Straight in front is a sort of three- sided column, every side of which is mirror and from which the various departments run in lines. On the right is the flower department, where, in long rows of glass cases....... there are flowers of every conceivable kind, forming

quite a lovely decoration for the shop. On the right comes next the needlework department and beyond that we reach the part of the shop where lace and flowers are a speciality. Nothing is more advantageous than having all departments on one flat".

"Starting again from the entrance to the left hand side we have the ribbons department where, in large cases with glass shelves, gay ribbons and trimmings of indescribable variety make a show. Beyond that is the glove department, while on the other hand there are found small wares in great variety. Right around the shop runs a light balcony painted white from which are attained many of the small wares. Furs have a suitably fitted room admirably lighted and having mirrors. Altogether, at 80 High Street, Mr Brown has made an establishment that has become a favourite resort for ladies bent on a day's shopping".

Brown was never one to stand on his laurels and constantly improved his store. In November 1896 it was reported that: - "The whole shop is now fitted with telephones, some twenty in number. Every department has been fitted with porcelain stoves and the newly fitted elevator makes it a pleasure to be sent upstairs. Brown liked to keep

D M Brown store in 1895

his staff happy and there were regular social events for the employees such as annual picnics, during which the store was closed, and staff dances. He chose the Annual Staff Dance held in Gray's Rooms on 20 February 1896 to inform all present that he understood the strain upon the feet of his female employees when waiting for customers to arrive. He therefore proposed to provide sprung revolving seats for all female counter staff.

Keeping the staff happy was one thing – expansion was quite another. On 1 March 1898 it was announced in the press that "D. M. Brown has acquired Nos.85, 86, 87, 88 and 89 High Street. The business was established only ten years ago but it is now beyond doubt one of the first of its kind in the country. Only in 1896 it was intimated that after large yearly extensions Mr Brown had quadrupled his premises."

By this time the Christmas displays at D. M. Brown's had become quite an event. The Courier of 6 November 1899 carried a review by their fashion correspondent, Annette, who reported that:-

D M Brown 1900

"The bazaar proper, which last winter was set out in the basement, occupies this year an immense room upstairs in the new building, where, in the brilliancy of the electric light everything shows to the best advantage". The rest of the article which comprised two whole columns of detailed descriptions of the wares available amounted to free advertising for the firm.

Looking towards the future Brown knew that women liked shopping to be a social event, and so, on 20 June 1900 he opened new tearooms designed by the local architect William Gauldie. These were clearly designed to be attractive to the middle class ladies whom Brown wanted to become regular customers at the store. A contemporary account described the tearooms as being:-

"panelled from floor to ceiling and enamelled purest white, The walls are hung with a number of exquisite coloured engravings. On the floors Axminster carpet is carried out in shades of gold. The pretty chairs are upholstered in green embossed velvet. And everywhere there are flowers. It is a feast of delight for weary eyes. There are fully twenty tables of different sizes. Adjoining the tearoom is the ladies' parlour carried out in a harmony of pink and green. The gentlemen's room is rather less luxurious and is fitted as a writing room with leather comfortable chairs".

D M Brown - The Pillard Tearoom

By now there were an increasing range of goods on sale and Brown became concerned that his cornucopia of offers was not visible to passers by. To overcome this problem an arcade lined with glass display windows was created that also provided a covered walkway from the High Street to Commercial Street. The first section of the arcade was opened on 5 July 1906 and it was completed in 1908. The arcade provided an additional 80 feet run of window space. A parcel room was provided as part of the alterations so that those ladies overburdened by their load of shopping could shop unhindered in the store.

All this obviously impressed Dundonians and in July 1906 the Courier reported on the opening of the arcade that:-

"The talk of the town has undoubtedly been the new Arcade constructed in the section of D. M. Browns commodious establishment. It can afford accommodation for a very large number of visitors for the extent of the Arcade which leads from the High Street right through to Commercial Street is much greater than could be imagined. Its windows are filled with wondrously pretty things. The entrances are all bowered in flowers on trellis-work, as are the archways leading to the main body of the warehouse. Miss Brown is to perform the opening ceremony. The band of the 3rd Black Watch will give selections of music from three to five and seven to nine".

Subsequent adverts generally made reference to "The Arcade" and described D. M. Brown's as the store "where the luncheon and tea rooms are". Competition from the other stores was stiff and Brown was continually trying to enhance the shopping experience. In the D. M. Browns June 1913 Semi Jubilee celebration he boasted that "There are many demonstrations including the use of the Gair Skirt grip and the Samson stocking suspenders, Shetland knitting and the making of dolls hats. There are flowers all the way."

Arcade opening 1906

When the First World War arrived D. M. Brown did his bit to support the men on the war front. He was involved with a number of fund raising bodies and notably became the chairman of the Dundee Tank Fund. In 1916 he personally provided funds for the erection of a hut in Flanders for the war wounded with instructions to spare no expense as "only the best would do".

After the war Brown, if anything, increased his activity in the community. On 14 May 1920 he was elected to the board of the Dundee Mission to the Blind. But this was only one of the many charities to which Brown gave his time and his money. Among their number were the Dundee Horticultural Society, the Dundee Indigent Sick Society, the Royal Victoria Hospital, the Board of Dundee Dental Hospital, the Board of Dundee Savings Bank and the Dundee Temperance Society.

Brown was also heavily involved with Dundee Royal Infirmary where he was not only a Board member but also served on various committees associated with the hospital. In September 1926 he made a gift of £3,000 to upgrade the admissions area at the DRI. He was also a great supporter of the establishment of the Sidlaw Sanatorium for Children, which he formally opened on 7 June 1926 and was a founder member of Dundee Dramatic Society,

In addition Brown supported causes outwith the City. For example he offered to match any staff contributions to the 1929 Relief Fund for Mining Areas, and he also made contributions to a fund for the relief of the many Greek refugees who had been expelled by the Turks in 1923.

Brown's benevolent attitude to his employees was exemplified by the staff outing that took place on 22 May 1924. In the evening just over 300 staff departed by the sleeper train from Taybridge Station bound for London. On their arrival breakfast was provided before they went on a morning charabanc tour of the City followed by lunch. After lunch and a visit

to the Empire Exhibition at Wembley, dinner was provided before an overnight trip back to Dundee. At Tay Bridge Station special trams were provided to take the staff home.

But by now Brown was in his sixties and it had become apparent that his offspring did not see their futures as being in the retail business. In November 1926 the press revealed that - "A new public company, with the name of the Scottish Drapery Corporation Ltd, is being formed...for the purpose of acquiring controlling interests in the well known Scottish businesses of Pettigrew & Stephen, Glasgow, Patrick Thomson Ltd, Edinburgh, D. M. Brown, Dundee and Watt & Grant, Aberdeen. The managements of these firms will remain undisturbed and there will be no change in personnel".

Only four days later, on 15 December 1926, the business was under the ownership of the Scottish Drapery Corporation run by Clarence Hatry. The store was then turned into a private limited company with Mr D. M. Brown as Chairman.

After the new arrangements were in place something seemed to have changed. Brown was still in the chair but the company seemed for a time to have lost its taste for innovation although it was active in promoting itself to the Dundee public.

David Millar Brown died on 11 January 1934. What is particularly noticeable in the tributes paid to him not only in Dundee, but also in Forfar and Brechin, was how highly he was regarded by his staff, his competitors and the public. His obituary in the Courier commented that: - "remarkable as were his talents, success in business was far from being the primary and chief element in the estimation of Mr Brown by the citizens of Dundee. He was admired and loved for the fine humanity that at all times in all relations informed and ruled his life. He was among the rare few of whom nobody ever had an ill word. Kindness and helpfulness were the constant expressions of a modest and unassuming nature".

That this might in any way have overstated his reputation was belied by the fact that there were over 2,000 mourners at the cemetery when he was interred.

During his lifetime he had constantly given money to Dundee charities, and this was continued in the bequests he made when he died. Monies were given to the Dundee Royal Infirmary, the Dundee Original Secession Church, the Royal Victoria Hospital, the Sidlaw Sanatorium, Dundee Orphans Institution, the Childrens Free Breakfast Mission, Dundee Sick Poor Nursing Society, the Salvation Army Eventide

Nursing Home, the Curr Night Refuge, the YWCA in Dundee, and the YWCA in Lochee.

New Management

Subsequent to the death of David Millar Brown, John Campbell of Glasgow became chairman and Robert Adam McEwan took up the post of managing director. McEwan was a childhood friend of Brown with whom he had attended the 'penny' school in Lochee. He was the first male assistant taken on by Brown and had had a variety of roles in the firm, including being a buyer and a traveller. Albert Adamson Fyffe was the new Assistant Managing Director.

The new management team proceeded to improve the shop in August 1935 by creating a new main entrance with a bronze and glass canopy and a new central staircase inside the building. And this was just a beginning, for on 16 November they embarked on a second phase of alterations that included the installation of a new heating system.

In 1937, probably in reaction to the success of the Fashion Cavalcades held by Draffens, the company decided to hold a special Mannequin Parade. This finally took place on 26 March 1937 and went rather better than they hoped as instead of the 250 expected over 1,000 customers arrived. Always equal to a challenge they managed to round up some 600 chairs from various places, including other shops.

Keeping up the pace in May of that year they decided that a touch of Americana was called for and installed "The Golden Fountain Buffet" to provide milk shakes to their customers.

All in all things went well for the new management team in the late 30s and by the eve of the Second World War they employed over 400 people.

World War Two

During the Second World War the clothes rationing regime brought in by the government made things difficult for all the department stores and D. M. Browns were no exception. Quite apart from blackouts and air raid alarms, they also had to deal with shortages of goods and the conscription of staff. Nevertheless in September 1941 they set up a new company, D. M. Brown (Wholesale) Ltd which was registered at Rankines Court.

In August 1941, somewhat bizarrely, but perhaps in keeping with the times, the store had an exhibition of rifles, shotguns, revolvers and automatic weapons. These were part of an armoury sent by private American citizens to aid the British in the war and attracted large numbers of viewers to the store.

Post war

In the immediate aftermath of the war rationing and shortages persisted. And it wasn't only goods for sale that were in short supply. The fuel shortages in the severe winter of 1947 meant that staff had to wear extra clothes in the store just to keep warm.

Things were a little better with the ending of some clothes rationing in February 1949, but the continuing shortage of goods meant that this had less effect than might have been expected. It was March 1951 before all rationing ceased.

In spite of this Britain was hauling itself forward and things did gradually become better. On 6 January 1948 a queue of over 2,000 was attracted to a 'one price' sale at D. M. Browns. The items for sale were costumes and coats which had previously been priced at up to £19 but were now on sale for 36 shillings (£1.80). The great attraction was that only nine coupons were required for each garment. One lady commented that "Y'ken it's no the money, it's the coupons", while another said "This just shows how hard up we are for coupons".

Although the sale opened at 9.00 am there were sizeable numbers waiting by 4.00 am, some of whom had come from Kirkcaldy and Arbroath. Even in Kirriemuir the first buses into Dundee were crowded. So many people arrived that around six hundred customers were disappointed even though some were present before 9.00am. The Courier reported that "Only two men were seen in the queue and they vanished before they got to the door".

Goods were still in short supply and in July 1948 the availability of men's flannel trousers at D. M. Browns generated a queue of over two hundred customers. On 22 September 1948 over four hundred eager customers crowded into the store to see the first post war fashion show put on by the firm.

All in all, 1948 was a year of change for the company and no more so than when Robert McEwan retired at the age of 81 as Chairman and then became the new Managing Director.

As post war conditions eased, commercial activity increased. This engendered a greater sense of confidence and in February 1949 the firm held its first post war dance in Kidd's Rooms with around four hundred present. The guests were entertained by Robert Wilson, a famous Scots singer of the time, who brought along sixteen members of his company who were appearing with him at the Palace Theatre.

In the early 1950s many aspects of the store differed little from the 1930s. Much of D. M.'s publicity was still themed around their restaurants with advertisements commencing "You will enjoy Lunch and Tea at D. M. Browns" or "Lunch and tea are delightful at D. M. Brown's - The store that satisfies". The meetings of the Soroptimists and the local Liberal party continued in the restaurant just as they had throughout the previous two decades.

When on 5 June 1951 D. M. Brown's cricket team was beaten by a team from Justices at a match held in Lochee Park it seemed that things were back to normal. But nothing could have been further from the truth, for the very next year D. M. Browns was acquired by the House of Fraser Group.

The Fraser group could be traced back to 1849 and the foundation by Hugh Fraser and James Arthur of a small drapers shop in Glasgow's Argyle Street. The company had an aggressive expansion policy and from its home in Glasgow Frasers had developed until it was the owner of a large number of department stores throughout Scotland. Initially the business was still carried on under the D. M. Brown title.

Fraser's intention was clearly to develop the business as on 20 November 1952 they acquired 70/74 Commercial Street from Boots for an extension to their premises. In December they reopened the carpet department that had been closed since the start of World War Two. This meant additional staff and in 1953 when James D. Findlay was appointed as manager there were enough employees to generate an attendance of three hundred and fifty at a staff dance in Kidd's Rooms.

Refreshing the public image of the firm was a constant task and in February 1954 the company undertook more alterations. These involved the removal of the much vaunted arcade created in 1906 so as to provide more floor-space and the installation of "a door-less entrance using curtains of hot air projected from floor and ceiling". Their publicity made it clear that at that time there were only two other examples of this technology in Europe and none in Scotland. The novelty of this inspired a Mrs. Dempster to camp overnight outside the store so that she could be the first in Scotland to experience this new wonder.

Working in D. M. Brown's in the 1950s
In many ways D. M. Browns was in its prime in the 1950s and the experience of two people who worked in the store at that time gives a vivid idea of what it was like to work in the store.

The first of these was Mr Ian Brown (no relation) who worked in the store from 1950 to 1957 as a sales assistant in the menswear department. He recalls that "every sales assistant was given a number and an account book in which they recorded their sales and from which receipts were given. Mine was E52". He worked on the ground floor of the shop and at 95 was still enthusiastic about the experience of working in the store. When asked about what it was like to work there he immediately replied, "It was exactly like the TV series "Are you being served".

Ian recalls that "everybody's boss" was "old Mr Fyffe" who could frequently be seen coming and going from the store - a small slight figure usually wearing a dark brown coat with an astrakhan collar. The company still took a paternalistic approach to their employees and staff dances regularly took place in Kidd's Rooms in in Lindsay Street. On one occasion there was an outing to Glasgow to see the Ivor Novello musical King's Rhapsody.

The managing director at that time was a Mr. Hunter who was well liked. His successor Mr. Findlay was thought by the staff to be rather stiff and aloof, but his son was much more popular. He was a slim and elegant man whose brown hair with shades of grey were thought by the female staff to be rather distinguished.

The men's outfitting department, where Mr. Brown worked, was located on the ground floor and had a separate entrance facing Castle Street. Mr. Bob Nairn, who was in charge at the time, later opened his own men's dress hire store at the top of Castle Street.

Ian started work in the morning at around 8.30am entering the shop through a pend, which led to a door at the back of the store, and via the reception and dispatch of goods area. The store opened at 9.00 and all members of staff had to be in position by 8.55am.

The store closed at 6.00pm after which general tidying and adding up could take him until 6.30 or to 7.00pm on a Saturday night. On Hogmanay it was often eight o'clock before he could get away. But that was the job.

Most goods were displayed in glass display cases and counters from which they were extracted to show to interested customers. There was a stair to a lower floor where all kinds of working clothes could be bought. This area was later rented out to Joseph May, a Leeds firm (later to become Maenson Clothes Ltd). There were also shops within the store where floor space was rented by Singer, the sewing machine company, and Lotus Shoes.

A stair at the back of the department led to the furniture department on an upper floor. On the stair were bay windows opening on to Rankine's Court which dated back to the early days of the business. Ian particularly recalls the restaurants in D. M. Browns – then called the Pillar Room and the Parlour Room, the latter of which he recalls as being like a gentlemen's club with two fireplaces.

Perhaps his fondest memories of his time working for DM's, were of the people who worked alongside him. There were many characters working in the store, including a Mr.Ballantyne, who was the oldest member of staff having joined the company just after the First World War. Mr Brown recalls him as being careful and polite, and that he always gave good service to the customers. He was "really one of the old school". He also recalls that the lady who ran the restaurant, although in her 70s, still wore high heels to work. He also recalled a brassy blonde in the haberdashery department who. when asked by a handsome male customer "Is this where I get felt" responded by saying " If it is up to me you will".

They must have had a somewhat mischievous personnel officer for Mrs Pottie and Mrs Kettle worked in the same department. There was also a Mr Walker who was the floor-walker. He, like Mr Peacock in the television series "Are you being served", wore striped trousers and a dark jacket with a red carnation in his buttonhole. Among his duties was the welcoming of customers into the store

Another with memories of working in D. M. Browns was May Strachan who started work there straight from school at the age of fifteen. Like all their young recruits she started working in the basement stockroom. After some days Mr Fyffe appeared to tell her that she would be assigned to the mantle (ladies fashion) department and she was given her sales number - 205 - which would stay with her throughout her employment in the store.

At that time it was the rule that assistants had to be at least five feet six inches in height so that they could easily help customers on with coats. It was also essential to be completely dressed in black although a white lace fringe around the neck was acceptable. She recalls that every counter was provided with a seat for customers. Her immediate boss was the head buyer – a Mrs Donaldson - who was very strict with her staff.

The fashion department was a large one and customers were very much treated on an individual basis. On busy Saturdays this sometimes resulted in waiting customers sitting on a row of chairs set down along the middle of the department. Clothes were individually fitted and the tailors, who were employed to make alterations and were located on an upper floor, were treated like gods.

The tea rooms were an important part of the store and models were employed to walk through showing off currently fashionable dresses. Ladies who had afternoon tea were invariably dressed up for the occasion. Surprisingly May recalls that in the 1950s the Dundee FC football team including Ian Ure and Billy Steele would visit the restaurant for tea

The Last Change of Name

Throughout the 1950s and 1960s Frasers continued to operate the store under the D. M. Brown logo but in 1972 they decided to change the name of the store to Arnotts. It was hard to see the commercial logic for this. The name Arnotts commemorated a Dublin entrepreneur of the 19th century who had absolutely no links to Dundee. Nevertheless with this arbitrary act the name of D. M. Brown was forever lost to the city.

In 2002 Frasers closed the store and the premises were vacant for a while before being redeveloped in 2003

D. M. Browns is now just a memory and yet something still remains. When in 2003 the former D. M. Brown building was to be redeveloped the new owners, Dawn Developments, were required to keep not only the A listed façade, but also the Edwardian Tea Rooms and Art Deco Rooms located above the pend in Rankine's Court. They are still there, a relic of the time when locally owned department stores were at the forefront of shopping in Dundee.

Former D M Brown Store

Alexander Caird & Sons

The founder of what was to become one of Dundee's most prestigious retailing firms was Alexander Caird, who was born in 1854 and started his career working as a tenter in Baxter Brothers jute mill. He found the dusty atmosphere affected his health and so he decided that he would become what was then known as a "packie", walking on foot with a pack on his back to sell textile goods. Certainly this was an occupation where he would have fresh air in plenty.

To start with the goods that he sold consisted chiefly of collarless shirts and household linen that were made by his wife Jean. Initially, he walked from Dundee with his pack upon his back around those areas of Angus and Perthshire that were within his daily reach from Dundee

However, he was very successful in his enterprise and it soon became apparent that the demand for his goods was such that the pack he carried was quite inadequate. He therefore acquired a pony and trap that enabled him to take more goods on his rural round.

The use of a pony and trap also greatly increased the range of his operations, and before long he began to visit places as far away as Kirkmichael, Blair Atholl, Braemar, Pitlochry, and Glenshee, often staying away overnight. Alexander was a natural salesman and his success continued. A contemporary comment was that "Caird's dear, but guid", and such was the demand for his goods that he soon had to invest in a large horse van.

During this period his family was expanded by the birth of his first two sons - Alexander Jnr and Thomas W. Caird. When his oldest son, Alexander Jnr, reached working age Caird sent him to work in Glasgow as an apprentice tailor and cutter. After Alexander Jnr. qualified and returned to the business, the younger son, Thomas, was sent to train in Draffen and Jarvies who were then a prominent

firm in Dundee. His apprenticeship completed, he too joined his father's firm. Caird was to have three more sons – James and Alfred, who later were to play a substantial part in the business, Harry who did not join the business but became a chemist, and a daughter Jean who, like Harry, did not enter the family firm.

With four of the Caird family now involved a permanent base was required for their operations. So in 1878, together with his sons, Alexander set up in business as a men's outfitters at 46 Union Street Dundee under the title Alexander Caird & Sons, Tailors, Hosiers and Hatters. Up until this time he had not advertised in the local press but by Christmas that year he had begun to place regular adverts in the Courier giving details of his stocks of silk scarves, silk handkerchiefs and fancy woollen vests.

However, the fact that Alexander Snr. now had a Dundee store in a good location did not mean that he had lost sight of the rural sales that had enabled the firm to grow. Thus it was that while Alexander Jnr. sat and made shirts in the shop in Union Street, his father and his brother Thomas continued their rural travels. The firm increased its sales by providing a service where goods could be bought and paid for at a rate of one shilling per week - an early form of hire purchase.

The First World War
During the First World War Cairds continued to prosper. His son James joined the forces while his third son Alfred entered the family firm in 1915. By this time the business had grown to the point where more space was essential. The result was the acquisition of a new and larger shop at 17, Reform Street. This was to be a permanent and happy location for their burgeoning enterprise. In the first year in their new premises turnover was to double, with sales at just over £1,000. The following two years saw a more gradual growth of revenues to £1,100. By contrast, sales from their country travels contributed over £7,000 in 1915, and reached over £11,000 in 1917.

James was invalided out of the forces and rejoined the family business in 1917. The firm then decided to venture further afield and opened a shop in Perth High Street. This was to be one of Cairds' most successful ventures. For many years, while the Dundee shop concentrated on the higher end of the market, the Perth business, which was managed by Thomas, focussed on the manufacture and sale of working clothes and the country rounds. These rural sales rounds were to continue until 1937 as an important part of the company's activities. Cairds' sales in Perth continued to grow to the point where they eventually became larger than that in Dundee - a situation that was to persist until the 1950s.

After the end of World War One Cairds needed more space in both Dundee and Perth. This would need more money and as a consequence, in 1919, the partners decided to launch their business as a private limited company with a capital of £10,000. In 1923 they gained a building warrant for the reconstruction of their Dundee premises which at this time was concentrating heavily on highland dress, tweeds and boys clothes. However it was not until 1927 that they finally carried out what were described in the press as "interesting" extensions to their Reform Street premises. These were completed in September and the reopening of the shop was reported in the Courier as follows:-

"The ground flat has been brightly decorated in light oak with an oak floor and panelling, the front shop being devoted to hats, ties and handkerchiefs and the back to the men's department. A wide oak staircase leads to the first floor to which the boys de-partment has been removed from the basement. Customers can also see a demonstration of the knitting of Braemar jerseys."

Given their new and enlarged premises it was not surprising that when, in 1927 the traders of Reform Street got together to produce a promotional brochure entitled "The Romance of Reform Street" Cairds were the only business to have a double page spread.

The extensions to the Dundee store were very successful in bringing in customers, to the point where it was again necessary to look for ways of expanding the shop. Accordingly in May 1928 they acquired the adjacent premises of the rival clothiers James Robertson at 23 Reform Street. They also expanded their operations upwards into the four floors above their existing ground floor shop.

However time was taking its inevitable toll and in 1928 Alexander Caird Snr. retired and moved to Meigle. Despite this the company was still seeking to expand their business. This time they looked south of the Tay and opened a new store in St Andrews, Fife. This was to be managed by Alexander Jnr.

They also decided there were other prospects for selling their products and in December 1930 Cairds were successful in winning the contract for the supply of uniforms, oilskins and boots to the Dundee Fire Brigade. They were to retain this contract for the next four years.

It was not only in Dundee that things were going well: the continuing success of the Perth branch of the company meant that more space was also needed there. The company therefore decided to acquire the three storey commercial and residential premises adjacent to their shop in High Street, Perth. The newly extended shop, which was to be managed by James W. Caird, opened in time for Christmas 1931. The new three-storey sandstone faced building featured a substantial arcade at ground level and a new entrance finished in bronze with pearl granite dadoes. Cairds earned great praise locally for developing such a substantial building in the midst of a severe economic depression.

In 1933 Thomas Spence Caird, the son of Thomas W. Caird, joined the firm at the age of 18. June 1934 saw Cairds embark upon a major alteration of their premises at 17/23 Reform Street. Interestingly for a company that up until then had always advertised itself as a men's outfitters Cairds boasted that the building had been extended to "devote more space to the dress requirements of their feminine customers and that the furnishings had been chosen to accord with feminine taste". However, they also pointed out that "The Highland department has also been extended where Cairds have a comprehensive range of Highland Dress wear".

In 1935 the founder of the company, Alexander Caird Snr died, and James Caird and Alfred G. Caird were appointed to the board. The new board took a time to consider the way forward and then in August 1937 Cairds commenced another major update of its Dundee store. This was designed by the Dundee architect William Wilson who, it turned out, had to deal with some unforeseen complications. These occurred because during building operations the contractor encountered the remains of the ridge of rock that had once run across Reform Street. The result was that fully six feet of stone had to be removed to attain the basement levels. The updated store opened on 5th September 1938 and a feature of the alterations was the creation of a new ladies department.

The Courier was very impressed and reported that:- "The front, with its twin arcades framed in three varieties of Aberdeen Granite - grey, dark grey and pearl - enhances the appearance of Reform Street as a shopping centre". It also noted "that a central heating system will replace the old arrangement of gas and electric fires".

In 1938, as the shadows of war began to loom, Alexander's grandson, William Small Caird, joined the company.

The Second World War

Like all other companies Cairds was affected by the conscription of staff and indeed, of family members working with the company. Thomas Spence Caird was called up and served in the 51st Highland Division in Sierra Leone, France and Germany, rising to the rank of Major. William Small Caird saw service in the Parachute Regiment in Norway and Arnhem, returning to the family business in 1946.

Despite this, the imposition of clothes rationing in 1941, and a lack of goods to sell, business went on. The stringency of wartime conditions was highlighted by an incident in the Dundee store. In November 1944 the theft by one of Cairds' shop porters of 1,400 clothing coupons resulted in six months in jail for the culprit.

During the Second World War the accommodation above the shop premises on the 3rd floor was made available for "The Officers' Club" - open in the evenings to all officers of the Armed Forces, and a place where they could meet socially local middle class ladies in their 20s or 30s. It was all very respectable and mothers had no fears for their daughters!

Post war

In the 1950s, after weathering the austerity of the immediate post war period, the firm began a strong period of growth that was to carry on right through to the 1970s.

Their initial moves were small in scale and they first decided to make better use of the property that they already owned in Reform Street. In 1946 when Stewarts the hairdressers on the other side

Cairds - Reform Street in the 1940's   D C Thomson

of Reform Street closed down, Cairds, to the relief of Stewarts' male customers, decided to convert their top floor into a hairdressing salon with eight chairs for men and five for ladies. This arrangement

continued until the closure of Cairds when some 4 or 5 hairdressers and the receptionist, who had all originally been with Stewarts, were given accommodation on the first floor of Winters in Dock Street lasting for a few years.

At this time Cairds sold a range of school uniforms and in a curious incident in November 1947 an unnamed miscreant broke into the Reform Street premises ignored the general stock and the safe but stole ten Harris Academy caps and nothing else!

In 1949 Alexander Caird Jnr. and Thomas W. Caird retired, and William S. Caird and Thomas S. Caird were appointed as Directors. In the early 1950s William Caird's brother, Gordon who was a Chartered Accountant, and Alfred's son Forbes, entered the firm.

Perhaps because of this there were signs that the company was looking further afield for business. In December 1950 they signed up for a Scottish trade exhibition touring Canada and USA. As part of their exhibit the company ordered a model of a Scotsman from Holland of all places. The result was somewhat less than satisfactory. They complained that the model that they were sent was "nothing but a replica of a continental spiv". This occurred somewhat late in the day, but fortunately Duncan of Jordanstone College of Art came to the rescue with a more acceptable model.

In the same year Cairds looked across the Tay and acquired a small shop in St Andrews owned by J. C. Smith. Following alterations the premises were opened with Alexander (Sandy) W. Caird as Manager. The shop was a great success and by 1959 its takings had risen sevenfold.

Success for Cairds was not confined to their Fife enterprise. Their store in Dundee was doing particularly well. The January sale in 1950 attracted a queue of over two hundred waiting to get into the shop where four guinea check waistcoats could be had for one pound. By the time that the January 1952 sale took place there were over four hundred impatient customers waiting to be admitted. More sales meant more staff and at their 70th anniversary dinner and dance held in Kidd's Rooms in 1952 there were over two hundred and sixty guests present.

As the 1950s went on, business continued to improve, and in 1953 Cairds ventured north and established a new store in Elgin. This was to be managed by Forbes, an outgoing man, who became very involved with the local community and eventually became a member of Elgin Town Council. The Elgin operation was so successful that in 1959

Cairds bought premises at 82 High Street in order to create a Men's and Boy's department and a special section for teenagers.

Earlier, in 1954, Alfred G. Caird had died. When, in 1957, James W. Caird retired their respective sons, Forbes W. Caird and Sandy Caird became directors of the company.

In 1959 the Perth Store organised a Fashion Parade focussing on Fashion, Nightwear, and Corsetry, featuring as models staff from their Aberdeen store. The Courier noted that between nine hundred and one thousand women and two men turned up for the show. Style Parades were also organised in the store to show off Cairds' range of menswear.

In the late 1950s the company had a lively social club that organised outings to Glasgow shows, and held staff dances in Gray's Rooms. It even held golf matches with the employees of other stores, and put up the Caird trophy as a prize. Management still seemed to have a hand in these matters as evidenced by a note in the staff newsletter that stated, "The organisation of the forthcoming staff dance in February is now under way. Mr William has found it necessary to crush some wild schemes originated by the organisers".

If the 1950s were good for the company the 1960s were even better. Cairds had set the scene in 1959 when they had negotiated an arrangement with D. W. Meldrum, who had the adjacent shop, to acquire the three floors that lay above Meldrum's shop and, in due course, the shop itself. They also acquired the business of the furriers Arthur A. Miller, one of their neighbours in Reform Street.

In 1960 they completely gutted and refitted the properties to create space for a new fur and gown department and also took the opportunity to increase space for their tailoring operations. It was a mark of the size of the market in which Cairds were now operating that after the new premises were open Cairds had eleven staff working with furs and provided summer storage facilities for over two thousand fur coats.

In 1963, as a springboard for further expansion, Cairds became a public company and doubled their capital base. This enabled them to acquire the premises of Henderson and McKay in Whitehall Street, Dundee. There they established a new branch of the business by setting up Cairdsport. Surprisingly the shop boasted its own (very) small dry ski slope in the premises. Elsewhere in Dundee, Cairds opened a store in the new Overgate shopping centre and another in Broughty Ferry.

Encouraged by the success of their Elgin store the company looked north again and in 1964 Cairds opened a store in Inverness. They also decided to take advantage of the expanding market for skiing and outdoor pursuits in Scotland and opened Cairdsport shops in the Spittal of Glenshee and the new Highland resort of Aviemore.

In 1968 William S. Caird became the sole Managing Director. In 1971 he was succeeded by Forbes Caird, after which William acted as the Dundee store Director until he retired in 1980. W. S. Caird was a man of many and varied interests including golfing, angling, painting, chess and bowls. He was also involved with the community, becoming a Director of Dundee Repertory Theatre, Chairman of the Chamber of Commerce and a member of the board of Dundee Trustee Savings Bank.

Expansion seemed to be the main policy for Cairds at this time but not all of their initiatives worked out. In 1966 they added a major extension to their store in Perth but the larger premises were found not to be viable. In March 1970 they sold their existing store in Perth at 143-159, High Street for £225,000. It closed in August of that year when they moved to new and smaller premises at 21, High Street where, although they reduced the number of departments, they still had sections devoted to men's clothing and outfitting, ladies fashion, hosiery, and fashion accessories.

CAIRD FLAIR

A. Caird & Sons Ltd., of Reform Street, Dundee, is a family-run store with some very up-to-the-minute ideas on fashion for both men and women. It is a lively store which has become well known over the years for quality and friendly service. Caird Flair, is a feeling for fashion which is carried through every department from furs and bridal wear, to men's hairdressing and shoe departments. HONEY is a special department for the younger woman, packed with swinging fashions, and for the well-dressed man about town, the 05ive shop has a good range of international menswear.

Shoppers will also find a comprehensive selection of sports wear, sports equipment and a toy department. There are Caird's branches in Perth, St. Andrews, Elgin, Kirkcaldy and Inverness.

Caird's has been established for almost 100 years now and has seen many changes, but the good service and personal welcome extended to customers have always remained the same.

CAIRDS

Reform Street   Dundee

75

Interior of Cairds Reform Street store   *D C Thomson*

The statement made by the company explaining the reasons for the closure of the Perth premises gave a clear indication of the future direction of the business. "The Perth store was not profitable and our current policy is to extend the number of number of branches but in smaller units which are more economical and profitable". At that time they already had stores in Aberdeen, Dundee, Perth, St Andrews, Elgin and Inverness and were shortly to open another in Kirkcaldy.

By March 1969 the company was going well and had become very large. Its fashion buyer Betty Kennedy was being sent as far abroad as Copenhagen and was giving the fashion tip for the year - trouser suits and cat suits for evening wear. In 1970 the Courier described the Honey Boutique that Cairds had set up in their Dundee store as "packed with swinging fashions".

The 1970s were a time of change for the Cairds business. In 1971 the firm embarked on another programme of expansion – this time in the north and the west of Scotland. In 1972 a new store was opened in Oban and very next year a second shop was opened in Inverness as well as a new shop in Troon. Meanwhile Cairds undertook a major modernisation of their store in Reform Street.

Cairds Sports, Glenshee

Cairdsport

The 1970s also saw the emergence of Cairdsport from under the wing of the parent company. Although it started as a part of the Caird business, Cairdsport was very much the child of Alexander (Sandy) Caird. Born in Perth in 1930, his two years' national service took him to Austria where he had a spell with the Artists Rifles, a part of the 21st Special Air Service (SAS) regiment

On his return to Scotland, Sandy helped run the family stores, initially in St Andrews, later in Perth and Dundee. In the mid-1960s, foreseeing the potential for winter sports in Scotland, he opened the Cairdsport shops and ski schools at the Spittal of Glen-shee. More importantly he was the man who brought the first ski shop and ski school to the fledging ski resort of Aviemore and was regarded as one of the founding fathers of the Scottish ski industry.

In October 1970 Sandy bought Cairdsport from the family firm, and it was not long after that the business really took off - thanks to what he later referred to as a "diabolical" snowfall that year. Skiers from all over the UK descended on Aviemore and once a few stars had been photographed sipping pints in the local pubs Cairdsport was on a firm basis.

At its height, Cairdsport had 35 full-time ski instructors and dozens of part-time ones and rented out hundreds of pairs of skis and boots a day. Sandy was assisted by Derek Brightman, his friend and co-director who was an accomplished Alpine skier. To ensure year-round employment for the staff, they set up a sailing school and out-door activity centre on Loch Morlich.

In 1994 Sandy sold his interest in Cairdsport. From then on he occupied himself with serving his various charities and going fishing, golfing, sailing, and above all walking. He served on the Cairngorm Mountain Trust, the Aviemore and Spey Valley Tourist Board, the Cairngorm Recreational Trust, the Badaguish Outdoor Centre in the Cairngorm National Park, and the Crossroads charity, which supports care workers. Sandy died in 2008.

Demise

In January 1980 William Small Caird retired and in June of the following year there was speculation that the Cairds Reform Street store employing almost 90 people was to be closed, at least in part. In response Cairds indicated that they were intending to sell off part of their Reform Street premises and four months later announced that the southern half of their building had been sold to the Bank of Scotland. This followed the announcement of the closure of the Caird store in Troon and was a part of the general retrenchment of the business.

However, in spite of this Cairds continued to be in a financially precarious position. In June 1982 Cairds announced that they were to sell a 37% share in the firm to Parque Investments, a firm based in London. In April 1983, Christopher Parker of Parque Investments took over as Managing Director from F. W. Caird. Matters did not improve and in March 1984 Parker was forced to deny that he was in negotiations with Sir Hugh Fraser relating to a takeover of the firm.

In the way of these things it was not altogether surprising, that on 12 July 1984, Harrods Stores under the direction of Sir Hugh Fraser acquired the main Caird business for £500,000. The only exception was the Sports Locker. Cairds was wound up as company on 19 July 1984.

What was surprising was that less than two years later, in March 1986, Fraser attempted to sell all the stores as a going concern. There were no buyers and in May 1986 the Reform Street store closed. On 6 June 1986 Sir Hugh Fraser announced the closure of the remaining Cairds stores. He explained that "all the stores were losing money when I bought them in 1984" and went on to say that matters had worsened since that date. With these closures the Caird business, established over a century before, came to an end.

Postscript

Strangely, a belated epitaph for the company, so long a part of Dundee's shopping scene, appeared in the Daily Record of 11 September 2013. It is set out below.

"Howard Renwick started wearing his cosy red socks which had been bought in Cairds when he was just 12. Now 55 years on he's still using them for hillwalking and metal-detecting expeditions. The sturdy red sports socks have seen service on the school hockey pitch, hillwalking trips and metal-detecting expeditions. Howard, 67, fills them with presents for his grown-up kids every Christmas.

Howard, of Dundee, said: "They're very much part of the family. I don't think they've ever been repaired. I have no idea how or why they've lasted so long. They've ruined quite a few sets of underwear, white shirts and T-shirts over the years and they're not allowed near the washing machine any more. I wash them carefully by hand, which is maybe the reason they've lasted so long.

They've never even been near a darning needle since my mother bought them from Cairds Haberdashers back in the 50s."

As the founder Alexander Caird might well have said, "Quality always counts."

When a Scotsman wants to look his best . . .

He wears the one form of dress which is admirable for every occasion. Scotsmen throughout Britain have come to rely on Cairds for the finest quality Highland Dress (both Day and Evening wear) hand made by experts in the finest traditions of Scottish Craftsmanship

THE COMPLETE FAMILY OUTFITTERS

REFORM STREET, DUNDEE

Also at PERTH, ST ANDREWS and ELGIN

Cooper & MacKenzie

This business was founded in 1874 by Adams and Cushnie who were both potato merchants, and who jointly employed a working tailor to make clothes, kilts and highland wear for them and their families. When Cushnie retired, the firm developed a tailoring side to their business. They then traded in the dual role of tailors and potato merchants, under the name of J. D. Adams and Company. Eventually it was decided that the future prosperity of the company lay in the tailoring and highland wear, and in 1884 in pursuance of this aim the company acquired premises at 42, Reform Street.

In 1895 the firm was taken over by J. D. Mitchell who had been head cutter with J. D. Adams up to the time of Adam's death. At this time Reform Street was the 'Saville Row of Dundee', with well over a dozen tailors businesses situated in various locations on either side of the street. At that time

*"**KAYDEE**" Caps designed by Cooper & McKenzie*

working tailors could be viewed going to work suitably clad in morning tails and silk hats! But Mitchell, who had been born in Alyth, had always been more interested in the Dundee community than in silk hats, and in August 1898 the company made donations of clothing to the disadvantaged children at Baldovan School.

When, in April 1924, J. D. Mitchell died, David Henderson Mitchell took over the business and, in 1946, made a bold move by successfully concluding the purchase of the well-known Dundee furrier George Cooper at 43, Reform Street, thereby greatly enlarging the shop. A limited company was formed and the Cooper and McKenzie name we know today was adopted as its title.

Competition was intense in the postwar period and at that time there were as many as 44 tailoring and outfitting shops in and around the city. Of these at least 12 still had a hand-made facility for the making of suits on the premises. But things were changing and there was an increase in the popularity of ready to wear clothes, in which speed of delivery was of prime importance. Cooper and McKenzie set out to make the radical changes necessary to accommodate the increased demand for made to measure clothing. David Melville Henderson Mitchell joined the company in 1949, and his ability to combine tailoring skills with entrepreneurial awareness saw him mastermind the transition of Cooper and McKenzie into a powerful retail operation.

In 1978 Grant Mitchell joined his father in the company to learn the trade. In 1985 he won a Travelling Scholarship funded by the Mens Trade Association which gave him the opportunity to spend a month in the U.S.A. In New York, Los Angeles and San Francisco, he witnessed a form of retailing in which stores were successfully utilising secondary sites, often one or two levels above the street but still situated within a stone's throw of internationally renowned stores and newly created shopping malls. He also found that the American retailers were dynamic and exciting, full of new ideas, and overflowing with enthusiasm about their marketing skills!

Grant found all this enthusiasm for change very infectious, but he returned to a retailing scene where many shops were moving to out-of-centre locations and many city centre shops were closing. Standing still was not an option. But any plans for continued growth were being hindered through a lack of space!

In 1994 an ambitious £1.5 million expansion plan was instigated, with the purchase of the entire six floors of the block in which they traded. A complete gutting and refurbishment of the entire premises saw an impressive large first floor showroom being opened which included a greatly extended, and modern, highland section.

The original main retail floor was reconstructed incorporating a modern open plan layout and the lower basement floor was extended. A suite of offices on the second floor was demolished to facilitate the creation of a 1,500 square feet state of the art warehouse. A modern alteration workroom containing the very latest in modern sewing machinery was also created as part of the scheme.

The result was over 7,000 square feet of fully modernised, comfortable air-conditioned surroundings located a few minutes stroll away from the City Square and the bustle of the Overgate Shopping Centre!

In 2004 the company's progressive approach was recognised when it was awarded the inaugural prize of Most Professional Buyers at the Independent Menswear Company Awards. Innovator and survivor the company continues to operate in its city centre location some 140 years after the firm was first set up.

Joseph Sawiamiak and David Mitchell

Dundee Eastern Co-operative Society

D E C S - Seagate Store

The Dundee Eastern Co-operative Society (DECS) was, for a time, the largest retailer in the city. Its store in the Seagate was a very large and popular department store, with around twenty departments and a well patronised restaurant. It was also the management centre for a large number of branches located throughout the city.

However, the story of DECS is a rather complicated one that cannot be understood without a brief account of the history of the co-operative movement in Britain and in Dundee.

The co-operative movement started in 1844 when a group of artisans established a small profit-sharing co-operative store in Rochdale. Whilst this was not the first Co-op it did set the rules for future co-operative retail stores: open membership, member control, political and religious neutrality, profit sharing related to purchases made from the society.

The movement grew, and in 1863 some 300 cooperative societies combined to found the North of England Co-operative Agency and Depot Society. This eventually became the Cooperative Wholesale Society (CWS). The CWS supplied cooperative societies and stores but did not initially carry out any retailing itself.

The Scottish Co-operative Wholesale Society (SCWS) was formed in 1868 for the purpose of purchasing or manufacturing goods for supply to local co-operative retail societies. In 1873 it became a partner with the CWS in establishing a surprisingly wide range of co-operative ventures. These included grain mills, timber suppliers, a tea plantation in Ceylon, and a factory complex in Glasgow which produced a wide range of foods, furniture, clothing and metalware.

As time went by the SCWS moved into direct retailing, and either opened local branches or took over existing local co-operative societies.

Dundee

Although co-operative shops and stores soon began to be opened throughout Scotland, in Dundee the development of co-operative shopping was somewhat slower than might have been expected. By 1867 when Dundee had only one short unsuccessful experiment Angus could boast at least ten societies in operation. In July 1873 the Dundee Co-operative Association was set up and in December of the same year the Dundee Co-operative Fishing Association was initiated. However, the first of these was closed down in the early 1880s whilst the second only survived for twelve months.

The prospect for co-operative shops began to look up when, in November 1873, the Dundee Eastern Co-operative Society opened their first shop in Erskine Street. At that time they had 89 members and a share capital of only £84.00. Nevertheless the shop prospered and so in November 1875 the DECS opened a second shop this time in Ann Street. By this time the DECS had increased the number of members to 205 and their share capital to £305 and decided to appoint a General Manager in the shape of William Phillips.

Many Dundonians will remember that the great attraction of the DECS was "the divi", or dividend, that was paid in respect of all purchases made in the DECS shops. This could only be obtained if you were a member and registered at the store in which you shopped. All members had a divi book and on entering the shop this would be placed in a box on the top of a pile of divi books belonging to shoppers who had arrived earlier. The shop assistant took the bottom book out before serving the customer, thereby ensuring that everybody got their proper turn. There were rows of chairs provided to ease the legs of weary shoppers while they waited to be served. This was all a little bureaucratic but for many families the dividend was a great attraction, as with its twice yearly payments it was found to be an ideal way of saving for Christmas, summer holidays, or for particularly expensive goods.

This idea proved to be a great success and growth was rapid. By 1878 the DECS had 565 members and share capital of £671. Thereafter things proceeded more slowly, but by 20 February 1885, when DECS held a public meeting in the Weavers Hall to test the possibility of opening a shop in Lochee, they had over £1,000 in the bank. The store was duly opened and two years later DECS opened a Boot Department in Victoria Road. In 1897 business had increased to the point that they decided they had to open their own bakery at Kings Cross.

By the end of the century the DECS had enough members to hold annual sports meetings where competitors could take part in races, the high jump and throwing the cricket ball competitions. They even held a five a side football tournament and were running their own football team –the Ardmore Strollers. In 1900 they started up the Arnhall Swimming Club, although this was also open to those who were not co-operative members.

Expansion continued in the period up to the start of the First World War. By 1902 the DECS had 15 shops and extensive bakery premises and were looking to expand further. Two years later their properties included twenty shops, a bakery and an office in Albert Square. On 27 October 1904 the DECS placed an advert in the press that all working families could now buy their household requirements at their new store in Brook Street, Broughty Ferry. They also pointed out that on payment of 1/3d, anyone could become members and participate fully in the profits of the business. By April 1905 additional stores had been built in Broughty Ferry and Milnbank Road and a site for a new shop had been acquired at the corner of Hilltown and North George Street.

The DECS had by now become a very large business and in 1913 decided to establish a central office and store in the Seagate. This included their first drapery department and a new head office.

Competition and Controversy

The Scottish Co-operative Wholesale Society was Glasgow based and did not have a local depot. As a consequence the DECS started to acquire its goods from other firms. From early on this led to considerable antagonism between the DECS and the SCWS. This became open hostility when the SCWS decided to support the creation of other co-operatives in Dundee.

It first became involved in the establishment of the Dundee West Co-operative Society but this failed in 1881. The cause according to the SCWS was "the imbecility of the management committee who had allowed themselves to become mere tools in the hands of a manager who ruled supreme." This was followed two years later by the failure of the Broughty Ferry Co-operative Society in which the SCWS had also become involved.

The SCWS then decided to open its own stores in the city thus setting themselves in direct competition with the DECS. The first SCWS store to appear was a shop that opened in Trades Lane in July 1882 and this turned out to be a great success. This intensified the bad feeling between the SCWS and the DECS and on 20 January 1897 the SCWS in a public meeting in Dundee condemned the activities of DECS as "spurious co-operation". In March 1897 this resulted in a total parting of the ways between the two co-operative organisations, with the SCWS deciding that it was no longer willing to supply goods to the DECS.

It did however, supply goods to the rival City of Dundee Co-operative Society that was established in 1897. This was very successful and by 1914 had twelve shops and a bakery. It also had a children's choir, ran outings, produced its own newspaper and provided educational classes.

In 1906 the SCWS suffered a setback in Dundee when their Trades Lane premises were gutted by a fire that had started in the bonded whisky warehouse situated next door. It is a measure of the bad feeling between the two organisations that, over a quarter of a century later, the DECS in a publication celebrating their Jubilee in 1933, commented that "the Wholesale paid the penalty of its evil association, for in 1906 a fire destroyed completely their building."

The First World War

While, during the First World War both co-operative societies continued to expand, the success of the DECS was much the greater. When in February 1915 William Phillips, the general manager, retired he could look back on a period when he had presided over a considerable growth in the DECS which was now one of the largest in England and Scotland. It was a mark of his success that the DECS, not the most open handed of organisations, felt that they could pay a salary of some £400 to Phillips' successor, Mr William Crooks.

The DECS could not of course isolate itself from the effects of the war. When in 1916 the Government increased taxes, the DECS had to find an additional £1,600 and had to reduce the level of the dividend from three shillings and a penny in the pound to two shillings and tenpence. This caused great controversy among the members but matters became even worse when in November 1917 the dividend was reduced to two shillings in the pound. By the end of the war the dividend had been further reduced to one shilling and a penny.

The war also brought management problems for the DECS and there were a number of instances in this period when doubts were raised by members as to whether the elected committee, or its permanent officials, ran the business, In addition the DECS also had to deal with absence of the 148 DECS staff who had enlisted and of whom 15 were killed and 26 wounded. Its efforts to cope with this were not helped by the anti-feminism of the Society's management which strongly resisted the employment of women to fill wartime vacancies.

The interwar period

At the end of the war the DECS like all the other stores in Dundee had the task of re-accommodating the staff who had served in the forces but this was soon dealt with. The DECS then embarked upon a period of growth much of which consisted of new branches, some within the inner parts of the city and some located to serve the spreading suburbs of Dundee.

The DECS also widened their field of operations. In 1920 they decided to start selling furniture and in March 1925 the DECS bought a four storey tenement plus a double and single shops at 264 Hillltown in which they created a shoe shop and a drapery department. In the same year they opened a drapery branch in High Street, Lochee.

A major expansion and the elimination of a rival concern occurred in 1926 when the City of Dundee Co-operative Society was taken over by the DECS. By this acquisition the DECS acquired branches in Princes Street, Hawkhill and Strathmartine Road. At the subsequent Annual General Meeting the Society demonstrated both its economical approach and its democratic management credentials by narrowly defeating a proposal to increase the general manager's salary from £900 to £1000.

The following year saw more property acquired for new shops at 73 Nethergate, 83 Albert Street, and, in a move out of town, in Invergowrie. This programme of expansion meant that by 1928 the numbers of members had grown so great that it was necessary to hire the Caird Hall for the DECS half-yearly meeting.

Another branch was opened in 1929, this time at Strathmore Avenue, where a smart new building housed a grocery, butchery, bakery, and a confectionery section. This was followed by a major expansion of the DECS central store in 1930 when the Society took over the adjoining Fairweather Tobacco Factory premises, and in 1932, another modern store was opened at the junction of Clepington Road and Caird Avenue. In 1933 they commenced daily milk deliveries.

DECS - Clepington Road Branch   D C Thomson

By 1933, the Society's Jubilee year, the DECS could look back with some satisfaction. From starting in 1873 with virtually nothing, they had created the largest retailing business in the City, and between 1927 and 1933 they had increased their sales from £463,000 to over £1,000,000.

The Second World War

During the Second World War there was a pause in any major advances by the co-operative movement in the UK but the English based CWS became deeply involved in sourcing overseas goods for UK consumers and in manufacturing wartime goods.

However, the antagonism between the DECS and the SCWS had not gone away and in 1939 the SCWS opened a number of branches in Dundee so as to compete head to head with the DECS. Most notably in 1940 they opened a major store in the Cowgate extending to some 14,000 square feet. This was to be managed jointly by their Edinburgh and Dundee offices and was to be their main store in the city centre. The store incorporated departments dealing with footware, hardware, drapery, and house furnishings. This was a substantial modern store externally finished in black pearl granite and stainless steel.

During this time the CWS began planning for the future as even then those who ran the business could see the potential disruption to the retail market that the new multiple grocers could have in the future. In 1944 the CWS published a report entitled 'Policy and Programme for Post War Development' which focused on methods for revitalising the co-operative movement after the war had ended. The report suggested merging the CWS with the Scottish Co-operative Wholesale Society.

Post War

At the end of the war John Leese, the general manager of DECS, retired. He was replaced by James Fyffe who had started working with DECS in 1925. In the immediate post war period, in a period of difficult trading conditions he managed to maintain the level of the dividend at two shillings and five pence in the pound. But as the city moved into the 1950s the main task for Leese was not only to establish new branches to deal with the rapid decentralisation of Dundee's population to the peripheral housing estates, but also to ward off the threat posed by the SCWS.

By 1961 the DECs had around 1,000 staff and was involved in selling groceries, meat, boots and shoes, drapery, tailoring, hardware, floor coverings, china, cosmetics, stationery, travel goods, electrical equipment, sportswear and toys.

Whilst the SCWS now had some 26 branches in the city and an annual turnover £766,000 it began to have trading problems and had closed some of its smaller stores.

For the DECS on the other hand things seemed to be going well and in February 1962 they opened a 10,000 square feet store and bakery at Ardler and followed this two months later with a new store in Beauly Avenue in Kirkton.

However, in the wider world of retailing things were changing fast. More people had cars and were using them to travel to larger stores which was not good news for the large number of local stores operated by the DECS. The increasing need to compete and the narrowed profit margins on branded goods following the abolition of Resale Price Maintenance in 1964 meant that "the divi" had had to be progressively reduced to the point where it had lost most of its value as a marketing device.

In 1964 the DECS had come to the view that serious changes had to be made to the company if it were to keep up to date. They therefore decided in April to appoint a new manager, Mr J White, whose primary task would be to initiate a programme of modernisation of all their stores. His first announcement was that "we shall be opening a food hall at Peter Street. Prices will be keen". He also announced that DECS would be opening their first self service store and would be ceasing to bake bread on their shop premises as they would be opening up a central bakery unit.

November 1964 saw the opening of a DECS store in Charleston Drive which was to sell a curious mix of bakery goods, meat, clocks, nylons, cosmetics, hardware and gardening goods. Plans were also announced for the upgrading of the existing branches at Caird Avenue, Craigower Road, Brook Street, Broughty Ferry, Downfield, Strathearn Avenue, Balmoral Terrace and Fintry Road.

Although the DECS was clearly leaving the Dundee operations of SCWS in its wake the announcement on 14 June 1968 that the SCWS would no longer operate its 15 shops in Dundee came as something of a shock to the wider public. The SCWS spokesman said that it was hoped that the DECS would be taking over at least some of their stores. In September 1968 the DECS made its first move. It rented the SCWS store in the Cowgate with a view to its later purchase and connection to their store in the Seagate by means of a bridge at the rear of the property.

By October 1968 the DECS had taken over the former SCWS stores in Ballindean Road, Arbroath Road and Muirhead. In that month they also opened a completely new store in Balmuir and announced that their Strathmartine Road branch would become a self service store.

Their expansionist approach was maintained in 1969 when in February the DECS announced that it would cease bread production at their Clepington Road bakery and would be introducing bakery units in the Seagate and Cowgate premises. It also announced that it would be converting its store at Ardler to a supermarket and an on site bakery unit.

However it soon become clear that although much time and energy had been expended on the modernisation of the company, things were not going according to plan. In November 1969 the DECS closed its branch in Princes Street and this was followed by the closure in December of its premises in Main Street and Tannadice Street. January 1970 saw its shop in Victoria Road closed while in February and March it closed its stores in Milnbank Road, Benvie Road and Albert Street.

The DECS announced that another six stores were to be closed by 21 November 1970 and then gave out the news that it was going to merge with Scottish Co-operative Retail Services Ltd. All assets, property, and stock would be transferred to SCRS including the DECS's twenty-six grocery branches, its central store and its two restaurants.

Although co-operative stores have continued to operate in the city since 1970, that decision spelt the end of the "Sosh" - Dundee's own co-operative society.

Draffens

The business that was eventually to become known to all Dundonians as Draffens, was established in 1834 in a small shop at 10 Overgate. The owners were William Moon and John Langlands. When opening their shop they decided to take a new approach to retailing and became the first shopkeepers in Dundee to sell goods on the basis of fixed prices rather than by bargaining, which was then the current practice.

By 1837 Moon and Langlands were selling a wide range of materials and clothing. Silks of various varieties such as Gros-de-Naples, Ducapes and Satinettes were a speciality, and bonnets were on sale from makers as far apart as Dunstable and Tuscany. Ladies could buy fashionable items such as Sarcenet ribbons, Paisley shawls, French merinoes and chintz from London.

At this time clothes for men were seemingly much more colourful than was later to be the case. Men's suits could be made in cassimeres (cashmeres) and buckskins and in a wide range of colours - blue, claret, dahlia and olive were all available. Even trousers were available in such exotic materials as printed moleskin and lavender canton.

The two partners' approach was so successful that only three years later they were looking for larger premises. They eventually decided on a move to a shop at 27 Overgate. This they considered an attractive location, situated as it was on the corner with Tally Street. Even in this new shop they were still squeezed for space. So much so that the male outfitting part of the business had to remain at 10 Overgate. Seeking to add to their business they also opened a branch at the West Port.

Five years later, in 1842, the business was on the move again, this time moving to premises known

as Albion House, on the corner of Union Street and the Nethergate. This move signalled a change in ownership when Mr Langlands departed from the firm to be replaced by a new partner, Mr John Robertson.

The firm prospered in the new location and in June 1845 was awarded the Town Council contract to supply uniforms for the police force. They also had more and somewhat unwelcomed contacts with the police as they found shoplifting an on-going problem. In 1847, for example, a Jane Robertson from Edinburgh was arrested for stealing a shawl, while on another occasion a Mr James Cowan was given sixty days in prison for smashing one of their plate glass windows.

Moon & Langlands, as they were still known, had a very entrepreneurial approach and, in August 1847, seeing a gap in the market, opened a room exclusively devoted to the sale of mourning goods. Eighteen months later they were selling Paisley shawls stated to be "similar to that presented to Queen Victoria". In the same year they opened a new carpet warehouse in Albion House. To heighten public anticipation they even publicised the buying of goods for the store and on 28 September 1849 an advertisment to that effect appeared in the Dundee Courier.

A change of ownership

By 1877 the business had been operating for a third of a century. The last of the founders of the business, Mr William Moon died in that year and the business was passed on to his son, James Stocks Moon. It would appear that James Moon was not really interested in retailing and by the end of the year the firm had been sold to two new partners - Thomas Blakeney who 'had experience in the colonies' and a Mr Steele who came from Glasgow. To mark the change of ownership a great sale was

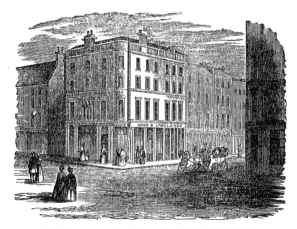

NEW ALBION WAREHOUSE,
NETHERGATE, DUNDEE.

held in January 1878 at which demand by customers was such that the doors had to be closed to prevent more people entering the store.

At the start of March 1879 an advertisement gave an indication of the range of household goods that the company was selling:- "Curtains of all kinds, Brussels Carpets, Scotch carpets, hearthrugs, doormats, Chinese Mattings, Linoleum, Floorcloths. Black silks at 3/6 to 10/6 per yard, Calicos and the best American Cottons".

As the company grew it began to look for opportunities outside shop sales and in 1881 Moon & Langlands gained an unusual contract. This was for the supply of dress uniforms for the Forfar Light Horse to wear when they took part in a march past celebrating the visit of Queen Victoria to Holyrood.

The new owners had initially traded under the title of Moon Langlands & Co, but in June 1882 the partnership between Steele and Blakeney was dissolved. From September 1886 the business traded under the name of Thomas S. Blakeney & Sons although little is known about Blakeney's sons. However such was the reputation that the company had built under its previous owners that nearby retailers, such as a bookshop in Crichton Street, described themselves in their adverts as being "three doors down from Moon and Langlands". Even some years after the business had moved out the new occupiers described their location as being "In the premises formerly occupied by Moon and Langlands".

Retailing was changing rapidly in the late 19th century and Blakeney, not wanting to be left behind, decided to upgrade his premises. An architect – Mr Hutchinson - was engaged, and on March 7 1879 a scheme of alterations was put in hand. Completed by the middle of May that year, a new, and very large, plate glass window was installed where the previous entrance had been. Two new entrances were created at the east and west corners of the building and to improve the rest of the shop front, new plate glass windows were installed. Inside, the store was completely redecorated and "to secure effective illumination in the evening improved gas pendants with large and brilliant sunlight reflectors have been installed". The handrail to the new staircase was finished in black and gold and the general effect was described at the time as"chaste, rich and cheerful".

On 2 November 1886 there was a serious fire at Albion House, and Blakeney transferred the business to new premises that he had had built on the corner of the newly formed Whitehall Street and Nethergate. This was a substantial and elegant building accommodating all the functions of what was now a major department store.

The Draffens take over

On 14 August 1889 Blakeney leased the building and sold the stock to George Draffen and John Jarvie. Although the business had been in operation for some 55 years it was only when the store was taken over by George Draffen and John Jarvie that it really took off.

George Draffen was the son of a draper, and was born in Coatbridge in 1849, He trained in his father's business and, at the age of 21, together with John Jarvie, he opened a shop in the same street as his father. Remarkably, both he and his father were happy with this situation.

In 1872 he married Jean Jarvie, the daughter of his business partner, John Jarvie, also a native of Coatbridge. He was 40 when, together with Jarvie, he took over Blakeney's business in Dundee. The family set up house at Duneaves in West Queen Street, Broughty Ferry, later moving to Hamewith in Glamis Road.

George Draffen turned out to be a man who was deeply involved with the community. He was a strong supporter of the Unitarian Free Church foreign mission, the Dundee branch of the Scottish

Blakeney's Buildings Doorway

85

Society for the Prevention of Cruelty to Children, the Royal Institution for the Blind, Dundee Royal Infirmary, and served on the committee of Broughty Ferry Bowling Club.

Draffen and Jarvie, although not yet the owners of the building, immediately set about changing the way the business operated. Their priorities were to look after the existing staff and get up to date on the fashion front. In March 1890 they held a picnic for their workers providing transport to Glamis Castle and dinner in the Glamis Hotel. The same month they entered an agency agreement with Liberty's of London to supply their latest and most fashionable goods. November saw the reporting in all the local papers of the opening of an elaborate Christmas show. This was to be a feature for years to come.

By the January of 1891 they had held the first Annual Dance for their employees. The employees for their part held the first of a series of musical evenings performed by members of the staff, this taking place on the evening of 26 November in the Upper Hall at Gilfillan Church in Whitehall Crescent.

Although trading as Draffen and Jarvie, the business seems to have been run almost entirely by George Draffen. Frances Simpson (George Draffen's granddaughter) recalls " When I was about fourteen I asked my grandfather who Mr Jarvie was (he was my Great Grandfather's brother-in-law), Grandpa replied 'he was the sleeping partner - positively somnolent", I didn't know the meaning of the word in those days, so I wasn't much the wiser."

Perhaps not able to keep up with the pace of change John Jarvie was bought out and retired in 1891, leaving George Draffen as the sole proprietor although the business continued to trade under the name of Draffen & Jarvie. This change seemed to encourage George Draffen to continually make innovations to keep up with what was a very competitive trading environment.

In November 1892 the company instigated the first of their Annual Fashion Shows. The timing of the show was designed particularly to show evening wear for ladies. Marie – the Courier's fashion writer – commented at length on the up to date fashions on display, noting:- "Such a thing as large sleeves is not to be seen. Little puffs of lace, tulle, net or silk have superceded the bundles of fibre chamois we have lately had to drag about on our shoulders".

When in the early 1890s an electricity supply was inaugurated in the city, Draffen and Jarvie were among the first to install this new source of light and power and used the fact that they had installed

DRAFFEN & JARVIE, DUNDEE.

Latest Fashions.

Business Hours: 9 a.m. to 7 p.m.; Saturdays, 9 a.m. to 4 p.m.

electric lighting as an incentive to shop in the store. For example on 7 November 1894 Draffens introduced what was a lengthy article about goods featured in their Annual Fashion Show in the following fashion:-

Overheard after dinner
"Did you go to Draffen & Jarvie's this forenoon?" she asked.

"Why yes", was the reply, "I wanted a gown for the dance".

"Isn't it good," chimed in a young lady, "to have electric light? It changes the colours so much that an evening gown bought by daylight would probably be a failure".

From early on the company seems to have had a good relationship with its staff. In January 1896 an Annual Dance was held in Gray's Rooms in Perth Road, and in October of the same year, Draffen's employees gave a concert in the YMCA hall. This must have been a success as in March 1897 a vocal and instrumental concert on behalf of the Indian Famine Relief Fund was given in the City Assembly Rooms by Draffen's employees.

Always looking forward, in 1896 George Draffen decided to do something about the future management structure of the company and took his sons – John Jarvie Draffen and William Stirling Draffen - into partnership. After this he took more time to indulge in his love of travel visiting South Africa and India, and voyaging twice to Australia.

Both John and William had been born in Coatbridge before the family had moved to Dundee - John in 1875 and William 1881. William turned out to be the most prominent of the two brothers. As early as May 1894 he was mentioned in the press when it was recorded that "Master Stirling contributed a collection of birds eggs in a mahogany case to a benefit for the Dundee Orphan Institute".

In April 1898, to cater for their increasing levels of business Draffen & Jarvie took a long lease of the adjacent printing works of William Kidd, situated on the floors above Kidd's shop at 7, Whitehall Street. It was not until over fifty years later that Draffens were able to purchase Kidd's shop.

A new century dawns
The period after the turn of the century was one of great prosperity for the middle classes in Dundee and for the department stores that catered for their needs. But Draffen & Jarvie by now had aspiring competitors such as D. M. Brown to think about. More facilities were required for ladies of leisure and on 12 December 1902 the company opened a new suite of tea-rooms, advertising the event as follows:-

DRAFFEN & JARVIE have very much pleasure in intimating that they have
Opened LUNCHEON and TEA ROOMS in connection with their extensive Warehouse.
Together with the restaurant Proper, which is conveniently situated on the Second Floor, a
LADIES BOUDOIR AND GENTLEMEN'S SMOKING ROOM

Have been provided with Spacious Cloakroom Accommodation Adjoining and the firm feel sure that these Rooms will be much Appreciated and Used by Visitors in the Restaurant.

Everything served in First-Class Style at Moderate Prices, the Linen and Table Appointments kept Scrupulously Clean, and the Menu varied according to the Season.

The company's approach at this time was to appeal to the middle classes aesthetic sensibilities and at the same time taking into account their customer's desire for economy. This was clearly illustrated in a contemporary report that noted that the new tearooms "are decorated with exquisite taste in soft tones of ivory, pink and yellow, the effect being particularly cheerful and artistic. The aim of the new tearooms is to provide recherché viands at strictly moderate price".

Continuous improvement now seemed to be Draffen's motto and in April 1910 an elevator was installed to improve access to the upper floors of the store. In late 1913 a new lounge was created for men and women where a musical trio entertained during afternoon tea. The Courier's fashion editor, Norma, wrote that :- "a fine comfortable lounge has been established at Draffen & Jarvies overlooking Whitehall Street. It is a very cheery and bright room furnished in perfect taste with comfortable lounge chairs of the artistic 'Dryad' make, while the beautiful Turkish colourings of the rich carpet harmonises perfectly with the colour tones predominating in the tapestry wall paper".

Draffens made much of the fact that although this was not a smoking room, smoking was permitted throughout the day. They were clear that, "to have tea in the lounge with a lady and not to be debarred the privilege of a cigarette is a consummation for which many men have devoutly wished".

The First World War
The outbreak of war at first had no impact on Draffens retailing operations, although an increasing number of situations became vacant as the war went on. Draffen & Jarvies's Christmas show in 1914 featured "war and naval games of all kinds and a huge army of soldiers of all kinds together with castles and forts –all British made. A side counter is specially devoted to the needs of our soldiers and sailors". The 1915 Christmas show still featured war games and soldiers but, not surprisingly, there was a noticeable lack of German products such as mechanical tin toys and dolls. By Christmas 1917 they were advertising for sale toys and games made by disabled soldiers and sailors in Lord Robert's Memorial Workshops.

During the war the Draffens became very involved in raising funds for the troops, Mrs Draffen in particular becoming an active member of many support groups. In December 1916 George Draffen donated a 'Patriotic Barrow' to be located at Bridge Station to supply soldiers passing trough with coffee, buns, sandwiches and cigarettes.

The interwar period
The cessation of hostilities and wartime restrictions in November 1918 saw the company's enthusiasm quite unabated. It was in good shape and eager to further develop the business. But creating better facilities and increasing the range of goods carried was difficult to do within the shell of the existing store. So in October 1919 the company acquired the Overseas Club at 29 Nethergate, in order to accommodate their wholesale department.

In October 1920 a serious fire broke out in the linen department of the store that effectively closed

Draffens for a considerable time. This could have been a real setback but the firm decided that the opportunity afforded by the need to reconstruct part of the store should be used to their advantage. The works were completed in March 1921 and featured the introduction of glass cabinets to hold goods, rather than the behind the counter shelves which had formerly been in use. A sprinkler system was installed together with central heating throughout the store. Another innovation was the introduction of the Cottage Tea Room on the top floor to provide snacks "at a very reasonable price"

Outside the confines of the retailing industry the wider world was changing fast. In 1922 the British Broadcasting Corporation was set up and started broadcasting. Initially their transmissions could only be heard in the south of England but by 1925 programmes could be listened to in Dundee. Draffen realised that whilst the programmes were being broadcast to the city, as yet few Dundonians had radios to receive them. They decided to broadcast the BBC's musical programmes in their lounge and tea rooms. So popular was this innovation the firm advertised on a daily basis the list of programmes that could be heard in the store.

Continuing success resulted in a need for more floor space. In November 1927 the firm acquired the Swan Electric premises at the corner of Coutties Wynd and the Nethergate. These were used to create a new men's store with a separate stair. This was specifically advertised as 'not passing through the ladies department'. The new department opened in October 1928.

Dining in Style

Draffens seeing the success of the restaurant opened in D. M. Browns, their chief competitor, decided to open one of their own. Situated on the top floor of the building it soon became a very popular venue for middle class ladies. To facilitate the catering the company employed a chef and restaurant manager called Mr Orr who had his own office on the top floor in the turret room on the corner of Whitehall Street and the Nethergate.

Dennis Collins recalls that in the late 1930s and early 1940s he would be expected after school to join his mother and aunts at their almost weekly gatherings for tea in Draffens.

Neil Hynd remembers that "One of the distinctive features of visiting the Cottage Tea Room (or the main dining room), was the constant clatter of silver service. Teas and coffees were served in proper silver (plate) coffee and tea pots, along with all

matching accoutrements, trays, salts and peppers, sugar basins, and cream jugs etc., all in the art deco style".

The acquisition of the silver service is an interesting story. At that time the head chef came to Stirling Draffen to say that in his younger days he had served on the stylish liner L'Atlantique, which plied the Bordeaux to South America route, under the flag of Le Compagnie de Navigation Sud-Atlantique. After only three years of service she was destroyed by fire and eventually towed to Smith & Houston at Port Glasgow for scrapping. The head chef persuaded Stirling that he should go to salvage the silver service from the ship. This he did and that is how Draffens acquired such stylish silver service! I have two coasters and a tray from the service. Each of these sports an art deco logo "SA" for "Sud-Atlantique."

Art deco on the Nethergate

When George Draffen died in May 1929 his sons, William Stirling Draffen and John Jarvie Draffen, took over as owners of the business. In the early 1930s the new management team determined to expand their premises yet again and commissioned architects Thoms and Wilkie to design a new block on the Nethergate to replace the former Swan Electric building. This was to accommodate their Menswear department. The new block opened in 1934 to great acclaim. Although now occupied by a café it is still a handsome addition to the townscape of the Nethergate.

The four storey block was designed in the fashionably modern Art Deco style and finished in a combination of the local Leoch stone and polished granite. Internally the building featured large areas of walnut panelling and cut glass, and chrome plated lights. Virtually all the work was carried out by local firms with exception of the lifts that were installed by Weygood Otis. Interestingly the structural steelwork was supplied and erected by the Caledon Shipbuilding and Engineering Company based in Dundee Harbour.

But Draffen's expansion plans went far beyond the construction of the new building. They also acquired the offices and flats above the adjacent British Linen Bank in the Nethergate, partly as workshops for the making and altering of clothes, and partly as a staff entrance via a bridge over Coutties Wynd. The scheme also involved an expansion into the third and fourth floors above their neighbour, Rattrays the Jewellers. This space was used for administrative offices for the store.

Draffens were determined that the opening of the new premises would be a special occasion and timed it to coincide with the centenary of the founding of the business. They also laid on a special programme of events associated with the opening.

Of particular note among these was the Cavalcade of Fashion, consisting of a series of dresses and fashion items covering the period 1834 to 1933. The clothes involved had been obtained from a museum in Canada and were to be modelled by Dundonians. It was reported in the Dundee Courier that "some trouble has been caused because the waists of ladies are not what they were". Fortunately the efforts of the in-house dressmakers were able to overcome the problem. Also on view was a dress that had actually been worn by Queen Victoria.

To accompany this display, and to show that Draffens was really about up to the minute fashion, they laid

1834-1934

Centenary Dinner

Given by the Directors

of

DRAFFEN & JARVIE
LIMITED   DUNDEE

October 15th, 1934

on a modelled display of current fashions that was widely reported as a great success.

Staffing

The growth in the company meant taking on many more employees. To keep contact with them and to guide their conduct an internal house magazine was set up entitled, rather ominously Watchdog. This was quite a comprehensive mix of social matters - listing in every edition the names of new staff and those leaving - and numerous exhortations to the staff to do better. In the immediate post war period it also listed those members of staff resuming their position after being on active service. Every edition had "A Motto for the Month" that was mainly composed of homilies such as "If truth won't sell it, don't sell it" and "If you can't make a sale, then make a friend".

But there was another side to staff relations. Daisy Haxton, who started with Draffens as a junior eventually becoming a departmental buyer, recalls that in the inter war years "One Saturday afternoon each summer we had the staff outing to the The Gows , the Draffen's family home at Invergowrie.

This was quite an event as everyone went - right down to the workroom assistants. We played games on the lawn and Mr Stirling Draffen would sit down at the piano beside the window and play and sing to us."

An indication of the scale of the company in the late 1930s was that on 29 February 1936 over three hundred guests attended the Draffen's Dramatic Club dance held in the new Palais ballroom.

Draffens was by this time "the store" in Dundee, and, indeed, in Angus and Perthshire. It was not altogether surprising that Elizabeth of Glamis, (who was later to become Queen and subsequently Queen Mother), often visited the store. Royal visits, such as that on 15 October 1936, when the Duchess of York accompanied by the Princesses Elizabeth and Margaret toured the store, occasioned great excitement. The Royal connection was kept up over the years and in 1958 Draffens were awarded a Royal Warrant as Linen Merchants to the Queen Mother.

World War Two

During the Second World War all plans for expansion were put on hold. Draffen's were seriously affected by the restricted range of goods available for sale. Dealing with the effects of conscription of many of its staff was another problem. It nevertheless managed, in April 1940, to field a football team to play a match against staff from Justices to raise money for the Dundee Royal Infirmary.

George Stirling Draffen

Meet "The Pringles"

PRINGLE Sportswear

Introduced by

Draffen's OF DUNDEE

Post War

In the post war period the firm continued to operate a strategy of further developing the business and in November 1948 renamed the company as Draffens. In the 1950s, to emphasise their status as Dundee's top store a fashion evening was held in Kidds Rooms where Barbara Goalen, one of the worlds top models of the time, showed off examples of fashion wear available at the store. This event was attended by over 350 guests.

William Stirling Draffen died on 22 September 1958, leaving his son George Stirling Draffen as Chairman of the Company and his daughter Marjory as a major shareholder. George S. Draffen and George Symington were the joint managing directors.

George Stirling Draffen was born in 1910 and although he worked in the company throughout his career he had many other interests. In 1940 he became Commandant of Dundee Auxiliary Fire Service. He was subsequently promoted to Assistant Regional Inspector of Fire Brigades in Scotland and later Deputy Inspector of Fire Brigades in Scotland. He was awarded an MBE in 1946 in connection with this work. George had many other interests, becoming a Fellow of the Society of Antiquaries in Scotland, and a Member of the Scottish Historical Society.

Although generally mild in nature, Stirling could be firm when it was required. On one occasion Hugh Fraser (of Fraser Stores who had long wished to buy the firm) elbowed his way into Stirling's office and rudely demanded, "How much do you want for your shop?" Stirling Draffen's answer was to call the security man and have Fraser ejected from the building.

After this incident Fraser was persona non grata as far as the Draffens were concerned. The animosity was such that when George S. Draffen died he specified in his will that none of the shares were to be sold to Hugh Fraser.

In April 1961 Draffen's were still expanding and acquired the premises of Henderson & McKay on the opposite side of Whitehall Street, which they developed as an annexe to the main store.

However, behind the scenes all was not well. When John Draffen had died in 1949, a considerable number of his shares had been sold to pay death duties, and a further block was sold when William Stirling Draffen died in 1958. The joint managing directors, George Stirling Draffen and George Draffen Symington realised that the business was slipping out of the family's control.

In September 1961 the shareholders accepted a takeover offer from Blyths Ltd of Edinburgh which was a subsidiary of James Grant & Co (East) Ltd. The firm continued to trade under the name of Draffens, and George S. Draffen remained in charge until he retired in April 1962. Thereafter Mr Harold Oppenheim of James Grant took over as the head of the business.

In 1963 the firm acquired the Whitehall Printing Works located in Couttie Wynd and owned by William Kidd & Sons. They then added new departments in the store for Carpets, Electrical Goods, Hardware and Toys.

In the late 60s Draffens modernised the store, closing the two restaurants on the third floor thus releasing a complete floor for retail space. Although the Cottage Room continued as a restaurant, these alterations signified a big change to the pattern of retailing in Dundee's department stores.

In February 1970 Draffens was merged with Smith Brothers who were also under the control of the James Grant organisation. As a result the Smith Brothers store in Commercial Street was closed and the business was moved to Whitehall Street.

As the store continued to prosper it needed more space, and in 1976 took over the premises of their neighbour, Justices. This was a substantial expansion and meant that Draffens had now come to occupy virtually the whole of the western side of Whitehall Street.

But whilst the shop continued to trade as Draffens and Smiths throughout the 1970s and 1980s, it had lost its aura and atmosphere. The end of Draffens as a company name came with the dissolution of the company in 1992 when the store was sold to Debenhams plc. In 2000 Debenhams moved their Dundee operations to the newly redeveloped Overgate shopping Mall where they continue to trade at the present time.

After a period when the premises in Whitehall Street remained vacant, the ground floor was let to a variety of small shops and restaurants. Today at ground level it is not the grand store it once was but, if you lift your eyes to look above the ground floor, the upper stories are redolent of a time past when a great store called Draffens was the place to shop in Tayside.

Draffens Whitehall Buildings Doorway

Thomas Justice & Son Ltd

D C Thomson

Although Justices was an important and prominent store in Dundee's shopping hierarchy it was not a department store in the fullest sense of the term. The company saw itself primarily as a business designing and manufacturing furniture, even when it was in fact selling a wide range household goods.

The business was established in 1872 in a shop with a single window in Tally Street. The founder was Thomas Justice, who was born in Dundee but had trained as an upholsterer in Glasgow. When, in 1873, he married Jane Henderson he was described as an upholsterer and journeyman. He had three sons, Mathew Low Justice, Thomas Jamieson Justice and Alexander Justice, the last of whom was not involved with business.

Originally the company sold only furniture designed to order, using catalogues and display samples, but by 1882 they were also selling a range of rugs, and linoleum. This approach proved to be successful and by 1890 it had to acquire additional premises in Tay Street.

However even this additional space did not suffice to accommodate the burgeoning business and so, in June 1892, it opened machine workshops in South Ward Road with some 70,000 square feet of floor-space. While this gave it ample space for the production of furniture the firm still needed larger retail premises and so in 1894 it built, and in 1895 opened, a new 30,000 square foot building in Whitehall Street.

This allowed Justices to greatly increase its turnover and in 1898 Justices turned the business into a limited company with a share capital of £100,000. This in turn enabled it to acquire the ironmongery business of Messrs Gray & Sons in Whitehall Street. After this it ventured into the provision of fireplaces, grates and tile hearths. fenders and fire irons. Perhaps inspired by all of this, in 1899 it was describing itself as "Artistic House Furnishers".

The first of Thomas's sons, Matthew Low Justice started working for the family firm in 1902, when he was 23 years of age. He was described as a cabinetmaker when he married Lilian Sear Smith in January 1908. Together they had two sons, Thomas Low Justice who was born in 1909 and Roland Sear Justice who was born three years later.

By 1907 Justices had increased their assets to £115,000 and were looking around for new areas of business. They decided that in addition to making bespoke furniture for the wealthy, Justices would compete in the contract furniture market. The company soon made progress in this field and in September 1909 was successful in winning the furnishing contract for the new diphtheria ward at Kings Cross Hospital. This proved to be the first of a continuing stream of contract work which would last throughout the century.

Despite the publicity that surrounded the gaining of such contracts Justices were anxious to stress that the core of the business was the making and selling of domestic furniture. In particular the firm placed regular advertisements in the Dundee Courier indicating that it specialised in selling furniture.

However, this in no way inhibited the company from expanding the home furnishings side of the business and nor did the onset of World War One, for in December 1915 they had a special display in their store of the quilts, cushions, tables, and the wide range of fabrics that they had on sale. It seems that Justices were little affected by wartime conditions and the firm continued its steady growth into the 1920s.

The size of the business at this time was clearly illustrated when, on 26 June 1922, Justices celebrated the Jubilee of the company by taking around 300 employees and friends for a visit to Monikie where the guests were treated to a lunch. At the lunch, the staff presented an illuminated address in a silver casket to Mr Justice. It was, unfortunately, a somewhat rainy day but seems to have been enjoyed by all in spite of the weather.

At the start of October 1924 Thomas Justice, the founder of the company, died in Dundee leaving Matthew Low Justice and Thomas Jamieson Justice to run the firm.

Matthew Low Justice's first son, Thomas Low Justice, who had trained as a chartered accountant. started working in the family firm in the late 1920s. His younger brother, Roland Sear Justice, gained a degree in mathematics from St Andrews University in March 1931, after which he too joined the family business.

The company continued to develop throughout the interwar period and they exhibited in the 1932 Dundee's Own Exhibition held in the Caird Hall. There it had on display, not just furniture, but also ironmongery, fireplaces, boilers, china, crystal ware and floor coverings.

In December 1932 Thomas Jamieson Justice died leaving Mathew Low in charge of the firm. Mathew brought his son Thomas Low Justice onto the board in 1934. This seemed to generate a more creative approach to advertising and in April 1934 there was a week-long demonstration of "the art of oriental carpet weaving" that took place in the firm's shop window.

Unfortunately Mathew Low Justice developed a chest complaint that resulted in him leaving Scotland in 1937 and going to live in Lausanne in Switzerland. Although he visited Dundee in the period up until the outbreak of the Second World War, his position as the owner of the firm living in another country complicated matters. Nevertheless the firm was still increasing its retail business and in May 1936 the company applied to the City Council for permission to extend their premises northwards in Couttie's Wynd but this was refused. This was a real setback requiring a significant rethink of the company's plans for the future. Despite this the company continued to increase the range of their activities and by 1938 were also advertising themselves as:-

'Thomas Justice & Sons Ltd Cabinet makers, upholsterers, ironmongers, funeral undertakers, removal contractors 9-15 Whitehall Street & Whitehall Crescent Cabinet Works South Ward Road'

By 1939 the company was selling silver plate, cutlery, and china and had opened a new electrical department plus a Children's Corner where bikes toys and rocking horses were for sale.

World War Two

During the Second World War Justice's manufacturing business was seriously affected by the lack of raw materials and, in its retailing side, by the lack of goods to sell. But they had more than that to contend with for Mathew Low Justice died in Lausanne on May 29 1942. His son Thomas Justice

then became Managing Director and held that position until he retired in 1978.

Early in his career with the firm Thomas travelled to Scandinavia and started importing Danish furniture. Thomas Justice who was of medium height, was softly spoken and possessed a sharp wit and a good sense of humour. He was a family man, keen on cine-photography, golf, gardening, skiing and travel.

Post War

The post war period was a good one for Justices who, in the early 1950s, developed their own brand of inlaid flooring which they named Justoid and for which they provided a design and installation service. Roland Sear Justice who ran the Justoid section of the firm was rather gung-ho and outgoing in attitude and adored angling but he was no designer, and the firm employed a Dundee artist, Joe Paterson, to design patterns for Justoid.

In February 1955 there was a major fire at Justices warehouse in Ward Road but they seem to have quickly overcome the problems that this caused for from the mid 1950s they carried out some surprisingly wide ranging contract work. This included in 1955 carrying out the refitting of the electrical system in the Skerryvore Lighthouse, the tallest in the UK at the time, and located twelve miles off the west coast of Scotland. Eight years later, and somewhat closer to home, Justices executed the contract for the electrification of Bell Rock Lighthouse in which the power of the light was increased from 734,00 to 3,000,000 candlepower.

In the 1960s Justices rode the national building boom by engaging in the contract side of furnishing for hotels and schools throughout the country. In Dundee they furnished the General Post Office and the Bank of Scotland's premises in Bank Street and also the branch of Royal Bank of Scotland in the High Street where mahogany and walnut were extensively used. They also established a design and contract furnishing office that won contracts with Scottish and Newcastle breweries and many private hotels and pubs.

Roland Justice died in March 1963 and later that year Alan Justice, the son of Thomas Justice joined the firm.

In 1976 the store was sold to Draffens which had itself fallen under the control of James Grant & Co, an Edinburgh based firm, but the furniture manufacturing business was carried on separately, concentrating on the design, supply and installation of institutional, and later, hotel bedroom furniture.

This was very successful and furniture was shipped to many destinations, the most exotic being a shoreside village complex in Barbados.

The firm had moved its manufacturing facilities from South Ward Road to a warehouse in Balgray Place formerly occupied by Valentine of Dundee Ltd. In November 2005 they moved again, this time to premises in Brunel Road in Gourdie Industrial Estate. Here the company continued to operate a showroom and factory until it went into receivership in 2007 and finally closed.

Lawsons Ltd

Lawsons was from the very start a family business. It was founded by a packman - Robert Lawson, who was born in Fife in 1828, the son of a coal miner. He started his drapery business touring the small villages and the farms of southern Fife, most of his wares being sold on a credit basis. In 1856 he opened a small shop in Stirling but still continued his rural sales tours. These went as far as the Dundee area and 1873 he sold the Dundee part of the business to his brother James.

In 1900 the firm in Dundee was operating from two small shops in Union Street and the first floor above. The two brothers decided to amalgamate their businesses as a public company under the name of Lawsons Ltd with Robert Lawson's son, William, as its managing director. The firm adopted a policy of recruiting their travelling salesmen from members of the Temperance Society, which, given their lack of immediate supervision and their peripatetic existence, was a shrewd move.

In 1906 William Lawson died at the age of 44 and was succeeded by James Lawson's fourth son Robert, who had trained as a schoolmaster but had a good knowledge of accountancy. However, he too died at a very early age and was succeeded by his brother Daniel who also owned the Star Boot Co. Ltd. His time in post was also short, for in 1910 he retired in favour of his elder brother Archibald Lawson.

In 1926 the third generation took control when J. Douglas Lawson, Archibald Lawson's son, became the new managing director. Within one year the headquarters of the company had been established in Whitehall Crescent, Dundee and a branch opened in London. In 1930 the Sheffield firm of George Binns was acquired.

J. Douglas Lawson seems to have been made of stronger stuff than his predecessors and remained as managing director until his death in 1951. The firm was then taken over by his cousin, Dr James Lawson, and Mr A. S. Lowson, the son-in-law of Daniel Lawson. In 1955 Mr Lowson died leaving Dr James Lawson in control.

By the early 1960s Mr W. P. Lawson had become Chairman, while the post of Managing Director was held by Mr H. D. Lawson, the great-grandson of the founder. The business was now at its peak and ran a separate manufacturing company. Overall it employed some 1,100 staff in locations throughout Scotland and in Portsmouth, Brighton, Reading and London.

Credit trading was by far the major part of Lawson's business – in the case of the Dundee branch this almost 99%. As the branch covered a very wide area bounded by Inverbervie and Blair Atholl in the north, Aberfeldy, Crieff and Milnathort in the west and virtually all of Fife in the south, nearly half of the one hundred and nineteen sales staff based in the city were travellers equipped with cars to cover their extensive beats.

Lawsons Ltd. managed to attain its centenary but in 1981 the family sold the company although the name Lawsons continued to be used until the final demise of the business in the 1990's.

Potters

Potter's shoe shop was established by Alexander Potter in 1888 at 12-16 Murraygate. Alexander was born in 1869 and died in August 1958. He had four sons, George, Alexander Jnr., James and Frederick.

The premises in Murraygate had previously been a substantial 18th century house and Alexander was of the view that something more stylish was required. He therefore commissioned architects Gauldie and Hardie, and in 1911 the front was transformed by remodelling the facade in an Arts and Crafts style. Four storeys in height it had a workshop on the top floor and a basement, and proved to be a location in which the company would prosper.

Potter's liked to keep up to date and soon installed a Lanson pneumatic tube system to move money from the tills to the office. From the late 1930s each department was equipped with a Pedoscope. This amounted to a small-scale x-ray machine that was used to ascertain how well customer's feet fitted inside shoes. Norrie Robertson recalls, "once a year my mother took me to Potters for my annual dose of radiation." However the increasing concerns over the use of radioactive devices in shoe shops led to their banning in America and an increasing level of regulation in the UK. This became so onerous that they were effectively banned in this country and were no longer the highlight of a visit to Potters.

Of the four sons, George died during the Second World War, Alexander Jnr. did not go into the business at all, and Frederick was only briefly in the firm before emigrating to Australia around 1950. And so it was that the job of continuing the business fell upon the shoulders of James Potter.

James was born in 1900 and was a qualified chiropodist. He had served in the Army during the Second World War, but fortunately he was stationed not too far away on the island of Inchcolm in the River Forth. James was an active man with a wide range of interests, both sporting and social. He was a member of Rotary and of the East of Scotland Health Board. He was also a keen sailor and an enthusiastic skier as were all of the family. It was therefore no surprise when James became a member of Dundee Ski Club.

As a result of his enthusiastic approach to skiing Potters began to sell and to hire out skis. These generally went out of the store on Friday night and were returned on Monday. Most of the first floor ski department was kept under the watchful eye of Alec Baxter. As this was a time when shoes were made to last Potter's had a workshop on the fourth floor and employed three men who were exclusively engaged in the alteration and mending of shoes.

James's son George was born in May 1943 and joined the business in 1960. He was then sent to work in Clarks Shoes to learn about the children's footwear trade. After two years he returned to work in the family business and set up house in Broughty Ferry.

Sheila, daughter of James Potter, was involved with the work of the shop from an early age. She recalls that there was a lift in the four storied building which, latterly, was operated by a Bert Coull from Bowriefauld in Angus. When Sheila became involved in the business at the age of about 13 her first duties were to cover for Bert when he was not available. Thereafter she worked on the repair counter and as a sales assistant.

Sheila recalls that "there were three sales held each year when the shop was very busy, and it was "all hands to the pumps", Christmas time was another busy period. Slippers were a favourite gift, and they went off the shelves like snaw aff a dyke. Later I was taught how to manage the till, which was serviced by the Lanson tubes that went to all the departments. The money generated from sales was sent to the office by the pneumatic tubes. At that time Mr. Thow was Manager, and a lady called Miss Don, and latterly a Mrs. Fimister were all part of the office scene; they kept me busy all day long."

In 1966 the shop moved from its Murraygate home to the former premises of the Dundee Supply Company in Commercial Street. This was a large shop but, unlike the Murraygate shop, was all on one floor. A new manager was installed, Mr. James Neil. George was now fully integrated into the business. He took on a number of roles, and was gradually "taking over the reins" of the whole business. All seemed to be going well until George suddenly announced that he no longer wanted to work in the business and was going to study law at the University.

James Potter was quite devastated by this development. By this time the firm was finding that trading was becoming more difficult as shoe suppliers now required payment up front for the whole of each season's stock. Faced by increasingly difficult trading conditions and with no heir to take over the business, in 1978 James sold the firm to Peter Lord Ltd, a national chain of shoe shops. After the closure James retired and died in January 1993.

Smith Brothers

Smiths Store Murraygate

The founder of Smith Brothers was Daniel S. Smith who was born in Dundee in 1849, the son of David Smith, a letter carrier. In 1865 he left school and took up employment as a messenger with the clothiers firm of Mr J. P. Smith (no connection). Other than this little is known about Daniel S. Smith but in 1909 he was described as "a cheery and reliable guide to getting a suit", and having a very hands on approach to managing the firm.

Seven years later Daniel was joined in the firm by his brother, James Luke Smith, who was seven years his junior. James was a strong supporter of the Scottish Temperance movement and a non-smoking abstainer who never went to the theatre or cinema.

Both brothers were active and capable workers and by 1879 Daniel had become a partner in the business whilst his brother James had become the manager of the J. P. Smith's branch in Montrose.

Given that they were both ambitious and confident in their own abilities, it was no surprise that they decided to set up their own business. After searching for suitable premises they settled upon 35, Reform Street, Dundee, and it was there that they opened on Saturday 9 February 1884. It was a leap in the dark for the brothers, who had engaged some fourteen members of staff to start their operations. These comprised a commissionaire and, less surprisingly, an expert cutter and twelve tailors and tailoresses.

Soon after this the two brothers strengthened the firm by taking on their brother George K. Smith as a third partner. Before George K. Smith joined his brothers he had started work as grocer's message boy and then, like his father, became a letter carrier in Dundee. He then acquired a post office business in Alyth where he became known for his radical political views. When he lost the post office concession he ran the shop as a drapery business for about five years and then decided to move it to Dundee. However he was persuaded by his brothers to join them in their store at 35 Reform Street.

Smiths store in 1880s

The opening of the Smith Brothers' store in Reform Street proved to be a great success. Although this was an omen for the future of the business it did not happen by chance. In addition to supplying a high level of service the brothers realised that in a competitive business such as tailoring, good publicity was essential. And for this they proved to have a natural flair.

In the summer of 1884 they organised a convoy of around sixty horse cabs that drove to the Smith Brothers shop. There, each cab driver was given a new bowler hat. Not only was this a well reported event at the time, it also meant that in the cab drivers Smith Brothers now had a fleet of ambassadors who provided transport for the middle and upper classes, the very market at which they were aiming.

A year later they were again in the news, this time presenting each of 150 poor boys, selected by the Dundee Free Breakfast Mission and Dundee Police, with a warm overcoat to ward off the chills of winter.

Development

The four successful years that followed left the firm needing additional accommodation. As a result in 1888 they took over Coopers & Co.'s business and premises at 7 Reform Street thereby, at one and the same time, giving themselves room for expansion and increasing their customer base. However the acquisition of the shop at 7 Reform Street had been made on the basis that they would be able to further expand by taking over the flat immediately above Cooper's premises. Unfortunately this did not prove possible and so they again began to look around for larger and newer accommodation.

Thus, when in May 1890 a six-year lease of a building at 4 High Street became available from the Royal Bank of Scotland, they had no hesitation in taking up the offer and they moved into their new premises on 14 August 1890. The building had previously been occupied by the Globe Public house and was located at the top of Castle Street and to the east of Tyndal's Wynd. This was a prominent location and the building was more than three times the size of their original premises in Reform Street. In 1892 David Smith Snr., who had trained both as a tailor and a furrier, joined the family business.

The Globe - High Street

However, despite the fact that they were successful in increasing business at the Globe, there was a downside to the deal. The reason that the building was on a short lease was that the City Council needed part of the site for road improvements that would necessitate its demolition. The Royal Bank of Scotland wanted the remainder of the site for the construction of a new Bank, and neither the bank nor the Council was prepared to extend the lease.

In spite of this the brothers went ahead with substantial alterations of the Globe premises. The revamped building was opened to great plaudits from the Press who noted that a new safe weighed more than a ton and that the shop was to be lit by 'brass gasoliers'. The grand new staircase that had been installed as part of the upgrading of the interior led to the first floor where the cloth and cutting shop was situated. The floors above held the workshops for the making of clothes.

In spite of further pleas from Smith Brothers, the City Council were adamant that they would go ahead with their road improvements on schedule and were not minded to extend the lease. Once again the brothers were looking for new premises. Luckily the City Council at this time had just made available a site in the Murraygate with a 95 feet long frontage. However, this would require Smith Brothers to build their own premises but to a design by the City Architect – Wiiliam Alexander. The brothers decided to take up the offer, and on 23 May 1896 the Town Council approved the plans for their new building.

Whilst this was a big step forward, the new building could not be finished for occupation until the end of July 1897, threatening the firm with having nowhere to carry on trading.

To avoid this unwelcome situation, the company took a short-term lease of the Kinnaird Hall in Bank Street. However this was decidedly less than satisfactory, as Smith Brothers frequently had to remove their stock to the adjacent Argyle Hall to allow previously booked entertainments to go ahead in the Kinnaird Hall. In these trying circumstances it was really surprising that the business managed to survive.

Nevertheless, survive they did, and in August 1897 they opened their shop at 7-9 Murraygate. The development included the studios at the rear of the shops at 13-15 Murraygate. These they let out, together with the first floor offices and the flats above.

Staff

Smith Brothers were very well aware that having happy staff was a great asset for the company and from early on they paid attention to the welfare of their employees. The company was a strong supporter of the Half Day Closing movement that eventually resulted in shops closing on Wednesday afternoons.

They were also anxious to encourage a social side to the business. For example, on 6 February 1892 they held an Annual Dinner for their employees. Those present were entertained by the Globe Choir, which was totally composed of members of staff. On 16 August of the same year the store was closed to allow for the staff outing to Kinclaven Castle, an event that also included boat trips on the Tay. Such outings came to be regular events with the exception of the war years, and were carried on into the late 1940s.

Moving on

In 1900 Smith Brothers took over the business of William Thomson & Son who were woollen merchants. The acquisition of the Thomson firm represented a major expansion of Smith Brothers. Accordingly a revised administrative structure was put in place, and Daniel S. Smith became responsible for the management of the firm's wholesale department.

This was a real move forward, but the company experienced a significant setback when, on 22 December 1900, there was a gas explosion in one of the ground floor workshops. The explosion caused considerable internal damage, and blew out every window in the building. There were a number of minor injuries inflicted on the staff, but more seriously a Richard Cameron was killed in the blast, as was a Mr Ferguson, the latter having caused the explosion by working with a candle at a gas pipe. Three seamstresses - Nellie Slogie, Susan

Cameron, and Mary Adams - suffered severe burns. Smith Brothers were later faced with an action for damages from the three women, but eventually the firm was absolved of all blame.

This setback did not dampen the company's enthusiasm for developing the business for in the very next year Smith Brothers became aware that Malcolm Brothers were moving out of their premises at 21 Commercial Street. They decided to purchase the building to accommodate their wholesale department. However, it transpired that Daniel S. Smith was not happy in his position as manager of the wholesaling side of the business, preferring to be in the thick of the retailing side of the firm. As a consequence he moved back to the retailing operation and put his son D. K. Smith in command of the wholesale department.

In 1902 the company set up a clothing factory. As this expanded more space was required and a storey was added to the Commercial Street property. The wholesale side continued to grow and traded in woollen goods, ready made clothes, blankets, flannelettes and trimmings. The firm continued to make many of the clothes that they sold until 1922 when the clothing factory was sold off.

The company was doing well and looked around for further possibilities for expansion. One area that attracted them was Reform Street, which, by the turn of the century, had gone somewhat downhill. They noted that the large drapery store that had been owned by James Spence had lain vacant for some time. In 1902, Smith Brothers took over the premises to expand their drapery operations. Daniel S. Smith and his son David Smith were put in charge of the new extensively restored and re-equipped shop. The new premises were opened by Lord Provost Barrie and Sir John Leng, and proved to be another great success.

The Murraygate branch was also thriving and such was the success that Smith Brothers decided that rather than continuing to lease the two shops that they occupied there they would acquire the freehold and this they did.

The firm's expansion continued apace and in January 1909 they decided to purchase the block at the corner of Murraygate and Commercial Street that separated their existing premises. However part of the property that they had acquired was occupied by the Bodega Public house. When the proprietor, a Mr Paul, was issued with a notice to quit by the new owners, he simply ignored it. Subsequent attempts to change Mr Paul's mind proved useless and on

10 September 1909 workmen employed by Smith Brothers arrived outside the Bodega and started to erect a wooden barricade around the premises. During their lunch break a party of workmen employed by Mr Paul arrived on site and proceeded to dismantle the barricade. An altercation then occurred that was only stopped when the police arrived. After some discussion the barricade was re-erected but this time with a door in it to allow the patrons of the Bodega to leave at a time of their own choosing.

Apart from this things went smoothly and by January 1910 they had occupied all the shops in the block. By May 1913 Smith Brothers were also in occupation of the former offices and flats above the ground floor.

They then undertook a major reconstruction of the premises including the opening up of the main saloon to a 'magnificent' dome. Two storeys were devoted to showrooms and the fourth storey to a new luncheon and tearoom with seating for two hundred and finished in panelled mahogany. An alcove was provided where a band could play and the third floor rest room and smoking room were very comfortably furnished. The finished building was opened on 18 December 1913.

Smith Brothers' concern for the social side of working continued with annual staff dances and even extended into sporting activities as they supported a staff football team that played in charity matches. An example of this was a game played at Balgay Park on 24 April 1910 in aid of the Dundee Royal Infirmary.

After almost three decades of expansion and improvement the onset of the first World War in 1914 saw them having to cope with the loss of experienced staff who were in the armed forces. Apart from this the war years were a period of

SMITH BROTHERS' NEW TEAROOMS OPENED TO-DAY.

Smith Brothers Tearoom

relative calm for Smith Brothers and on 30 January 1919 the company celebrated their first forty years in business.

For Smith Brothers the next decade was to be marked by family events that brought about significant changes in the management of the company. On 26 August 1924 the brother of Daniel S. Smith - David Smith who had left Dundee in 1866 - died at the age of 78 in Edinburgh. In February 1926 James L. Smith Senior retired from the business.

In the same year Mr G. K. Smith and his son Edwin requested that their interest in the business be bought out. It is not totally clear as to what the circumstances were that brought them to this decision. However in the light of their subsequent actions it is more than possible that there had been some kind of family rift, for only ten months later they bought the four storey block at 16-22 Panmure Street at its corner with the Wellgate in which Edwin and Wilfred set up in business as "The New Smith Brothers". They remained in these premises, trading in direct competition with Smith Brothers, until December 1935 when they moved to a Corporation owned shop in Crichton Street.

This left Mr Daniel S. Smith, the only original partner, and his three sons David Jnr, Daniel, and James to run the business. Unfortunately this situation was not to last, for in September 1927 at the age of 78, Daniel S. Smith died of a cerebral haemorrhage while visiting his daughter in Australia.

Although on 6 March 1929 there was an outbreak of fire in the Murraygate premises that caused considerable smoke damage to their stock, the 1920s were a good decade for Smith Brothers. The firm's flair for publicity was still alive and well. This was illustrated by their innovation just before Christmas 1928 of the "Dundee Juvenile Speedsters Competition", an event using model cars and held in the basement of their store, by then known as Toyland. This became an annual event and was very successful. So much so that the number of entries became so great that, rather than being a one-day event the competition extended from Thursday to Saturday!

In 1930 they added to the pre-Christmas activity by putting on a Meccano model building competition. Just like the Juvenile Speedsters competition this attracted so many entries that it became an annual event in Dundee's pre-war shopping calendar. Smith Brothers innovative approach could also be seen in their advertising. On one occasion the firm paid for a large advert in the Courier that was totally blank apart from the words:

> "This space belongs to Smith Brothers who are too busy to write adverts"

On 16 March 1934 David Smith, Daniel K. Smith and James Luke Smith were made Life Governors of Dundee Royal Infirmary in recognition of the support they had given to the hospital over a very long period. When on 22 March 1934 the company publicly celebrated their Jubilee with an elaborate dinner in Kidd's Rooms, two of the third generation of Smiths – David Smith Junior and George Bell Smith were both working in the business. The occasion of the company's Jubilee was marked by a donation by the partners of 1,000 guineas to the Dundee Royal Infirmary. Needless to say, at that time such a sum was a very considerable amount of money.

The company were still looking to expand their business and in 1935 the company made plans for a new annexe to be built at the rear of premises. However they were delivered an unwelcome Christmas present when their scheme was turned down by the Town Council on 20 December of that year.

Maybe because of this, Smith Brothers decided to divest themselves of part of their property portfolio and on 25 April 1936 James Grant & Co (of 11-15 Cowgate) took over part of Smith Brothers premises in Murraygate. Grant's made major alterations to about half the existing frontage and successfully extended the rear of the property. Just over a year later, in May 1937 George K. Smith died at his home Roinneach Mor in Strathmartine Road.

Wartime
After the high level of activity in the 1930s for Smith Brothers, the years between 1939 and 1945 were very quiet. It seemed as if the war years took all the firm's energies just to cope with the problems of staff shortages, clothes rationing and the lack of goods to sell.

After 1945
In the immediate aftermath of the Second World War, Smith Brothers, like many others in the retail business, had to cope with both family members and staff returning to work in the firm and the ongoing problems arising from the rationing of clothes which were to persist until 1949.

Perhaps surprisingly in the difficult conditions facing the company in the post war years they found the money in October 1948 to open a canteen and social club for their staff. Their staff were certainly important to them, and Joan Cowley the daughter of George B. Smith, recalls that it was a tradition that at Christmas the male employees went to the office for a drink with George Smith.

Perhaps because of this approach Smith Brothers was a store that tended to retain its staff. As time went by presentations to staff for long- term service with the company became a regular occurrence. In September 1947 for example, forty-six staff – some of who had been with Smith Brothers for over four decades - were presented with cheques at an event in Kidd's Rooms.

Serving the public for such long periods of time meant that some employees such as Mrs Sword who was in charge of the knitwear and haberdashery department, Mrs Stewart who ran the cosmetics department and Mr Scott the manager of the boys department, became well known characters in Dundee.

At the top of the company too, some long serving characters were about to leave the stage. In 1947 David Smith who had been working in the firm for almost 55 years, and Daniel K. Smith, who had been in the business for around half a century, announced that they were entering semi retirement. It was clear that changes had to come about. So on 27 September 1947 the directors decided to make the business into a limited company and at the same time to take Mr George B. Smith onto the board.

Expansion was clearly on the agenda of the new board and in October 1947 Smith Brothers bought the Trades Hotel at No 55 Commercial Street to form an extension to their premises. Their plans did not stop there and in March 1949 the company acquired a furniture business that had premises at 22/26 Seagate and these were enlarged together with part of 56 Commercial Street.

As the 1950s opened the company experienced more change at the top. In October 1950 Mr James L. Smith retired after working in the firm for almost 50 years. Less than a year later Mr George B. Smith, became the Managing Director of Smith Brothers while at the same time his brother, Mr David Smith Jnr. became a director. In May 1952 Mr David Smith Snr. died, having been with the business for 60 years. Only two years later, at the age of 41, David Smith Junior died.

After all this the later part of the decade was a more settled time for Smith Brothers. "It was the store where I was always taken to get my school uniform" recalls Iain Wilson. "Their restaurant, which was arranged around a gallery that looked down onto the haberdashery department below, became patronised by the Countess of Airlie". It also became a regular haunt for lunching businessmen from all around the town centre. The waitresses knew their customers and even decades later Murray Thomson recalled that his regular waitress was called Mabel. Katherine Leslie, the daughter of David Smith Jnr remembers that in his retirement her "Great Uncle Dan stood at the door of the shop welcoming customers into the store. He was a very quiet man."

Journeys End

At the end of the decade, in July 1959, Smith Brothers were taken over by James Grant & Co (East) Ltd. For a while the firm continued to be run under the Smith Brothers name and George B. Smith remained as managing Director. But in 1961 after working in the business for 39 years George Bell Smith went into semi retirement and this was the end of the Smith family's involvement with a company they had started almost eighty years earlier. Nevertheless the firm continued to be one of the landmark stores in the city for another ten years.

In January 1970 a press announcement was made that the Smith Brothers store would be closing on 28 February, and on that date it would merge its trading operations with Draffens of Dundee. The new company would operate under the title of Draffens & Smiths Limited. The owners in their closure statement said that this was not due to lack of trade, but to the effect of rising business rates and Special Employment Tax, together with significant increases in their operating costs. Whatever the reason, it was the end of a company that had been a landmark in the shopping scene in Dundee for the best part of a century.

G. L. Wilson

Gavin Laurie Wilson was born in 1852 in Strathaven, South Lanarkshire and was one of nine children in the family of John Wilson, a Lanarkshire farmer. On leaving school he served an apprenticeship with Mr Cochrane, the local draper, after which he worked with a Glasgow wholesaler as a travelling salesman selling hats and caps. Having gained experience of the clothing business he then set up the Popular Warehouse in the Crossgate in Cupar, Fife.

He married Jessie Dunlop McCulloch in 1881. They had two sons, John, born in 1884 and Garnet born in 1885. They also had a daughter - Jessie who was born in 1888 but unfortunately Wilson's wife died only three weeks afterwards. Four years later Gavin married Alison Johnston Russell.

The Popular Warehouse was a successful enterprise but with a new family and an awareness that the Cupar market was limited in its scope, Wilson began to look at his options elsewhere. The rapidly growing city of Dundee was an obvious possibility and so on 26 June 1894 he opened a drapery store in the city. This was located on the corner of Murraygate and Commercial Street and was popularly known as 'The Corner'. Rather boldly Wilson opened the store with some 20 staff, a goodly number for a new and untried business.

A report of the opening in the Dundee Courier mentions that the alterations were very comprehensive and that the walls were covered with Morris wallpaper in yellow and pale brown tones. "At the turn of the staircase a handsome glass showcase with a mirror back finishes the blank wall. The goods on sale were hats and clothing exclusively for women. The corner door led right into the shop where drapery goods are on sale." Upstairs the new workrooms for the dressmakers and milliners were the beginning of what was to become a big department in later years.

The first years went well and by July 1896 he felt confident enough to pay for his employees to go to Glenfarg for a picnic and then journey to Newburgh, where tea was served before returning to Dundee.

However in 1897 the business began to lose money. Typically Wilson decided to expand rather than contract. He borrowed money from his father and extended the shop. He also modernised the shop front and upgraded the interior of the premises. This turned the business around and sales began to increase. To accommodate the extra customers he took over the two floors above the shop. Turnover increased yet again, and when the top two floors were acquired the business owned the entire building from basement to roof.

The extended shop was now selling a range of goods that went far beyond drapery. An advertisement in the Courier just before Christmas 1897, offered "Japanese bronzes, inlaid screens fancy brass, wrought iron and art metal work of all descriptions for sale".

G. L. Wilsons had now become a prominent business in the city, and this was underlined by the scale of the exterior decorations celebrating both Queen Victoria's Jubilee in August 1899, and the coronation of her son George in August 1902.

Wilson's way of running his shop seemed to have struck a chord with the citizens of Dundee, and in September 1903 he felt sufficiently confident to expand his premises once again. This time he took over Lipton's adjoining store and incorporated it into his shop. He also made extensions to the rear of the building where a large cupola was installed. On the re-opening of his shop the fashion correspondent of the Dundee Courier reported that: -

"The interior is delightfully light and airy, a considerable area having been added to the rear of the shop in which the beautiful ornamental cornice is tinted in pink and white. A new single entrance has been created paved with mosaic tiles, and from the roof which is panelled with mirrors hangs a large electric light cluster cornice."

In 1903 G. L. Wilson decided to take his son Garnet into the business. Customer numbers continued to increase and by April 1905 the workforce had grown to over one hundred. The extension of the premises was urgently required. This expansion was made possible by taking over the premises of the hairdressers shop next door. The Courier noted that:-

"During the past two years Mr. Wilson has added a spacious and handsomely fitted mantle and costume saloon, two stairs up, access being gained by an electric elevator of the most improved type".

Business steadily increased and in 1911 G. L. Wilson's oldest son, John, joined the business. G. L. Wilsons had now reached the point where their Christmas shows were reviewed by all the local papers. Looking back on this period Wilson remarked that the most important word to describe the goods they sold was "durable".

With his two sons now installed in the business, Wilson perhaps felt that he could relax a little, and in the summer of 1911 he took a long tour of Italy. It must have impressed him, for on his return in November he gave the shop's staff a Magic Lantern show of his tour. This took place in the Forester's

Hall and some years later he was back in the same venue, this time giving a slide show to his staff entitled "The Peoples of the New World". He followed this up in the same evening with a lecture to the members of the Hibbert Literary Club on "Odd thoughts on American Life".

An extensive article in the Evening Telegraph in December 1912 could not have made it clearer that by now this was a store for the better off. It ended "mistresses who wish to remember their maids at the glad season should not leave without having a look at (the) neat Dalhousie wrappers, afternoon dresses, aprons and caps."

The First World War

If one judged the effects of the onset of hostilities upon the store by the regular advertisements that G. L. Wilson placed in the press, little changed when war was declared. In 1914 the Christmas Bazaar still merited a half column in the Courier and much space was given over to their Toyland display. However the columnist did point out that:-

"not all the toys are representative of peaceful times and signs of these strenuous days have even invaded Toyland. One sees all the necessary materials of warmaking forts, guns, howitzers, drums, and bugles. There are boxes of soldiers all regiments being represented, and there are cannons that actually shoot bullets. Nor is the little girlie forgotten, for among the dolls is one in Red Cross uniform."

Among the gifts for grown ups one could find the Cul de sac - " a knee high felt bag, thick and warm that adds little to the weight of marching equipment". Advice was available in the store as to how parcels should be addressed for the fighting forces on land and sea.

As increasing numbers of men joined the forces gaps began to appear in ranks of the workforce. More and more adverts began to appear for women to join the sales staff. Events at the front pressed upon everybody and G.L.'s wife became the Treasurer of the Newport Soldiers Club.

The initial popular enthusiasm for the war was exemplified by a G. L. Wilson advertisement in 1915 for "Regimental Hat Bands - the latest ladies fashion". But the mood soon changed and significantly the review of the 1916 Christmas display made no mention at all of the War. This was to be the case for the rest of the duration of hostilities.

However, in 1915 the store had been operating for twenty-one years and this was an occasion to be celebrated. On 30 November the staff made a presentation to Wilson of a silver tea and coffee service and a set of gold studs and links. Mrs Wilson was given 'a handsome pearl pendant'.

A party of G. L. Wilson's employees visited the Dundee War Hospital in January 1918 where they held a whist drive involving many of the patients and provided entertainment during an interval. In October the Hospital were again visited by a group of the store's employees. This time the visitors were from the mantle department who put on a concert for the wounded soldiers and provided them with cigarettes and sweets.

In March 1918 Gavin L. Wilson - G. L.'s nephew, who had by this time achieved the temporary rank of Major, was awarded the Military Cross for conspicuous gallantry. (He was later also awarded the DSO, the Croix de Guerre and the Legion D'Honneur). But any good feelings that the Wilson family felt on receiving this happy news were swept away by the tidings that on 31 August 1918 GL's youngest son Gavin Arthur Wilson who was serving in the London Scottish Regiment in France had died of wounds received in action. Matters were made worse when Gavin L Wilson, GL's much decorated nephew, who had survived the war, died of meningitis in 1919.

The Inter war Period
In the post war period Wilson, perhaps because of the deaths of his son and nephew, was drawn more into the field of politics and pursued his interest in the affairs of the Liberal Party in Fife. In 1921 he could be found at Fife Education Authority putting the case for schoolchildren to be released from their studies to work harvesting potatoes. However his views on the children's working hours did seem to be a little less than liberal as he advocated that schoolchildren should work on the farms for three 48 hour weeks each year. In 1922 he declared himself against raising the school leaving age.

On the other hand he was still concerned with the staff in his store. In May 1924 the company arranged a Victoria Day trip to London for one hundred and fifty of its employees. They left by special overnight train and had their breakfast at Lyons Corner House. They then had a charabanc tour of London followed by lunch at Selfridges. In the afternoon they toured the British Empire Exhibition where they had tea, then went to a show at the Coliseum Theatre after which they embarked on the overnight train, arriving back in Dundee at 10.30 the next morning. The following year the company arranged another Victoria Day trip to London but this time for only seventy four of their staff.

The annual staff dances continued to be held, although it was now noticeable that Gavin left the job of Master of Ceremonies to his sons Garnet and John, the latter of whom regularly entered the guests with "humorous recitations" and talks in verse. In 1930 there was another intimation of change. For all of the success of his store in Dundee, Wilson had kept his original shop going in Cupar. However in May 1930 he finally decided to sell the Cupar store to Hepworths the tailors.

Although he had shown no signs of ill health Gavin Laurie Wilson collapsed on 14 October 1932 at the Scottish Liberal Federation Conference in Perth and died shortly afterwards. He was 80 years of age. The many tributes to him made much of his involvement with the Liberal Party at both a local and national level. In his will, among a number of charitable legacies, he left £1,000 to the Church of Scotland, £1,000 to be distributed to the staff, and £1,000 to be put into a staff pension fund.

New Management
After G. L. Wilson's death his sons, John and Garnet now took over the running of the business. Later John's son Gavin L . Wilson became involved.

John Wilson had joined the company immediately he left Dundee High School but was not taken with the work and left the family firm. He gained a degree in Engineering after which he worked in England and in the United States. In 1913 he returned to Britain and rejoined the family business. On 22 October 1914 he married Allison Gibb from Downfield. They had two sons - John Basil Wilson and Gavin Laurie Wilson both of whom would later join the firm and become members of the board, and both of whom died before the age of sixty.

John was very active in the running of the business and had a more hands on role than Garnet. Outward looking in nature he liked meeting customers and was very experienced with handling their problems and requests. While about his duties he liked to smoke a cigar and always wore a rose or a carnation in his buttonhole. John also always carried a bag of sweets in his pocket that he distributed to the children of customers in the store.

He lived at BalnaCraig in Hillpark Road, in Wormit and was an active bowler and a supporter of both the Newport Tennis Club and the Wormit Boating Club. Interested in both people and learning, he took evening classes at the Dundee College of Technology in subjects as varied as modern physics, botany, plumbing, metallurgy and nuclear physics, a practice that he continued up to the age of 78.

John also had the habit of strolling about the town and chatting with his wide range of friends and acquaintances. When he died at the age of 80 in May 1963 the Dundee Courier described him as "one of the city's characters in the best sense of the word".

G. L. Wilson's younger son, Garnet Douglas Wilson, was born in 1885. He had joined the family business in 1903. Like his father he was active in politics at both a local and national level and a member of the Liberal Party. In 1925 he married Gladys Johnson with whom he had two sons, Guy and Ian, and a daughter, Jennifer. Garnet moved to Dundee in 1929 where he became a member of the City Council, continuing to be an active member of the community until he died in 1975 at the age of 90.

The new management team did not make significant changes to the way the business was run. The Spring Fashion Mannequin parades still took place each year as did the Toyland exhibitions at Christmas. However to celebrate the Silver Jubilee of King George V and Queen Mary in June 1935 the partners - John Wilson and Garnet Wilson gave a personal Jubilee gift to all of their staff - every employee receiving a banknote. In July of the next year the company initiated their staff pension scheme. Rather unfortunately the first payment needed to be made within 5 days to an employee's widow whose husband unexpectedly died.

In May 1938, in an echo of the 1924 staff trip to London to see the Wembley Exhibition, the company paid for a special train to take their staff to visit the Empire Exhibition that was being held at Bellahouston in Glasgow.

War again
In the store, the onset of the Second World War was greeted with weary resignation. Like all the other stores in the city G. L. Wilsons was affected by the wartime shortage of goods and the rationing of clothes. Staff shortages were also a problem but the company helped itself to some degree by keeping on its older staff. It, like the other stores in Dundee, had to provide air raid shelters for staff which, when a review of shelters was undertaken by the Council, were described as excellent. On a somewhat bizarre note, in 1940 the firm let it be known that a barrel had been provided in store where staff could put old bones as these "could be used to make aeroplanes"

It is interesting to note that wartime problems not withstanding, Garnet found plenty of time to devote to politics. In 1940 he became Lord Provost of the City of Dundee, a post that he held until 1946.

On 21 October 1942 he was to be found presiding over the Tay Road Bridge Conference that was held in Dundee.

Garnet was a very dignified man but could appear remote at times and sometimes even pompous. Once in 1944 when he was working at home on his biography his son Iain asked him what he was doing. The answer was "I am marking my steps on the sands of time." In retrospect he was right as his book became quite popular and remains as a good witness to his life and times. He also made his mark upon the city in other ways.

Garnet was deeply involved with Dundee University and played a central role in bringing the National Cash Register factory (NCR) to the city. He was knighted for his public service and in 1952 became Chairman of Glenrothes Development Corporation. When a time capsule originally placed in the main post office was opened in August 2014, one of its contents was an essay by Garnet on the League of Nations.

The Post War period.
When the war ended it was a time of celebration rather than change, as the rationing of clothes and the shortages of goods to sell were to persist for some years. But things were slowly improving, and in April 1946 the company's Staff Dance resumed in Kidd's Rooms with over 200 present.

In 1947 the light began to appear at the end of the tunnel, when on 25 February the firm staged a fashion show entitled "New dresses to by-pass Austerity". The Courier reported that:-

"Over 600 women thronged the salon to learn what they may buy with their coupons next month, and many gasps of admiration could be heard."

Business was now beginning to perk up and on 30 April 1947 the company, "at the request of their commercial travellers," held a second staff dance in Kidd's rooms. As things got better confidence grew, and on 27 January 1949 Garnet announced at the Annual Dance at Kidd's Rooms that a day off for the Spring Holiday would be given to all staff. The growth of prosperity was now becoming evident throughout Dundee and later that year huge crowds were queuing to get in to see Santa Claus and the stores display of toys in the G. L. Wilson Christmas Grotto.

In the late 1940s a new generation of the Wilson family began to join the firm. Garnet's son Guy, after service in the Parachute Regiment in the Second World War, worked for a while in Wolverhampton

In 1950 the company decided to improve further on their arrangements for Christmas and so in late November a small parade of vehicles carrying Santa Claus left Garnet's home in the Perth Road and proceeded to Green's Playhouse where an audience of 3000 adults and children saw a free film show sponsored by the store. Afterwards the parade proceeded to the G. L. Wilson store where large crowds awaited the arrival of Santa. This was such a success that the event was repeated each year well into the 1950s.

Lynn Westbrook was one of those who eagerly awaited the Christmas Show. "It was a fairy tale come true, winding your way past fairies, pixies, lights, and glitter to see and get a wee gift from Santa."

A quite different initiative taken by the firm in the 1950s was to put on mannequin parades in the Caird Hall as part of a major exhibition of the fashionable clothes available in the store. The first of these events took place in 1950 and was attended by over one thousand people, a further two hundred having to be turned away. In 1951 the G. L. Wilson show was entitled 'The Spectacle of Fashion', and was opened by the Countess of Dalkeith who no doubt enjoyed the musical accompaniment provided by a string trio. Being successful, these events were continued on an annual basis.

before joining the business in 1949. Although Basil and Gavin, John Wilson's sons, both joined the company at about this time, it was Guy that had the most prominent role in the running of the firm in the post war period. He became acutely aware of the need to modernise both the store and its op-erations. This was not a view shared by other members of the company board but, as one of these later remarked, "In the 1950s and 60s. Guy was the driving force in the company." Guy fell out badly with his father over the matter of modernisation, but eventually won him over.

Another member of family recruited during this period was Iain Wilson, the younger son of Garnet Wilson, who entered the family business in 1951 and worked there until it closed in 1971.

The Smith Board - Garnet, Guy, Basil, Jenifer, Iain, Gavin and John

As in many other shops sales were used by the firm as a promotional device. In January 1953 their buyer Thomas Orr acquired a large, but limited, amount of sale goods that had been affected by water. The resultant sale of the goods at large discounts attracted huge crowds, and the stock on the floor was quickly sold. It was then decided to sell the last items from the shop windows. Unfortunately altercations immediately commenced as a number of customers each claimed to be first in line. Iain Wilson recalls having to decide on the fate of a blanket being claimed by two women each of whom held an end. Despite his diplomatic efforts to avoid trouble compromise was not on the cards and he eventually had to retire and leave them to resolve the argument themselves.

G. L. Wilson's Diamond Jubilee fell on 15 June 1954 and as part of the celebrations the company staged an exhibition in their store entitled 'Costume through the Ages'. They also put on a greatly enlarged version of their annual 'Show of Fashion' in the Caird Hall. Although staff were treated annually to a day out and a picnic, as a special treat for the Diamond Jubilee year buses and meals were laid on, not only for their employees, but also their wives, husbands and children.

The business was still being developed and in 1960 a hardware department was set up. By then the business floorspace had increased to 110,000 square feet, massively larger than the 13,500 square feet that were available at the first opening of their premises in Dundee. However, the interior of the store now needed upgrading, and in 1963 a new stair and lifts were installed as part of a general improvement of the premises.

But in the wider world of the 1960s retailing methods were rapidly changing and becoming much more competitive. The rapid expansion of chain stores such as Littlewoods and C & A, who were now operating in modern premises in the Overgate, made it difficult for independent department stores to compete. Fashions were now changing much more rapidly. Durability, once the watchword of the traditional department store was beginning to be less important than being right up to date.

There were other problems facing the store. In 1965 the company was complaining about the tax regime under which they had to operate. The introduction of Selective Employment Tax (SET) in 1966 meant that tax liability was related to the number of people employed in a business. This was described by Garnet as being 'a body blow' to the company that

Former G L Wilson Store

depended so much on the quality of service that it provided. If SET was a body blow, the introduction of Value Added Tax (VAT) in 1970 proved to be the final straw and the board decided that it was time to end their operations.

The decision to close the store was a difficult decision for the board to take for they had a reputation for retaining staff, many serving for periods of 50 to 60 years. Their slogan "The Friendly Store" was very much the way that former employees recall their time with the firm.

The store closed in December 1971 and the name of G. L. Wilson vanished from the city, ending an association with Dundee that had lasted for three quarters of a century.

Post mortem

After closure the G. L. Wilson store remained vacant for some while. Eventually the building underwent complete internal redevelopment in 1996 and is now occupied by small retail units. The exterior was refurbished and returned to its original state.

8 THE STREETS

Introduction

In the 1950s the layout of the main shopping streets in the centre of Dundee had changed little for over half a century. Each of these streets had its own particular character due to the combination of shops to be found there, and this contributed to the unique feel of Dundee as a city centre.

The main streets were clustered around a spine running in an arc from the Nethergate on the west, through the High Street, Murraygate, and the Wellgate, to the bottom of the Hilltown in the north. Running off the main spine to the north were the Overgate, and Reform Street, whilst Union Street, Whitehall Street and Crescent, Castle Street and the Seagate all connected to the southern side of the arc. The spine was bisected by Lindsay Street and by Commercial Street which was the major route from the Harbour to the rest of the town.

This chapter is based upon the entries contained in the Dundee Street Directory of 1955/6 and sets out a list of the shops operating in these streets together with comments and people's memories of them where they have come to the attention of the author.

The list of shops is confined to the main shopping streets within the central area of Dundee, roughly defined as the area lying within the current line of the Inner Ring Road. Although there were a very large number of shops operating in Dundee in 1955 lying outwith this area, they are not included here on the grounds that this would have required at least another two or three volumes to do it justice.

However this does mean that there is room for others to record the life and times of shops in such areas as the Hiltown, Lochee, Broughty Ferry and Albert Street, all of which had their own particular quality.

Castle Street

In the mid-1950s Castle Street was a busy street being the main route to the High Street from the harbour and the bus station that was then located on Shore Terrace.

1, Peter Speedie, tobacconist

This shop had been owned by R. G. Brown, Provost of Cupar but he had given it to his son Raymond Brown, who in 1955 was the owner of the shop.

2, Lindsay's, photo chemist

This shop was set up at this address in 1908 and in 1955 it was owned by Mr George J. Lindsay who ran the business with his son J. Bruce Lindsay When he died in in 1963 the shop was sold to Elena Mae.

5, Thomas Dunbar, clothier

R. M. Nairn who had worked in D. M. Brown's set up as a gent's outfitter at this address on 14 March 1953 but sold out to Dunbar in December of the same year. A good illustration of the way the city centre worked at that time was that David Blackadder a solicitor based in Castle Street, bought all of his suits from this tailor.

21, Lawleys, china merchants

The Lawleys china chain was set up by Edgar E Lawley in Regent Street in London in the early 20th century.

29, George Stephen & Sons, ironmonger

One of the oldest shops in Dundee this business was founded in 1814. In the early days goods were supplied by pony and trap to cartwrights and blacksmiths in Angus and Perthshire. In January 1953 John S. Agnew who had been running the firm since 1951 became Chairman of the Dundee Branch of the National Federation of Ironmongers. Although this store was nominally an ironmongers, in fact it sold just about everything in the way of garden and agricultural supplies as well as bicycles and bird scarers It even had a display of electric kettles on the top floor. It closed in March 1985.

44, J. W. Sutherland, tobacconists

A member of the Dundee & District Tobacco Traders Golf Club, Mr Sutherland was also a keen amateur film maker and he also had a tobacconists shop in South Union Street

38, Strachan & Son, jewellers

This firm, which was started in these premises in 1925 was owned by Lawrence Strachan and his son Wishart. Unusually it combined a jewellery businesss with an opticians. Lawrence was the jeweller and Wishart was a qualified optician. The jewellers occupied the front shop while the opticians were located at the rear. When Lawrence died in 1966 Wishart moved the business, now only an opticians, to Meadowside.

34, William Whittet, sewing machine manufacturer

The firm had been started by William Whittet in 1864 and by 1880 had a shop at 12 Exchange Street. By 1884 he had moved to this address. Apart from sewing machines the shop also sold knitting machines. Whittet died in 1903 after which the business was carried on by his widow and family.

32, Ronald Maconachie, confectioner

This sweet shop went under the name of The Honeycomb.

28, J. D. Brown, photographic dealer

This shop was set up here in 1919.

24, David Wallace, The Auld Pie Shop

The Auld Pie shop was owned by David Wallace, the grandson of David Wallace the founder of the business in premises in the Vault in 1892. He took over the shop in the late 1940s and it closed upon his retirement in in the late 1960s. Customers recall a warm cosy shop redolent with the smell of bridies and pies and long queues on Saturday mornings.

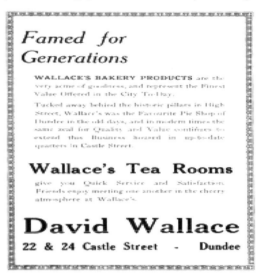

18, Stuart Patrick , bookseller

See 9, South Union Street

14/16, W. E. Dryden, fruiterer and florist

This firm was founded in 1873 by William Ellis Dryden. His son, William Alexander Spencer Dryden took over the business in 1918 and such was his success that the firm opened retail branches in Victoria Road, High Street Lochee, and Arbroath Road, a wholesale fruit business, and later a frozen fruit and vegetable service for schools and hotels. By 1955 the business was being run by the three sons of W. A. S. Dryden who eventually decided to split the business up between them, William Dryden taking over the wholesaleing business based in West Dock Street together with the Castle Street shop.

10, William Hazell & Son, grocer

This firm was set up in 1882 in 84 High Street but by 1901 it had moved to 38, Whitehall Street. It was a licensed grocer but sold a wide range of goods. In December 1930 it was advertising 'Christmas crackers of a novel design being presented as dolls dressed in Dutch, Irish and Welsh costumes or in the garb of household staff such as cooks, butlers, or housemaids'. In 1955 it was run by George Hazell. There was also a shop at 34, Commercial Street.

8, A Hutton, confectioner

6a, J. D. Gray, hairdresser

6, J. A. Braithwaite, tea merchants,

See Stores

D C Thomson

Commercial Street

Commercial Street was designed to be the main thoroughfare linking the harbour to the town and its hinterland. It was a street occupied by offices and commercial premises rather than shops. There were some important exceptions, particularly at its junction with Murraygate where the department stores of D. M. Brown, G. L. Wilson and Smith Brothers could all be found. Nevertheless the presence of the Dundee Supply Company, a delicatessen, David Low sports outfitters, Aitkens the grocers, and Malcolms furniture store combined to give it the feel of being a major shopping street.

7, David N. Crabb, electrical engineer

This was a small shop with few goods on show, but which seemed to stock every electrical accessory that had ever been invented.

9, David Carswell & Sons, grocer

This firm had been set up by David Carswell who died on 29 November 1930. In 1955 it was being run by his grandson, also David Carswell. It was not a retail shop but a wholesale grocer.

23, David Dickie & Sons, ironmongers

This business which had been operating here as early as 1905 was eventually taken over by James Lindsay and later his wife. However, they continued to use the DDD (David Dickie Dundee) logo. A little known fact about this firm of ironmongers was that it supplied coffins to joiners, who at that time often organised funerals. The coffins were kept on the fourth floor of the premises and amongst them were coffins wrapped in hessian cloth for transportation as far afield as the highlands and islands.

31, David Low, sports outfitter

This shop was 'the' shop in Dundee for golf and tennis equipment. David Low, a native of Carnoustie,

in 1920 started in business in the Wellgate as a tobacconist and newsagent. In 1926 in these premises he opened a golf school and sold golf clubs but later moved the whole business to Commercial Street. After the war he was joined by his son and went on to open shops in Carnoustie and St Andrews and to run the annual Scottish Professional Golf Championship. David Low Snr. who ran the chain of sports shops that bore his name, died at the age of 88.

35/39, Malcolms, house furnishers

Malcolm's Furniture Store was a substantial business describing itself as "upholsterers, house furnishers china and glass merchants, ironmongers, auctioneers and valuators". The company that ran this large furniture store had been started in Crichton Street in 1895 by two brothers, Adam and William Malcolm, as a firm of auctioneers and valuers The firm was successful and grew very rapidly necessitating two expansions of their premises. In 1898 William died, and three years later Adam Malcolm moved the business to 35 Commercial Street. The adjoining shop was acquired in 1906, restyled, and opened in 1907 as what was primarily a furniture store. In 1918 it was turned into limited company with Adam Malcolm and his son Ian, as the two shareholders. Ian Malcolm was an early advocate in Dundee of Danish furniture design, and remained in charge until the business closed in 1964.

Seagate here

57, Peter McLean, tobacconist

Peter McLean was born in in Glasgow. He moved to Dundee where in 1848 he set up a pipe making business employing 18 people in South Tay Street. His son Peter set up a tobacconists business around

1880 in the Nethergate. that employed his son James and his daughter Christina. This firm was both a retail and a wholesale tobacconist. In 1955 the shop was being run by the founder's granddaughter, Margaret Yule McLean.

61, J. Fyfe Ogilvie, tea dealer
This firm, dealing in tea and coffee was established in 1826 by James Fyfe Ogilvie at 61 High Street. In 1890 the business was moved to this address. J.F.Ogilvie was succeeded in turn by his son and his grandson, the latter dying in 1940. In 1955 the business was still being carried on under the same name, possibly by his daughter Helen.

63, D & W Croll, seedsmen.
Crolls were established at this address by 1881 and came to be famed all over Britain for their roses. At that time Crolls were selling around 2,000 rose plants per year but by 1955 they were selling over 500,000 roses per annum many of which were exported. In 1955 the shop was being run by Raymond Arnos who had joined the firm as a partner in 1921 and Alexander Lemon, a third partner, Mr James Young, having died in 1954.
See also 100, Nethergate

Murraygate here

73 The Corner, G. L. Wilson, draper
See Stores

89, Scottish Gas Board Showrooms
The Scottish Gas Board had been set up in 1949 as part of the post war government's programme of nationalisation. At that time the Board took over the gas functions of the Dundee City Council operations but was dissolved in 1973 when it became part of the British Gas Corporation.

IMPERIAL

"Good Companion"

Here is the most complete Modern Portable Typewriter. It can handle all classes of typewritten work — ordinary correspondence, stencil cutting and manifolding. The "Good Companion" will give years of good service and the appearance of the work it produces is outstanding.

T. M. SPARKS & SON

OFFICE EQUIPMENT SPECIALISTS
and COMMERCIAL STATIONERS.

91½ COMMERCIAL STREET, DUNDEE.

Est. 1908.   Telephone 3395.

91a, T. M. Sparks & Son, stationers
In 1908 the Cresswell Printing company was founded by T. M. Sparks in Peter Street before in 1928 moving to this address under the Sparks banner. In addition to carrying on a book binding business the firm was also the agent for Imperial Typewriters. Sparks also had sizeable premises in Meadow Entry where they sold office equipment and furniture. In 1955 it was being run by Alexander P. Sparks, the son of the founder.

95, North of Scotland Hydro Electric showrooms
The North of Scotland Hydro Electric Company was founded in 1943 to construct and manage hydroelectricity projects in the north of Scotland. In 1991 it was privatised by the government of the day.

Albert Square here

100/108, R. Buist & Sons, upholsterers
This was a very old concern having been established by Richard Buist in 1832. At one time it had had premises at 16/20 Castle Street where it also sold linoleum. In 1955 it was being run by G. A. Hamilton who was the grandson of founder Richard Buist.

86, Murdoch & Patersons, printers and stationers
George Duncan Paterson and James Murdoch were the founders of this business in the early 1900s and which had a branch in Blackness Road. One of their posters for a performance of 'The Eternal City' is in the collection of the Victoria & Albert Museum in London. One person who remembers the shop well is Jim Howie who recalls buying a revolutionary new kind of pen here – the Biro.

80, Dundee Supply Co., grocers
This shop was the nearest thing to a delicatessen to be found in Dundee. It was owned by Mr John B Miller who had started in the firm of William Miller & Sons at 75 High Street. He set up on his own at this address in 1950. John Miller was a keen skier. The shop closed in 1966 after which the premises were occupied by Potters shoe shop.

78, James Morton & Sons, clothiers
This business goes back to 1868 when it was owned by James Morton, born in Darvel. He died in June 1918, after which the firm was run by his son, James S. Morton who lived in Camphill Road, Broughty Ferry. In the 1950s the store was run by Frank Morton the grandson of the founder of the business.

68, D. M. Browns, drapers
See Stores

High Street here

54, Walker & Hall, goldsmiths

The business was established by George Walker in 1845 in Howard Street in Sheffield. In 1853 the firm was joined by Henry Hall and became Walker & Hall. The firm became a UK wide business and opened this branch in Dundee in the early 1900s.

52, Willerby & Co, tailors

This was a branch of a UK wide chain of tailors shops. They were more of an upmarket tailor specialising in bespoke suits and who, in the 1930s, had felt sufficiently confident of their position to publish 'The Style Book for Men'.

42, G. L. Dow, hairdressers

This was not only a hairdressers but also a tobacconists.

40, Wiliam Doig & Sons, chemists

William Doig was born in 1837 in Kirriemuir. When he retired the business was run by his son Willliam Doig Jnr who was born in 1875. After he died in the First World War the business was left to his son in law, John Lyall Doig.

38, Fraser & Son, picture framers

Fraser & Sons had moved into these premises in 1946. This firm, quite apart from being a successful picture framing business, were also dealers in art, particularly watercolours.

36, H. Gollan & Sons, jewellers

This Glasgow firm were engaged in both the retail and the wholesale jewellery trade. Founded in 1828 it had had a branch in Dundee since 1913. Thomas Gollan, the Managing Director of Hector Gollan & Sons, died in August 1934 after which the firm was run by Hector Gollan Jnr. The business was closed in June 1960.

6, Robert Adam & Son, ironmongers

This firm was founded in the Overgate under the title of T. Adams in 1874. Adam's son Robert moved the business to Commercial Street but by 1955 the firm was owned by a Mr. C. W. Scott. Although it advertised its services as a builder and ironmonger it was actually more of a locksmith and seller of safes.

2a, Milne & Son, hairdressers

This was a very old fashioned barbers. One customer recalls a large gas heater in the shop that in winter was used to warm the hair clippers.

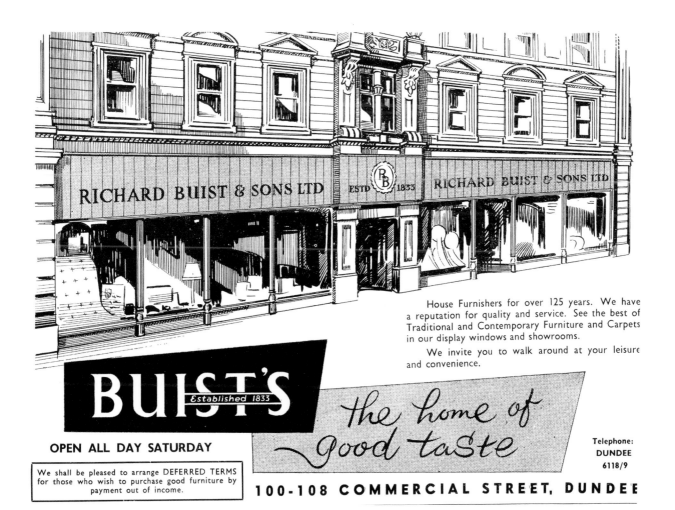

D C Thomson

Crichton Street

Crichton Street was the first attempt undertaken in the eighteenth century to improve the access from the centre of the town to the harbour. It was created by the widening of a mediaeval close, but only on one side, which accounts for the curved western side of the thoroughfare.

3, Alex Robertson, newsagent

Alexander Robertson and his son Ian started this shop in 1945 when Ian returned home after his service in the armed forces. Although a newsagents Robertsons was known for the high quality of the ice cream that it sold. The shop closed in 1980.

5, Mrs Betty White, tobacconist

This shop had been a tobacconists shop for many years, although under a variety of owners. In 1955 it was run by Mrs Betty White whose business had been founded in the Hilltown in 1928 by her grandfather, James S. Young. As well as this shop Betty White had ownership or part ownership of fruit and fish shops in Victoria Road, Hilltown and Reform Street. This shop was known for its window displays of a wide range of goods for smokers that included lighters, pipes of all kinds, blocks of pipe tobacco, and cigarette and cigar cases. When it closed in 1985 it was said to be the last true tobacconist operating in Dundee.

13, Clydesdale Supply Co, radio dealers

Clydesdale was a Scottish retailer of electrical goods and at one time the largest in Scotland. They opened a branch here in 1931.

17, Largs & Sons, music sellers

Alexander Larg was born in Perth but set up music selling businesses in Forfar and Montrose before opening a store in Dundee in 1895. When he died in 1927 the business was taken over by his son D. C. Larg By 1955 the shop was run by Eric Larg, the founder's grandson. It was a popular destination for record buyers in the 1950s. The firm, which also sold sheet music, had branches in Whitehall Street, Hilltown, and Lochee. In addition they had facilities, run by Willie Black, where would-be pop stars could make a record. Larg's also owned Low's music shop at 21 Crichton Street.

19, Grampian Paint & Wallpaper

This Glasgow based company had originally been set up in Aberdeen in December 1946 and opened a branch here in 1951.

21, Lows (Dundee), music sellers

This shop was in fact owned by Largs who were based in Whitehall Street but also had a shop at 17 Crichton Street. The shop was a popular one for those buying records and Norrie Robertson recalls that it was here that in 1946 he bought his first record - 'Sentimental Journey' played by the Squadronaires.

23, New Smith Brothers, outfitters
This business had been set up by Edwin and Wilfred Smith after they left Smith Brothers department store in the Murraygate. They first set up shop in the Wellgate but then, in 1937, moved to 12 Crichton Street before moving to this shop in 1950.

14, J. C. Johnstone, tailor
In 1955 this shop was owned by Thomas Mather Johnstone . He had in 1930 joined the firm set up by his father James C. Johnstone who provided "Exclusive Hand tailoring for Ladies and Gentlemen".

12, Stafford House, china & glass
In 1881 Thomas Jones set up a china and glass business in Stafford House in the High Street of Cardigan and traded there until 1914. The firm later expanded and opened a number of branches throughout the UK, one of which was established in 1954 at this address.

8, Wallace "Land O' Cakes"
This business was set up by James McHardy Wallace, born in Arbroath but who spent some years in New York in the bakery trade. When he returned to Scotland in the late 1890s he settled in Dundee where his whole family became involved. In the mid 1950s the shop was run by Andrew Wallace who had taken over the firm in the late 1940s. The Land o' Cakes was extremely popular and generated long queues outside the shop on Saturday mornings.

6, Roderick Tweedie, ladies outfitters
This was a Scottish firm with branches in Edinburgh, Inverness, Dundee, Aberdeen and Newcastle and set up at this address in 1936. It advertised under the slogan "for Town & County" and in addition to selling women's fashion also supplied dress uniforms to the armed services.

2, W. P. Laird & Sinclair, seed merchants
This was a very old firm having been set up in 1832 by William Pringle Laird when he took up the feu for the plot at 26 in the recently opened Union Street. The business grew and found itself short of space and moved, first to 46 Union Street, and then to 88 Nethergate. In 1899 the firm moved to these premises in Crichton Street. It was very much a local firm and Joyce Smart recalls her Uncle Roger gathering white heather on the moors around Ladybank in Fife, and selling it in bunches to Laird and Sinclair for sale in this shop.

D C Thomson

High Street

As one would imagine the High Street was at the heart of the city centre and had seen many changes. Not the least of these were the demolition of sections to enable the construction of Reform Street, Whitehall Street, Chrichton Street, Union Street and the City Square. After the 1950s the whole northern side was swept away for the first redevelopment of the Overgate.

1a, Halford Cycle Co. Ltd

This firm was originally founded by Francis Rushbrooke in Birmingham in 1892 as an ironmongers. In 1902 it moved to Halford Street in Leicester when the firm was renamed after the street. Here it started selling cycling goods and subsequently expanded throughout the UK, opening this branch in 1937.

2, Keiller, James, & Son, Ltd confectioners.

Keillers originated in Dundee 1797 when Janet Keiller created the first commercial brand of marmalade and the world's first marmalade factory. The firm were also believed to be the first makers of Dundee Cake. By 1955 they were owned by Crosse & Blackwell, having been bought out just after the First World War.

Castle Street here

6, Henry Adams & Son, glovers

Henry Adams was one of oldest firms in Dundee and dated from 1791 when it was founded by George Rough. In time he was succeeded by his son, also George Rough who became Provost of Dundee. By 1849 the business occupied a shop below the old Town House at 5 High Street. The firm was taken over in 1858 by Henry Adams from Yeovil. In 1889 he took his son, George Rough Adams, into partnership. In 1915 G.R.Adams died leaving the firm to be run by George Rough Adams Jnr. and his son Albert Edward Adams. Albert died in 1925 and in 1930 then owners moved to this address. This was a stylish shop and Liz Barrie recalls buying a pair of elbow length black gloves in this shop that "oozed sophistication".

7, Montague Burton Ltd., tailors

This was a branch of a tailoring firm set up in 1904 in Chesterfield by Meshe Osinsky, a Lithuanian refugee . When deciding to change his name he

chose Montague because to him it sounded posh, and Burton because Burton on Trent had been a town that he had stayed in and liked.

Burton's success lay in mass producing made-to-measure suits at a price the working man could afford. He was an enlightened employer, believing that success came from paying decent wages to employees. The company's factories had canteens, health and pensions schemes and even chiropodists and dentists on site. At one time it was the biggest tailoring firm in the UK and had over 30% of the market for 'demob' suits for those leaving the armed forces.

This branch opened in 1930 as part of the new city square complex. Two of the original black granite corner stones bearing the names of the members of the family who laid them are still there.

City Square here

26, Birrell, Ltd., confectioners
Birrells were a Glasgow based sweet maker founded in 1903 by John Stewart Birrell. They first opened a branch in Dundee at 18, Reform Street and in 1926 opened another shop at this address. The company was taken over in 1950 by Mayfair Products, a Sunderland firm. Even after the takeover this shop continued to be operated under the Birrell banner.

28, A. C. Little & Sons Ltd., costumiers.
This shop which had operated here since 1918 as a costumier and furrier used the slogan "The House For Value". Many Dundonians recall the spaciousness of this fashion shop.

Church Lane here

5, Church Lane
John Young, House Furnishers
This firm was set up in 1907 by John Young who had previously had shops in South Tay Street, Tally Street and 40/42 Victoria Road. When he died in 1932 the business was taken over by his son William, and his two daughters, Ann and Paula. William was a keen cricketer and played for Scotland. He died in 1966 after which the firm was run by his son, Logie Young. He later moved the shop to Dock Street where he continued trading until 1992 when he closed the shop.

4, Church Lane
The Penguin Snack Bar
The Penguin Cafe was opened here in September 1951 by Mr T. E. Morgan. Little is known about this establishment but the approximate site of this small cafe is now marked by a group of penguins on the wall surrounding the City Churches.

30, Dundee Institution for the Blind shop.

The Dundee Institution for the Blind originated in 1865 when Mrs Frances Mollison bought Dallfield House so as to set up an institution for the blind. This was eventually opened in 1869. The Dundee Institute for the Blind opened a shop at this address in 1886 where it sold a wide range of goods made in its factory on Magdalen Green. It later combined with Lord Roberts Workshops under the name Dovetail Enterprises.

32 James K. Sim, grocer

In 1905 a Mr Brennan set up shop as a grocer at 189 Perth Road and in 1924 he moved to these premises. He died in August 1927 after which the business was taken over by Mr J. K. Sim who also had a grocers shop at Stobswell.

34/36, The Treasure House

This was a gift shop set up by Miss Louise Bryant 1916. She sold the shop in 1946 to A. E. M'Millan, an Aberdonian,who still owned the shop in 1955. It was once described as "the Scottish Aladdin's cave, with an almost inexhaustible supply of old paintings, vases and other antiques". This shop's business may have been boosted by the presence of a tram stop right outside the door.

37, R. Bottler, hairdresser

This shop which had been here since 1940 was something of a specialist in permanent waving. In 1950 Bottler, who described himself as a 'Ladies Hairdresser and Posticheur', was advertising 'the latest Permanent Waving Equipment' at only 35/- for the whole head.

38, Andrew G. Kidd Ltd., bakers.

Since 1930 this shop had been owned by Andrew G. Kidd who was born in Brechin. At first he worked with Baillie Perrie's bakery in Lochee but in 1860 he set up in business with his family. He started by opening a bakery in Lytton Street and in 1897 opened their first shop in Reform Street. By the 1920's they had 19 branches and employed around 300 people. The firm also owned Kidd's Rooms in South Lindsay Street that was one of Dundee's best known function suites and a popular venue for teenagers as a dance hall.

40, William Chalmers & Son, bootmakers

This business was founded in 1824 under the name of David Scott. In 1837 it was awarded a Royal Warrant for the supply of boots to King William. William Chalmers took over the firm in 1882 and was succeeded by his son in 1908. The firm also had shops in Mid Kirk Style, under the name Out and About, and in Broughty Ferry and Blairgowrie.

When the shop closed in 1985 it was being run by Mr George Patterson.

41, Hardy's Furnishing Store

This shop, which opened here in 1939, specialised in credit sales with no deposits.

44, George Carrie Ltd, opticians

This opticians shop was established here 1939 on the first floor and had a giant pair of glasses on the outside of the building as an advertising gimmick.

48, Sixty Minute Cleaners, Ltd

This branch opened in 1944 and during the Second World War had a notice in its window somewhat ironically boasting of the availability of "a 24 hour Service".

Overgate here

51, Boots, The Chemists
See 2, Reform Street

Reform Street here

D C Thomson

62, Lamb, A. & R., newsagents

This was, at one time, probably the most famous shop in Dundee. This was due entirely to its diminutive size. With a floor area of three feet by three feet (under a square metre) it had once formed a part of an emergency exit to the billiard hall situated above. In 1888 Robert Lamb, a cabinet maker. rented it for the sale of cigarettes and newspapers. Later his sons Robert, George, and

Alexander came into the business with him. When Alexander retired in 1926 the business was carried on by Robert. In 1932 the Lambs bought the land for £1400 making it, for its size the most expensive piece of real estate in Scotland at the time. The firm prospered there but finally closed in 1962 . The firm also had two shops in the Overgate.

63, R. S. McColl Ltd., confectioners
R. S. McColl was originally a Scottish newsagent company based on the west coast. It was set up in 1901 by Robert Smyth McColl (a professional football player) and his brother Tom. It was successful and expanded across Scotland, later adding confectionery to its lines. in 1954 it opened a branch at this address. Its shops in Dundee were taken over by Birrells in 1970.

64, Maybole Dairy Co.Ltd.
This firm was operating in Dundee in 1895 from 85 High Street. The Maybole Dairy, which may have originated the in the Ayrshire town of that name, at one time featured an "egg testing machine' that consisted of a glass tank of water into which eggs were placed. If they sank all was well, if they floated they had gone off.

66, Wm. Timpsons, footwear
This Manchester firm was established in 1865 by William Timpson and Walter Joyce. Originally just selling shoes it expanded into a manufacturing business in 1884, and into repairs in 1903. A branch was established here by 1953. The firm was taken over by United Drapery Stores in 1978 but was bought back by John Timpson in 1983. As a result this business, with an annual turnover of £170,000,000 is still owned by the Timpson family.

68, James Keiller & Son, Ltd., confectioner
This shop had a restaurant above street level that was designed in an Art Deco style. Its windows still remain on the first floor façade.
See 2 above

70, G. & A. Stobie Ltd., tobacconists
This shop was opened in 1922 by brothers George and Andrew Stobie. They had run a number of shops in the past including a fruit merchants, florists, fish merchants and poulterers at 45 High Street, confectioners shops at 72 High Street and at 6 Whitehall Street, and a fishmongers at 13 Union Street. They also had a shop in Pitlochry.

72, G. & A. Stobie Ltd., confectioners
See above, but this shop was run by Sarah Elizabeth Stobie, a relative of the Stobie brothers, who spent her whole working life in this confectionery shop. She died in 1960.

73, Robertson & Watt, watchmakers
This Dundee jeweller was founded in 1841 by James Robertson and William Watt and had opened this shop in 1891. In 1946 it was taken over by Maurice Porter. The firm later took over the next door premises of G. & A. Stobie in 1960 and incorporated these into a redesigned store.

75, Wm. Millar & Sons (Dundee) Ltd., grocers
William Miller was born in Kirriemuir in 1848. After learning the grocery trade in 1876 he opened a grocers shop in Tally Street and moved to this property in 1898. After his death in 1913 the firm was run by his two sons William and John S. Millar. The shop closed in 1960 when the premises were acquired by the British Shoe Corporation.
Dennis Collins recalls "This was one of the few shops in Dundee with an overhead wiring system for the shop-assistant to send cash to the cashier while he dealt with another customer and the original customer, probably seated in a chair alongside the counter, waited for his change."

77, Kidd & Wallace, rubber merchants
Founded in 1901 by John S. Kidd and William Wallace by the 1950s the shop was owned by John B Kidd, the son of the founder. The shop sold a wide range of rainwear and sports goods. In the 1950s they also acted as a ticket agency and sold tickets for Dundee United games. In 1953 they sold the business to Connell & Sons who remained in charge in 1955.

78, Saxone Shoe Co., Ltd.
See 99, Nethergate

80, D M Brown, warehousemen
See Stores

94, Johnston & Adams, Ltd., chemists
See 38, Reform Street.

Lindsay Street

There were a number of smaller streets that connected to the Overgate but easily the most significant of these was Lindsay Street, which was divided into Lindsay Street North and Lindsay Street South.

Lindsay Street North

1, Andrew Birrell & Sons, bootmakers
See 107, Overgate

9, J. P. Shuttleworth & Son, weighing machine manufacturers
Shuttleworth was born In Angus in about 1863 and set up shop here in 1891. In 1955 his son Francis A. Shuttleworth was in charge of the business. The company supplied many machines to the textile industry and one of Shuttleworth's weighing machines is part of the display at Verdant Works Museum.

11, Muriel Clark, photographer
Muriel Clark who had previously operated from the Plaza Studio in the Hilltown specialised in Wedding portraits.

13, George G. Kirk, glaziers
This firm had been operating in Dundee at least since 1909, when it was located at 8, Johnston's Lane at the West Port. The firm was based in Ayr and all its branches were in the west of Scotland apart from the one in Dundee which it had opened in 1941.

Willison Street/South Ward Road here

43, John Menzies & Co. Ltd, newsagents
This company was founded in 1833 by John Menzies, a native of Edinburgh. The firm was a great success and was subsequently built into a national chain of shops and a newspaper distribution business.

49, St. Roques Automobile Co., Ltd
This company was set up in 1906 by David MacDonald in the remodelled premises previously owned by A. C. Scott, mill furnishers. In 1920 his son W. R. MacDonald took over the firm which, in 1922, he set up as a private company called the St. Roque's Automobile Co. Ltd.

72, Harry Key, newsagent
This business was set up in the 1930s by Harry Key. When, in March 1935, a bus station was established by W Alexander & Son in the adjoining premises he made an arrangement with them to supply newspapers to passengers. Later he branched out to sell leather goods and stationery items. The firm taken over in 1962 by his son Marshall Whitton Key, an extremely talented ice hockey player, who died on 9 February 2016.

70 W. Alexander & Sons, omnibus proprietors
This company had been started by William Alexander in 1913 to run buses in the Falkirk area. Alexander's grew to become the largest bus operator in Scotland and in 1924 began building buses for its own and others use. In March 1935 the company opened up a central bus station in these premises that included staff facilities and an overnight garage for buses. By 1955 it had been nationalised and was under the control of the British Transport Commission.

66. Dundee Pasteurised Milk Co., restaurant
See 27, Reform Street

South Ward Road here

32, W. S. McNab & Sons, leather merchants
This firm was founded in 1841 by William A. McNab. At the start of 1955 his grandson, William McNab, was in charge of the firm, but he died on May 15 1955, leaving his son and partner Mr W. S. McNab to carry on the business.

Lindsay Street South

24, James Cummings, fishmonger
This firm had been set up by James Cummings, a fisherman who operated mainly on the Tay estuary. In 1908 he introduced the first steam drifter on the Tay. He was quite a character and at different times sailed on Tay pleasure steamers and, in the first world war, served on a minesweeper. Cummings also had had one of his boats, the Elizabeth, sunk under him in a storm on the Forth. In 1955 the business was being run by Harold S. Cummings.

14, Handicraft Supplies
See 3 Queen's Hotel, Nethergate

12, Matthew Waddell, fishing tackle maker
From this shop Waddell sold not only fishing tackle but also guns, rifles and waterproof clothing.

10, Angus Shoe Works
This firm was a subsidiary of William Patterson & Sons who were based in the Overgate and opened a shop here in 1946 .

8, William Patterson & Sons, wholesale drapers
The founder of this company died in a car crash in Peterhead in 1929, but in 1955 the business was still being carried on at this address under the same name.

4, D. M'Innes, optician
This firm was operating from here from 1927 onwards, at first simply as an optician. However, by 1928 M'Innes was also developing films and selling cameras and wirelesses. In 1949 it became part of a public company controlled from Manchester.

D C Thomson

Murraygate

Throughout the last two centuries the Murraygate has been very important as a shopping street and, unlike some other shopping streets, its ground level was exclusively devoted to shops. In the late 1950s Jerome the photographer, who had a monkey as a prop, could be seen touting for trade in the Murraygate and buskers are still to be seen there from time to time.

1, Smith Brothers, outfitters
See stores

11, James Grant, house furnishers
This was a branch of a Glasgow firm that had some ten branches in that city when it established its first branch in Dundee at 11-15 Cowgate on 28 March 1928.

17/19, M. M. Hendersons, jewellers
Matthew McLaren Henderson, a native of Airdrie, in 1886 established in this business in Coatbridge and opened a branch in here in 1925. He had six sons and a daughter all of whom became involved in the business. Between 1923 and 1930 the firm opened five new branches culminating in the opening of a shop in Union Street, Aberdeen managed by David Henderson. In 1932 Matthew M. Henderson Jnr, took over the management of The Dundee branch of the business. He, along with his brother, Donald F. S. Henderson, became directors of the firm which moved to Commercial Street where it closed in February 2014.

23, Etam Ltd, ladies' wear specialists
Etam Développement was a French company founded in 1916 by Max Lindemann. The company was very successful and set up a company in the UK which opened a branch here in 1952. The British chain was developed separately until in 1997 the French chain bought out their British subsidiary. However in 2005 the whole business was taken over by Philip Green's Arcadia Group.

29, Paul & Matthew, printers
Paul & Matthews was a small locally owned printers that set up in the Cowgate before moving to the Murraygate. They described themselves as 'a very, very, busy firm' and were the original publishers of the Dundee Directory that was subsequently taken over by Burns & Harris. In 1955 the business was owned by Frank Lindsay.

45, Marks & Spencers
Marks & Spencers was founded in Leeds in 1884 by Michael Marks, a Lithuanian refugee (hence St Michael as a brand name)) and Thomas Spencer.

This branch was opened in 1936 and Sandy Melville recalls that in the 1950s M & S had a downstairs restaurant where music was playing.

55, Andrew G. Kidd, bakers
See 38, High Street

61, A. Harris, tobacconist
This was a Glasgow based business and had two other branches in Dundee, one in the Overgate and one in Union Street. This branch was opened in 1949.

63, W. H. Scott, furrier
This was both a manufacturing furrier and a shop selling luxury goods. It moved from the Murraygate to this location in 1927. For many Dundonians it was only a place for window shopping. It closed in 1955.

65, Fifty Shilling Tailors
Founded in 1905 in Leeds by Henry Price this was a very successful chain of tailors shops. Originally trading under the name Thirty Shilling Tailors it

prospered in the first half of the 20th century. It had two branches in Dundee one here - which opened in 1933 - and one in the High Street. In 1958 the firm was sold and then renamed as John Collier. Later it was sold to Montague Burton who discontinued the brand.

67, James Webster, tailors
This shop had been set up in 1900 by James Webster, but by the 1950s was owned and run by Peter Clark, his nephew, who had lost an arm in the Great War. Clark had become a partner in 1931 and retired in 1959, dying in 1960.

69, Claude Alexander, tailor
This was a originally a Scottish business and in 1930 opened a very modern branch at this address featuring an entrance arcade. It liked to use the slogan 'Scotland's National Tailors". The chain had 37 shops by the time that it was taken over by United Drapery Stores in 1950.

71, Vogue, ladies' fashions
Opened here in 1946, in spite of its name, this was not a shop that dealt in expensive fashion goods.

75/77, Jays Furnishing Stores
This store which opened here in 1946, sold kitchen furniture and units, electrical goods including radios, and floor coverings. It advertised in the press on a basis of hire purchase repayments rather than the purchase price of the goods it sold.

79, H. & J. Wilson, fashion specialists
A London based chain, Wilsons opened this shop in 1954.

78, Jackson the Tailor
This was a branch of the chain of shops set up by Lionel Jacobson, a self made Jewish immigrant. This store advertised itself as a hand tailor but in fact put all its alteration work out to home workers. The first branch in Dundee was at 16 Reform Street and opened in 1921. Later, in 1937, they opened a branch this address. In 1955 it was managed by Thomas Golden who had been working in the shop since 1937.

76, J. Hepworth, clothiers
This chain of tailors shops had been founded by Joseph Hepworth in Leeds in 1864, but it was not until 1937 that the company opened a branch here. The firm eventually became the biggest clothing manufacturer in the UK and is now known as Next.

72, Scotch Wool & Hosiery Stores
In 1840 John Fleming and James Reid started a worsted mill in Greenock. In 1883 they moved into the retail trade selling woollens and hosiery and in

1931 they opened a branch at this address. In 1957 the company rebranded their shops under the title of The Scotch Wool Shop. Shortly afterwards the firm ran into trading difficulties and in the 1960s it was acquired by Coats Paton.

70, True Form Boot Co.
In 1891 the True Form Boot Company was founded in London, by John and William Sears. The firm expanded rapidly, opening this shop in 1927.

66, G. A. Dunn & Co, hatters
This chain of men's outfitters was founded in 1887 by George Arthur Dunn, a Quaker who had started in business selling hats on the streets of Birmingham. By 1947 Dunn had a chain of around 200 shops selling hats and extended the range of clothing to include suits, blazers and notably tweed sports jackets. It dealt in quality wear with a rural slant and.traded in the Murraygate from 1947 to 1996 when the firm collapsed.

64, Stead & Simpson, boot manufacturers
This chain of shoe shops was founded in Leeds in the 1840s but was only registered as a company in 1863. At one time it supplied boots to the Confederate Army in the American Civil War. It opened this branch in 1915.

48/60, F. W. Woolworth
An American firm, Woolworths opened its first branch in 1878 in Utica, New York but the store failed. Frank Winfield Woolworth reopened in Lancaster, Pennsylvania in 1879 and the business grew to be one of the largest retail chains in the world. It went out of business in 1997. The Dundee branch, which opened in 1926 with the slogan "Nothing over 6d", with its island counters, was a great favourite with Dundee children. It carried a wide range of goods and one customer can recall buying a tortoise in the store. In 1984 it moved to the new Wellgate shopping mall.

46, Graftons, fashion specialists
This shop was owned by Morrisons a Glasgow company. Joyce Hendry, who worked in this shop, recalls that it sold mainly coats and dresses although it also carried out alterations which were done by a Mrs Auchterlonie.
See 51 Wellgate

44, Willam Barratt & Co., boot manufacturers
Barrats was established in Northampton in 1903 and was a very successful company. In 1936 they opened a branch at this location but in 1964 the Barratt chain was bought by Stylo, a firm based in Bradford. They expanded the chain but in 2008 announced that all Barratt shops would close.

40, Fifty Shilling Tailors (John Colliers)
This later operated under the John Collier logo with the slogan "John Collier - the window to watch". See also at 65 above.

2, Montague Burton, tailors
See 7,High Street

26, A. L. Salisbury Ltd, leather specialists
Salisburys, who styled themselves "The Handbag People", sold mainly ladies leather bags but also retailed quality costume jewellery.

20, Dolcis Shoe Co. Ltd.
This firm originated in 1883 in Woolwich Market where John Upson sold shoes from a barrow. However he soon graduated to a permanent shop entitled the Great Boot Provider. In 1920 the business went public and the shoes began to be sold under the Dolcis name. The company opened this branch in 1945. In 1956 the chain was acquired by the British Shoe Corporation. One Dundonian recalls that the shop assistants here "had a very superior air about them."

18, Stevenson Brothers, cleaners and dyers
This firm was set up in May 1820 in the Hilltown by James Stevenson and his brother John Stevenson. They were the sons of Baillie Francis Stevenson who was also a dyer. By 1938 the firm had been taken over by Associated Dyers & cleaners Ltd but was still operating at these premises in 1955 and under the same name.

14, Alexander Potter & Sons, shoe makers
See Stores.

Church's Church's

LADIES' DEPT. — THIRD FLOOR

Potters

MURRAYGATE — DUNDEE

2, G. L. Wilson, draper
See Stores

Nethergate

The Nethergate was one of the first streets in Dundee and was located at the very centre of the city. Unusually in its later life it has been, for much of its length, a one sided shopping street.

9, James Millar, mens outfitters

This tailor's business had been established by by James Christie Drysdale Millar who occupied a shop at 21, Overgate. When he died in October 1950 the business was carried on by his Trustees at that location until February 1951 when they moved to this address.

13, Thomas Cook, travel agents

Probably the best known name in travel, Thomas Cook & Son was founded by Thomas Cook, a one time Baptist missionary, in Leicester in 1841. Building upon his connections with the Temperance movement he started by arranging excursions from Market Harborough to Leicester. He retired in 1878 after which the business was developed by his son and three grandchildren. By 1890 it was selling over 3 million tickets worldwide. Cook's opened this branch in 1951.

15, Mrs George Nicoll, confectioner

This was a shop well stocked with all sorts of confectionery, mainly loose, and in glass jars. Mrs Nicoll also had a shop in South Union Street.

17, E. Littlejohn, newsagents

This was a very busy shop set up around 1909 by Mrs Littlejohn in the Pillars beneath the Town House. Having to move due to the demolition of the Old Town House it relocated to this address in 1932. In the 1950s it was run by three ladies who stood behind a wide counter on which the newspapers and magazines were laid out.

19, Miss Peebles, dressmaker

Miss Peebles, who also had a dealers business at 153 the Overgate, also had a 'saloon' in the premises above this shop prior to opening her dress shop here in 1943. When opened, this shop sold only made to measure clothing. Joyce Smart recalls,"this was a small shop which sold good quality clothes at moderate prices".

23, Miss B. Thomson, fish merchant

This shop was owned by Betty White and her brother

James White. White's son Forbes White also worked in the shop.
See 5, Crichton Street

25, J. Callaghan, cutler
Mr J. L. Callaghan, who opened here in 1933, not only sold cutlery but ran an ironmongers business from this address selling, sharpening, and overhauling lawn mowers and even sharpening skate blades.

27, A. W. Watson, motor hirers
This firm specialised in Scottish Coach Tours and in car hire for weddings and funerals. In 1951 the company planned to create a 12 day, 2,135 mile round Britain tour at a price of £26 - £30. However this was objected by W. Alexander & Sons and the Rail Executive. A hearing at the Scottish Licensing Authority decided in the objectors favour and so no such pioneering tour took place. Watsons also had a garage for their vehicles at Fairmuir.

29, Phins, ironmongers
This business which had been set up by James Phin in 1902 in the Cowgate sold fancy goods, kitchenware and china. Phin became a prominent politician, and was Lord Provost of Dundee for two terms. By the mid 1950s the shop was owned by David Gray who, in 1935 had moved the business from the Murraygate to these premises in the Nethergate. He was known for treating his staff well, providing outings to the Edinburgh and Dundee Tattoos. He was also very helpful in assisting staff to get new jobs when the store closed as a result of the opening of the new Overgate.

Frost Pine
a firm favourite in the range of
ROYAL DOULTON tableware

The beauty of pine woods .... softly expressed in tones of olive-green, white and mahogany against a warm grey background. In the versatile new coupe shape, this handsome dinnerware brings a contemporary grace to your table.   There are many other patterns to choose from

ON SHOW NOW AT . . .
Phins of Dundee
29 NETHERGATE —— DUNDEE
Telephone : 6094-5

33, S. Barbieri, confectioners
The owner of the shop was Stefano Barbieri Snr., who in 1929 had come to Dundee from the Borgo Val di Taro area of Italy. It had a sitting area in the rear and was a popular meeting place for youngsters to enjoy ice-cream, milkshakes etc. (the word "teenagers" had not yet been imported from USA). The firm traded under the title of the Washington Soda Fountain Co. but the premises were also known as the Washington Café. Stefano's son, Steve,with his wife Daphne took over the fish and chip shop known as the Crystal Bell in Union Street, while Steve's sister, Angela Schnell, ran the Washington Cafe.

35, Kinnear restaurant
This licensed restaurant was originally established by Mr William R. Kinnear in 1949 and after he died in the 1950s it was run by his wife. Horace Ianetta took over this restaurant from Mrs Kinnear. It was, allegedly, the first restaurant in Dundee to serve Spaghetti Bolognaise. It specialised in business lunches at 2/6d and also catered for weddings.

39, E. J. Allan, radio engineers
This firm had originally been a partnership between James Sturrock and Ernest John Allan but this was dissolved in November 1924 after which Allan set up business at 84, Nethergate. Allan also had a shop at 48, Seagate and a workshop in Long Wynd.

41, 60 Minute Cleaners
See 2, Overgate

57, G. Moncur, fruiterer
Although listed under this name, the shop was actually occupied by a florists called Imrie who also had premises in the City Arcade.

59, James Marshall, confectioner
This shop had been on a number of short lets in the 1950s having been occupied by Hogg and Ross and McNab's the cleaners. Marshalls, who also had a shop in Carnoustie arrived in 1953 and were still in occupation in 1955.

63, Malone Shoe Repair Co.
See 64 Overgate

73, Dundee Eastern Co-op
See stores

81, Charles Allardyce & Son, Surgical instrument makers
See Stores

91, Andrew G. Kidd, bakers
See also 38 High Street, 59 Murraygate and 64 Wellgate

95, Miss Mathers, costumier

Miss Mathers, who came from Fife, had opened this shop in 1923 boasting of a "Distinctive collection of dainty frocks".

97, E. W. Wilson, milliner

This business was opened in 1922 by Miss Wilson, but by 1930 the shop was actually owned by Miss E. C. Henderson.

99, H. G. Voice, tobacconist

This tobacconists shop also sold novelties and was owned by Hugh Voice. The shop was still colloquially known as "Tam Shepherd's" after the proprietor of the magic shop that had previously occupied the premises.

101, G. Anastasio, confectioner

Mr Anastasio took over this confectionery shop in 1951, but his family had been in the confectionery business since 1917 when he owned the Royal Arch tearooms in Dock Street. The shop had previously been occupied by another confectioner under the title of "The Ritz".

Tay Street here

109, George Robertson & Son, grocers

This shop was first set up by George Robertson in 1897. He died in 1958 but by 1955 the firm was owned by his son Andrew Birrell Robertson. He retired in 1971 at which time he closed the business down.

115, Kirkcaldy Linoleum Stores (Dundee)

The Kirkcaldy Lino Stores opened this shop in 1947 when it was run by a Mr George Duncan. The company also had branch at 224 Hilltown.

121, Miss M. Donaldson, milliner

Miss M. Donaldson had opened her hat shop at this address in 1932 when she took over the dress shop of Miss Brodie Wilson.

125a, Miss M. Millar, confectioner

127, Pickfords, removers

The firm of removers is believed to have been established in the 17th century by William Pickford, initially as a quarrying company, but later as a haulier. In 1776 it invented the fly wagon which could travel from London to Manchester in four and a half days. In 1816 it sold out to Joseph Baxendale who in the 20th century switched to road transport. Ironically it was taken over by a rail company and nationalised in 1947 as part of British Road Services. The company opened its premises here in 1949 and was still operating from this address in 1955 under the Pickford name.

129, Miss J. Robertson, ladies hairdresser

Morgan Tower

133, A. M. Weir, tobacconist

This shop was well patronised by those going to shows at the Palace Theatre.

135, Alex W. Barrie, chemist

This business was founded in 1905 by Alex Y. Barrie as the Morgan Tower Pharmacy.

139, Miss J. Shepherd, confectioner

Miss Jessie Shepherd, a Dundonian born in 1886, had been the occupant of this shop from before World War Two.

Queens Hotel Buildings

6/7, Queens Hotel Buildings
H. Pickles & Co, warehousemen

This wholesaling business was established in 1915 but by 1955 was being run by William Pickles, the son of the founder of the company. It sold a wide variety of goods to traders ranging from toys to to flags, linen, drapery, hosiery, underwear and small wares.

5, Ogilvies Bookshop

This bookshop was named after a Roman Catholic saint and was situated close to St Andrew's Cathedral and the University. It had a coffee-shop in the basement much frequented by students and priests. It was run by Roman Catholic intellectuals.

3, Handicraft Supplies

Among its other activities such as supplying schools with handicraft materials and selling kits for making jewellery, gloves and lampshades, this shop ran a Doll's Hospital and, somewhat surprisingly, provided occupational therapy for humans.

Nethergate House

158, Thomas Muir, coal merchants

This firm had been established by Thomas Muir in 1848 who later took a Mr Patton into partnership. Muir's coal yard was situated to the south at a lower level on railway ground to allow easy delivery from the goods wagons that came over the Tay Bridge. The coal was brought up from the yard on horse drawn carts for onward delivery by a rather steep drive.

152/4, Nethergate Garage Ltd, motor agents

Established in the mid 1920s in 1950 this firm was still selling cars made in the mid 1930s such as a 1933 Lanchester saloon.

134, Roneo, duplicators

Roneo, whose name was derived from Rotary

Neostyle produced rotary duplicators which had been invented in 1887. They opened a branch here in 1954.

134a, The Deep Sea Fish restaurant

Founded by Bruno Sterpaio in 1937 on the south side of Nethergate, the business moved across the street in 1966. It was later taken over by Bruno's sons – Raymond and Lawrence. During its lifetime Sean Connery, Joanna Lumley and Richard Todd have all been customers, due to the presence in the city of Dundee Repertory Theatre.

132, S. M. T. motor showroom

The Scottish Motor Traction Company was founded in Edinburgh in 1905. In 1928 it was acquired by the London Midland and Scottish Railway and the London and North Eastern Railway. and was eventually based in Motherwell as Central SMT. In 1948 the government became a major shareholder as part of railway nationalisation and in 1949 it became a fully nationalised company not only operating buses but also selling vehicles.

130b, Cecille, ladies hairdressers

This firm opened here from around 1940. In 1949 they boldy announced that those getting a permanent wave here could have "unlimited curlers".

130, Harley & Cox, printers

This firm was established 1907 by William Cox and George Harley, born in South Africa of Dundonian parents. Together they opened a shop here in 1909. In 1942 his son, William Thornett Harley, and Charles Smith became partners in the business and took over the running of the firm when George Harley died in 1944.

128a, Davidson & Gray, chemists

This firm was founded by James N. Davidson in 1870 who was joined by a Mr Gray in 1884. In 1955 this business was owned by Thomas Russell Brown who had taken it over from the founders in 1909.

128, Pettie & Co., surgical instrument makers

William Pettie had first set up in business in Commercial Street in 1890 as a partnership with Charles Allardyce and another entrepreneur called Whitelaw. Pettie and Allardyce later fell out and by 1911 had set up in opposition on opposite sides of the Nethergate.
See Stores

126, Hogg & Ross, surgical instrument makers

This firm was established at 14 Whitehall Street in 1944 by John (Jack) Ross who had been apprenticed to Charles Allardyce. The firm initially sold surgical instruments but when, in 1951, it began to manufacture them, it moved into these premises in the Nethergate. Hogg retired in 1946 and the business was sold in 1972.

118, Troup & Walkinshaw, linen drapers

In 1926 D. J. Troup and James Walkinshaw set up business here selling linen and soft furnishings and were still in business at this location in 1955.

112, Burns & Harris, stationers

This firm of Dundee printers was established in 1882 by William Burns who had worked for William Kidd. In 1884 he took his friend Mr William Harris into partnership as stationers. Behind the shop was a single storey building opening on to Yeaman Shore and it was there that the firms printing business was started. Their success was underpinned by the millions of labels that they printed for distillers and notably for Keillers marmalade. Burns died in June 1923, William Harris the son of the co-founder died in 1927 and four years later Burns & Harris purchased the printing rights for the Dundee Directory.

110, Birrell Ltd, confectioners

This business was founded in Anniesland in Glasgow in 1903 by John Stewart Birrell. By 1924 when the firm became a public company with Birrell and his two sons, James Burns Birrell and John Stuart Birrell Jnr as directors, it had 55 shops in Scotland and 5 in London.It opened a shop here in 1935.

102, Jean Black, milliner

This shop had opened in 1923 at this location when it took over the premises of James Smith, a jeweller.

100, Crolls Browns Flower Shop

Miss Catherine B. Brown who had worked in partnership with D. & W. Croll Ltd, nurserymen, had opened Miss Brown's Flower Shop at this address in 1938. It was still known as "Miss Brown's" in 1955 although it had had traded as Crolls since 1952.

98, James Keillor & Son, bakers

See 2, High Street

94/96, Morison, Pollexfen & Blair, travel agents

This firm of travel agents, based in Liverpool, only opened here in November 1954.

92, Sutherlands, tailor

James C. Sutherland was born in Edinburgh but in the early 1900s came to Dundee where he worked with shirt-makers J. M. Scott in Reform Street. In 1913 Sutherland set up on his own in Reform Street but in 1928 he moved to the Nethergate where he set up a tartan shop. His shop was highly personalised and set into one its walls was a space where he displayed his own collection of pomade dish lids. The shop also sold a wide range of souvenirs.

84, Canadian Fur Co. Ltd., furriers

In September 1936 the Canadian Fur Company, which had branches in Edinburgh, Glasgow, and Belfast, began selling furs from this shop.

82, The Hosiery Manufacturing Co., Ltd.

This retail branch of the Greenock Wool and Hosiery Stores was opened in 1897 shortly before it changed its name to the Scottish Wool and Hosiery Stores. At its peak in the 1950s the parent company employed over 1000 people. Its Nethergate shop was taken over by Matthew Hendersons in the 1960s.

78, Rossleigh Ltd, motor showrooms

T. F. Ross and William L. Sleigh, both Post Office employees and keen cyclists, in 1896 set up The Rossleigh Cycle Company Ltd in Edinburgh. The firm originally dealt only with cycles opening branches throughout Scotland and Ireland. It entered the motor trade as the car trade developed and opened a branch here in June 1930. The opening featured a $4^{1/2}$ litre Bentley saloon.

72, Steeple News Agency

This shop was owned by the Northern Furnishing Company but from 1950 it was leased to Mr Bruce Doig who also sold tobacco and fancy goods.

70, Robert Wilson, baker

This shop was owned by Robert Thomson Finnister Wilson with Agnes McNeil as a partner. In 1955, like their neighbour they were on a short lease from the Northern Furnishing Company.

66, Nelson Cream Ice Co Ltd, confectioners

See 10 Wellgate

60, Malone Shoe Repair Service

See 64 Overgate

56, Stuart Patrick, drugstore

Stuart Patrick took over the chemist's business of Mr Charles Duncan at this address in May 1955.

52, Scotch Wool & Hosiery Store

This company was started by John Fleming and James Reid in 1840 in Greenock. By 1910 they had over 200 retail branches across Scotland. In 1933 the company removed from their branch in the Nethergate and opened here. In the 1960s the company was acquired by Coats Paton who later who sold the premises to Matthew Henderson the jewellers.
See also 72, Murraygate

36, Draffens of Dundee, outfitters

See Stores

32, Rattray & Co, jewellers

This firm was established in 1850 by James Rattray. His son George David Rattray took over the business in 1907 and in 1916 established a shop at this address. He died on 22 January 1918. By 1935 the company was being run by Joan Kirkcaldy and John Shetland {Shilland}.

4, Nicoll & Smibert, bakers

This firm was set up in 1901 at this address by William Nicoll, Thomas D. Smibert and James Nicoll. At the rear of the shop was a restaurant much used by businessmen for coffee, lunch and tea. The basement was used for small dinner-dances and later as a tea-room. The shop closed in 1981.

Overgate

D C Thomson

The Overgate, formerly called Argyllisgait was a major shopping street from as early as the Middle Ages. In 1955 it had yet to be redeveloped for a new shopping mall and a Saturday Market took place at the top of the street. The street was very much a destination for the less wealthy and had always had a reputation for minor misdemeanours. On Saturday evenings a police wagon was stationed at the top of the Overgate.

1/3, James Scott & Co., electrical engineers

James Scott & Co. was established in 1902 as an electrical contractor and first worked from a wooden hut in Kirkcaldy. However as the firm grew it moved into retailing electrical goods and by 1955 it had major showrooms in Perth, Dunfermline, Edinburgh, Glasgow, Aberdeen and Dundee, the last of which was at this address and had been completely refurbished in 1953. In the 1950s it gave demonstrations of new electrical devices such as twin tub washing machines and television sets. By this time the company was run by a Mr I. Sinclair.

9, Petrie. Jeweller

William Petrie had started in business as a watchmaker around 1901 but by 1955 his son Eric Petrie was the owner. Joyce Smart clearly remembers the pain inflicted on her when she had her ears pierced in this shop using a needle and cork.

11, J. Durham, printer

John Durham, a native of Portobello, near Edinburgh, came to Dundee in 1835 and set up his printing business at 49 High Street, later moving to Argyll's Close. John Durham died in 1877 and left the business to his son James who was already a partner in the firm.

On John Durham's death, John Kinnoch, who had been with the company for several years, also became a partner.. For the next fifty years he was the active manager and did much to develop the business. When John Kinnoch died in August 1911, the business passed to his son George and his partner William Lamb.

15, Delnevo, confectioner

This was the Venice Café and sold confectionery from the ground floor while upstairs there was café and restaurant. It had been owned by Domenico Delnovo who had come from the Bogotara area in Italy to Dundee in about 1900. When Domenico died in 1941 the business was carried on by his widow Maria Zanre.

17, James Sturrock, tobacconist
In 1955 this small shop was run by two ladies, a Miss Thomson and a Miss Cameron.

21. Brighter Homes, wallpaper merchants
This firm which was based in Dunfermline had opened a branch here in 1949.

25. Delnevo, restauranteur
In 1916 this fish and chip shop, which had been started here by Domenico Delnovo in the early part of the 20th century, was selling fish suppers for 4d. By the 1950s it had become the Venice Fish Restaurant and was run by his wife Marie Zanre.

29, Levinsons, costumiers
Levinson Fashions which was opened in 1947 was owned by Hyman Levinson but by 1955 it was being run by his wife who was somewhat eccentric.

33, William Low, grocers
This iconic Dundee firm was founded by James Low who was born in Kirriemuir in 1849. He formed a partnership with William Lindsay and a shop was opened in Allan Street as Lindsay & Low. In 1866 Low invited his brother William to join the business. In 1879 William Low took over control of the business. His brother in law, William Rettie joined the firm and by 1899 some 22 stores were in operation.The firm was extremely successful and opened a large number of branches including this one in 1932. They went on to become the largest and most successful retail grocery chain in Scotland before being bought out by Tesco in 1994.

37, Meadow Dairy
The grocers shop which opened here in 1946 was part of a large chain owned by Home & Colonial Stores Ltd. who also owned the Maypole Dairy chain.

41, Becky Freedman, fruiterer
This shop had previously been owned by Edwards & Co, a fruiterers, of which Ann Edwards and Rebecca Freedman were proprietors. In 1929 Rebecca Freedman took over the business. By 1955 this shop was being run by Miss Freedman and her daughter who was now a partner in the business.

47, Morris Wallpaper Co.
This firm had originally been set up to market the hand printed wallpapers designed by William Morris but by this time supplied a wide range of wallpapers.

49, Franchis restaurant
Franchis Restaurant was an Italian sweet shop with a restaurant. It had been set up by John Franchi in 1912 and after he died in 1935 it was run by his son Joe Franchi. The sweets were sold from the front of the shop, which had a stair leading up to the very popular restaurant. The waitresses wore black with white aprons and white head bands. Mr Franchi stood in the front shop directing people upstairs. He also had a shop in Kirriemuir.

51/53, Alex Massey & Sons, provision merchants
This Dundee business had been established in 1898 and had a number of premises in the city. They opened this branch in 1922.

57, A Harris Ltd, tobacconist
See 61 Murraygate

59, Mrs S. Rosen, draper
Mrs Rosen had originally started in business with her husband Mr Isaac Rosen in a shop in Ann Street, but when he died in 1932, she carried on the business in her own name. By 1953 she was selling women' s clothes from this shop.

Barrack Street here

63/65, Edward Rowan & Co., pawnbrokers
This business had been here since 1891.
It's principal claim to fame was that Thomas Scobbie, the Kingennie murderer, was caught as a result of pawning his Balmoral bonnet in this shop.

71, J. R. Ingrams, bakers
See 18 Union Street

73, J. Greenhill, chemist.
Greenhills was a very popular establishment that had been founded in the 1890s by James Greenhill who died in January 1948. He was a native of Glasgow who was first of all a teacher and then became a chemist in Buckhaven before moving to Dundee. In 1955 this shop was being run by Andrew Greenhill, his son, who had worked for while in the Blackness Foundry before joining his father in the family business.

Greenhills was primarily a chemists shop but was famed in Dundee for its sarsaparilla soft drinks. The chemists shop was at the front of the store and sarsaparillas of different colours were laid out on a long counter that ran to the back of the premises. The record day's serving of 'sassas' was 9,000 during a heat wave in 1912.

One of the reasons for the popularity of this shop was that It was one of the few shops open on a Sunday. It was often busy on Sunday mornings as the sarsaparilla was allegedly good for hangovers.

77/79, W. Paterson & Sons, bootmakers
This company had been founded by William Patterson in 1871 in Glasgow and had branches throughout Scotland. In the early 50s the business was being run by the founders grandson, G. L.

Patterson who died in 1951. His brother William as the remaining partner took over the firm until his death in 1954 after which it was run by his son William Patterson.

95, The Shoe Box
These premises were occupied by Mr W. Patterson who was the proprietor of the shop next door and who had taken over these premises in 1949.

97, Wasilewski, bootmaker
This Polish artisan made boots to measure and Mrs Dino Barbieri recalls having shoes made in these premises.

99, Saxone Shoes
This company was formed in in Kilmarnock in 1908 by a merger of Clark & Sons and F. G. Abbott under the joint Managing directors, George Clark and George Abbott. During the Second World War most of its production was for military contracts and by 1948 it employed 1200 staff in its shops and over 1,000 in its factory. In 1962 it was taken over by the British Shoe Corporation. In Dundee Saxone Shoes were regarded by the young as glamorous and by the elderly as impractical.

105, Alex Munro, butchers
This was a branch of a firm based in Dunfermline who opened here in 1934.

107, Andrew Birrell & Sons, bootmakers
Birrells was one of the largest, if not the largest shoe shop in Dundee. The business was founded around 1890 by John Birrell who died in October 1925. Andrew Birrell, who took over the firm was a well known racing cyclist. This shop was always jammed in the week before the school year started and had a 'Pedoscope', an x-ray device for seeing whether shoes fitted properly. After the redevelopment of the Overgate, Birrells moved to a shop in the new development and located beneath the Angus Hotel.

North Lindsay Street here

119, A. & R. Lamb, Sports Outfitters
In addition to sportswear this shop sold knives of all kinds including sheath knives and flick knives. It also sold a wide range of gadgets and was described by one customer as "a Boy's Own kind of place."
See High Street.

121, A. & R. Lamb, stationers
See above

123, William Low, grocers
See 33 above

127/135, Wilsons Bonanza Stores, drapers
Set up by Mr James Wilson in 1933, although described as a drapers, this firm sold a variety of goods including upholstery, work clothes, drapery, and furniture.

143, Robert Smith, furniture
Robert Smith had taken over this shop in 1921 from a Mrs Carruthers, a dealer, and concentrated on the sale of low priced furniture.

149, William Sutherland, drapers
This business was set up by William Sutherland. During the first world war, he was joined by his son, William F. Sutherland who took over the firm in 1932 when his father died and subsequently ran the business until 1967. They also had premises in the Hilltown and the Hawkhill.

151, Fergus Young, fishmonger
This shop, previously run as Young's furniture store was converted to a fishmongers in 1950.

153, Georgina Peebles, general dealer
See Nethergate

155, Helen Wilson, restaurateur
This was a small café called "The Cookie" selling fairly basic food.

159, Leitch & Co., smallware merchants
Leitch & Co in 1937 had set up in this shop selling tobacco, newspapers and fancy goods and were still in business here in 1955.

163/165, Army & Navy Store
Originally established in London by a group of army and navy officers as the Army and Navy Co-operative Store, this firm became a successful limited company in in 1934 and opened on this site in the 1950s.

169, Ponsford & Co., radio dealers
Stephen J. Ponsford originally traded from a shop at 29, Crichton Street where he sold everything from cycles, toys, wringers airguns bells and lamps. He boasted of the largest selection of dolls prams in Scotland. In 1951 he moved out of those premises and opened stores here and at a shop in Ann Street, selling new and second hand cycles. In October 1955 the firm purchased large quantities of television sets, radiograms, and record players anticipating a a rise in purchase tax, and which they later sold at pre budget prices.

171, J. Zanre, fish restaurant
This fish restaurant was originally owned by Guiseppie Zanre but by 1955 was run by Joseph Zanre, the nephew of Domiinic Delnovo, who, at the age of nineteen had saved four children from a blazing house fire.

173, Mrs Elizabeth O' Neil, grocer

Set up by Martin O'Neill by 1926 this shop was later owned by his widow Elizabeth who sold her interest in 1953.

179, Geoffrey Wilson, baker

Wilson had taken over this shop in 1937 from a Mr Forbes who had operated the The Auld Dundee Rock Shop from these premises and also had a shop in the City Arcade.

181,James Frederick, china

Frederick took over this shop in 1951 and was still in business at this location in 1955.

185 John Donaghey, chemists

This business was started by John J. Donaghey in 1864. In 1904 his nephew, John J. Faulty joined the firm and became managing director and, later, the proprietor of the firm. Faulty, who was one of the founders of Dundee Hibs owned the firm until his death in 1954. His son then took over the business.

193,Johnston's Stores, grocers

This was one of a local chain of grocers founded in 1883 in 10 Stirling Street by George A. Johnston, a native of Airlie. By 1904 the firm had 5 branches located around the city. George A. Johnston died in 1932 by which time he was Lord Provost. Afterwards the firm was run by his four sons and comprised some 40 shops when, in 1959, it was acquired by the Rank McDougall conglomerate.

197, Maurice Rosen, furniture dealer

Maurice Rosen was the nephew of Mrs Rosen who had a shop at 59, Overgate.

203, Smiths Dog Shop

John Smith who advertised himself as "John Smith, original king of killers, the most experienced ratter in town" also ran this pet shop which sold monkeys, ferrets, pigeons parrots and mice. In 1948 he had taken over the City Dog Parlour which had previously operated here.

205, Wringer repair service

This shop opened here in 1950.

213, Waclaw Kulszynski, watchmaker

This shop had been opened here by Kulszynski in 1949 and not only repaired and sold watches but also mended jewellery of all kinds.

215, Quinns, wallpaper

Opened as P. & J. Quinn in 1923, by 1955 this shop was run by Vincent Quinn who was a keen fisherman. He died in 1966 shortly after the shop was bought by the City Council for the Overgate development.

217 S. & N. McNicoll, butcher

This firm was started as a partnership in the 1930s, but by 1955 this shop was run solely by Norman McNicoll.

221, Horatio Leslie, fishmonger

In 1955 this shop, which had been opened by Horatio W. Leslie in the 1930s, was being run by his son George Leslie.

223, Mary Buist, fish restaurateur

Mary Buist, the owner of this fish and chip shop, was married to a Polish man called Jurkiewicz.

227, Alfred Addison, newsagent

Addison who opened here in 1929 was, as well as being a newsagent, a tobacconist, confectioner and stationer.

231, Mrs M. Capitalli, restaurateur

This was a carry out fish and chip shop owned by Maria Capitalli, the wife of Tony Capitalli. Like many Italian families who settled in Dundee, the family came from the Bogotaro area of Italy near Monte Cassino.

233, Duncan Kerr, butcher

Duncan Kerr who came from Monifieth opened this shop in 1935.

245, Miss C. MCabe, grocer

During World War Two Catherine McCabe who had occupied this shop since the 1920s ran a Catholic canteen in this shop.

249, Wm. Hall, chemist

William Hall took over the chemists business of James Hardie at this address in 1950.

Tay Street here

212, PDSA

The Peoples Dispensary for Sick Animals opened their clinic here in 1946.

204, Two - O - Four, fruiterer

200, John Owens, antique dealer

This shop run under the name of "The Curio Shop", also acted as a ticket agency.

196, The Market Bargain Store

The Market Bargain Store which had located here in 1948 was actually run by the Barnes Clothing Store

Long Wynd here. This was area in which the 'buster stalls' ,so beloved by Dundonians could be found.

190, John Breslin, bootmaker

In 1955 John Breslin was a relatively new tenant of this shop having opened in 1953.

New market

168, M'Donald's, house furnishers
This shop owned by Mary M'Donald sold all kinds of furniture but a speciality was french polishing and upholstery repairs.

162 Mrs Mary M'Donald, dealer
Mrs M'Donald who sold second hand goods from this shop had been here since 1947.

156, Albert Lowe, furniture dealer
Lowe had set up here in 1927 and sold a wide range of goods from this shop, including wringers and pianos.

152, A, S, Sidhu & Co., drapers
This shop was owned by Achhar Singh Sidhu who opened his drapers shop here in January 1955. Grumman Hsing Sidhu also worked in the business which had other clothes shops at 75 Hilltown, and 10 Barrack Street.

148, Robert Smith & Sons, house furnishers
Robert Smith who had opened this shop in 1938 died in January 1950 after which the business was carried on by his sons Charles and Alexander. They made a feature of what they called "Smiths Babyland" selling prams.

118, A. & R. Lamb, fancy goods
See above

116, G. Zanre, confectioners
This shop which had been opened by 1935 was owned by Giuseppe Zanre but was run by Ginevra Zanre. (see below)

114, G. Zanre, confectioner
Giuseppe Zanre was born in 1899 in the Bogotaro area in Italy. After living in France for a while he arrived in Dundee in 1906 and set up the White Rose Café in these premises. Zanre also owned the White Rose Golden Crisp factory in West Wynd. He was helped by his wife Clementina and his nephew Peter Guillianotti in this family firm, and retired back to Italy in 1963 due to the acquisition by the City Council of the property for the redevelopment of the Overgate.

South Lindsay Street here

102, C. W. Carr, bootmakers
This shop was opened by Alfred L. Carr in 1925. A Dundonian recalls that during the war, one Ian Melville, who arrived in Dundee with only the clothes he stood up in after having been in a ship that was torpedoed, was given a pair of shoes by Mr Carr.

98, E. Wasilewski, bootrepairer
Mr Wasilewski operated here from 1950 under the title of "Steeple Leather Goods".

88, Mrs Agnes Saunders, grocer
This shop had been started by Richard Graham Saunders in 1927 but by 1955 was being run by his widow, Agnes Saunders.

82/86, Peter Fagan, broker
Peter Fagan was born in Dundee in 1860. He started up in business as a pawnbroker in 1893 in the West Port but by 1907 had moved to the large salesroom at this address. In 1915 he was advertising for, among other things, false teeth at 3d a tooth. He died in January 1940. In 1955 the business was advertising the sale of a variety of goods including waterproofs for cyclists.

80, Harry's, fruiterer
This fruit and flower shop was opened in 1949 by Harry and Nelly Freedman.

74/76, J. & H. Christie, drapers
This firm had opened here in 1935.

70, Petrie Bros., paint
This firm was started by David Mathers Petrie in 1893 in the Hawkhill. He then moved to this address where in 1899 where he and his brother set up business as Petrie Brothers. He died in 1949, and in 1955 the shop was being run by Jessie Cobban, his widow.

64, Malone Shoe, Repair Service
Thomas Malone was born in Perth but in 1883 came as a child to Dundee. He started his shoe repair business in the Hawkhill in 1896 before moving to 33, Mid Street in 1924. By 1926 he had a factory employing 70 men and dealing with over 1000 repairs per day. He opened this shop in 1940 from which he also sold bespoke and surgical shoes.

62, Mrs Helen Brown, grocer
This shop was set up in the early 1930s and run by Harry Brown until his death in the 1940s, after which it was run by his widow Helen.

60, W. D. Begg, tobacconist
This shop had been bought by the City Council in 1912 under its Garden City Scheme. It was thereafter let out on short leases and in 1955 was occupied Mr Begg.

58, W. Macgregor, fruiterer
As above this shop had been bought by the City Council and let out, in this case to Ann Macgregor.

56, Menzies & Sons, clothiers
See Wellgate

54, Kirk & Coutts, fireplace specialists
Kirk & Coutts was started at this address in May 1887 and were then trading as ironmongers. By 1899

they were selling tableware and lighting of all kinds and had a branch in Newport on Tay. In October 1955 Kirk & Coutts opened a new showroom at 28 Barrack Street and vacated this shop which was then occupied by Mr Joseph Koppel.

48, Mobile Caterers Ltd
This firm was set up in 1949 and was owned by James M. Wallace, whose property empire extended to dance halls, restaurants and hotels.

46, J. M. Wallace, baker
See 8, Crichton Street

44, G. P. Findlay, electrical engineers
This firm had been set up as ironmongers in 1877 by G. P. Findlay who died in August 1927 by which time the company was specialising in gas fittings. By the late 1930s his daughter Miss J. D. Findlay was a partner in the firm. In the 1950s the firm got into selling television sets in a big way. The owner in 1955 was Mr Norman K. Findlay and by this time the company were supplying TV sets to hospitals in the Dundee area.

42, J. Reilly's, Amusement Arcade
This was a simple amusement arcade owned by Sean Reilly that featured games at one penny a try and incorporated a rifle range.

40, James Marrs, fish restaurant
This shop had been a fish restaurant since 1924 when it was opened by Emilio Zuccone. In 1934 this fish shop was owned by Mary Garland and by 1955 had been taken over by James Marr.

38, G. P. Findlays, ironmongers
This was the store in which G. P. Findlay had first set up shop.

Thorter Row here

34, Wm. Wilkie & Sons, butchers
In 1955 the shop was run by James Ireland who had been with firm since 1919, first as a cashier, and latterly as owner. He died in 1959. Wilkies had written on their shop window "Wilkies sausages are world famous" showing a knack for publicity but perhaps a lack of understanding of the phrase "global reach." Inside the shop unrefrigerated carcasses hung along the walls. The sawdust that covered the floor was used as an artistic medium by the feet of bored children waiting for their mothers.

30. Keith Scott, outfitters
See Whitehall Crescent

16, T. Gibson, hairdressers
This firm was locally known as Jack Flash's due to the speed with which the barbers cut hair. One customer said it was a case of "How's your mother?, How's your father? How's that Sir? That'll be one and sixpence."

2, Sixty Minute cleaners
This was a branch of an American chain of cleaners. In the 1950s they provided an invisible mending service for nylon stockings. During WW2 they had in their windows here, and in Reform Street, a printed notice offering a "24 hour service" apparently being unaware of the contradiction in terms.

Reform Street

D C Thomson

This street was planned as part of William Burn's 1824 scheme for town improvements. Its construction required the blasting away of a stone ridge that ran across the line proposed for the street. Reform Street tended to pride itself in having the better class of shops but in fact there have been several times when the street has been a little run down.

1, H. Samuel, jewellers
The Birmingham based chain H. Samuel the Jewellers arrived in Dundee in 1909 when they acquired the premises of H. Tulloch, a firm of hatters. The pavement beneath the clock on Samuel's shop was a popular meeting place for Dundonians.

7/11. Arthur Miller & Son, furriers
Arthur Miller had moved into these premises in 1947 and were still in occupation in 1955.

13, D. M. Meldrum, rubber merchants
Meldrums specialised in rainwear, umbrellas and sports goods and was started by David Meldrum in 1820 in Cupar, Fife. In 1824 he moved to Dundee and opened a shop in Crichton Street. He then, in 1849, moved to these premises in Reform Street.

David M. Meldrum took over from his uncle in 1903 and was still running the shop in 1955. He died in 1966 at the age of 90.

17, A. Caird & Sons, tailors
See stores.

21, Caird's Hairdressers department
See Stores.

27, Dundee Pasteurised Milk Co.
The DPM, as it was known locally, was set up in 1923 at 34, North Street by James N. Robb. This shop and cafe was opened in the mid 1930s and featured a downstairs tea room. In the 1950s this was frequented by the boxer Dick McTaggart. The basement tea room was walled with mirrors that not only made the room seem enormous, but also gave great satisfaction to the more narcissistic Dundonians.

29, Morrison & Robertson, dressmakers
This firm had previously been located in premises at 9, Reform Street but in 1926 moved to this address. They made great play of describing themselves as "Court Dressmakers and Milliners".

33, Restaurant Wilson
This business was owned by Wilsons the Bakers who also had tearooms in Union Street and the Wellgate.

35, R. H. Lundie, stationer
This firm of stationers also produced post cards under the Elcho brand (now collectors' items) and stocked bibles, Sunday School tracts etc.

37, Sixty Minute Cleaners
See 2, Overgate

39, Hector Powe, tailors
A London based tailor, Hector Powe was founded in 1910 and specialised in made to measure suits. When the new Overgate was opened they moved from these premises to a shop located beneath the Angus Hotel.

43, Cooper & McKenzie, furriers & tailors
See Stores.

45, Dickson Travel
This firm was set up in 1919 by Robert Dickson, a Fifer, who had originally come to work in Dundee as a chauffeur. The firm had started as a coach hire business but soon moved into providing coach tours. Dickson's first vehicles were motor lorries to which charabanc bodies were fitted at the weekend. The business went well and by 1926 he was operating fourteen vehicles which he garaged in Dundonald Street. This firm not only arranged luxury coach tours around Britain but also organised continental holidays by bus and air.

47, D. M. Allen, wine merchant
Opened at this address in 1911, this shop sold not only wines and spirits but also a range of teas and spices.

49, The Abbey National Building Society
The Abbey National was first established in London in 1849 as The National Freehold Land Society by two Liberal MPs. The Society opened a branch here in 1953.

53, Scottish Amicable Building Society
This building society was founded as the West of Scotland Life Assurance Company in Glasgow in 1833. In 1948 it merged with the Co-operative Building Society and in 1954 established a branch at this address.

55, David Laurie, ladies outfitter
David Laurie's who opened here in 1947 described themselves as being "in the mantle trade".

63, Jaeger Co Ltd, wool specialists
Jaeger was set up in 1844 as Dr Jaeger's Sanitary Woollen System Co. Ltd. and initially specialised in woollen long johns. The company had a Royal Warrant and was the inventor of the camel hair coat. This came about as a result of its decision to use only natural fibres such as cashmere, angora and alpaca. The Dundee branch of Jaegers was opened here in 1926 and eventually became a fashion shop for the better off in Dundee.

58, Dunfermline Building Society
The Dunfermline building society was founded in Dunfermline in 1869. Before it merged with Nationwide it was the biggest building society in Scotland. Its Reform Street branch opened here in 1954 after moving from an office in Meadowside.

48, Callenders, hair specialist
This shop which was opened in 1930 was primarily a ladies hairdressers but also operated a gents department in the basement. It also sold a very large range of cosmetics.

42, H. Logan, tobacconist
Hugh Logan opened this shop in 1952 where he not only sold tobacco but also provided afternoon teas.

38, Johnston & Adams, chemists
This was a Glasgow firm of chemists set up in 1934 and who opened a branch here in 1937. By the 1940s the firm was owned by a Dundee family. It successfully marketed Lavapine floor and furniture polishes, much used in the cinemas of the time.

32, James Ramsay, goldsmith
James Ramsay established his business at 8, High Street Dundee before moving to Reform Street in 1885. One of the up market jewellers. it had a number of curtained cubicles where customers could discuss the style and cost of the articles they were seeking to buy.

30, Watt & Sons
This firm was set up in 1899 and in 1900 notably took photos of Dundonians in the 3rd Battalion of the Black Watch when they left for the Boer War. It was a shop that dealt in photographic goods but it also sold prints of paintings and photos. It specialised in taking formal photographic portraits.

26, Andrew G. Kidd, bakers
These premises had a finely panelled restaurant on the first floor and a restaurant in the basement, both well patronised by businessmen for coffee, lunch and tea. The first floor restaurant was also available for formal dinners. In the shop, cold meats were sold at a counter on the right of the door, bakery items at a long counter on the left, and on an oval island in the centre were Kidd's own make of chocolates and boilings, all kept in large glass jars. See also 38, High Street and Overgate.

22, Methven Simpson, music sellers

Methven Simpson who started up in 1865 had, in 1909, moved into this shop from 122, Nethergate. They later opened branches in Edinburgh, St Andrews, Forfar and North Berwick. In 1927 they boasted a Royal Warrant as Piano and Music Sellers to H. M. the King. Among other musical instruments they sold player pianos. Within the building was a lift, one side of which had been removed to accommodate pianos.

18, Birrells Ltd, confectioners

See also 110, Nethergate

16, Saxone Shoe Co.

See Overgate

14, Paige Ltd, gown specialists

In 1934 this shop was bought by Morrisons Associated Companies Ltd who were based in Glasgow. In Dundee they also owned Irene Adair (see below) and Graftons.

12, Irene Adair, gown specialists

This shop was also owned by Morrisons Associated Companies, a Glasgow firm that owned about 200 fashion stores, They were thought by a number of Dundonians to "have a bit of class and style about them'. Liz Barrie recalls that in 1958 it was here that she bought her wedding dress for the princely sum of £10.

8. Singer Sewing Machines

First established in 1851 by Isaac Merritt Singer and lawyer Edward Clark as I. M. Singer & Co, the firm was by 1860 the largest manufacturer of sewing machines in the world. In 1867 Singers opened a factory in Glasgow. The Scottish factory was so productive that in 1905 Singer set up a separate UK company. Singer introduced domestic electric machines in 1910 and was also a pioneer of hire purchase. The company also ran local competitions for primary school pupils. The prize was, somewhat inevitably, an electric sewing machine.

6, Manfield & Sons Ltd, boot manufacturers

This was a Nottingham based chain of shoe shops who were seen as one of the higher quality shoemakers. Their first branch in Dundee was established in 1900 at 28 High Street. In 1913 they moved to Strathtay House in Reform Street (where Boots now stands), and 1924 they moved again, this time to this address.

2, Boots the Chemists

Boots the Chemists, a Manchester based but nationally known multiple chain, arrived in Dundee when they took over the premises of Adam Small, clothier in 1929.

Union Street

D C Thomson

This street was constructed by the Burgh Council in 1824 to a layout designed by David Neave. In time it became the main route between the city centre and Dundee West Railway Station and also the Tay Ferries Terminal. For over a century, on the Tuesdays when the livestock market was held in Dundee, this street was a regular haunt for farming folk.

1, Matthew M. Henderson, jeweller

Matthew M. Henderson who was the chairman of this business had originally joined the family firm but, in 1937, he struck out on his own in these premises. He proved to be successful and in 1954 Matthew's son Scott joined the firm. The two worked together until Matthew died suddenly in 1960. Subsequently the shop took over the adjoining premises of the Scotch Wool Hosiery shop. In 1989 Scott Henderson was joined by his son Matthew and shortly afterwards they extended their premises further along the Nethergate.

11, W. A. Gilbey, wine merchants

This was a branch of a London based chain that had been set up by Walter Gilbey and his younger brother Alfred. They established their business, which specialised in London gin, in 1865, when they returned from the Crimean War.

13, Sawyers, fishmongers

Sawyers took over this fishmongers from Stobies in 1948.

17/19, S. Barbieri, fish restaurateurs

This shop was owned by Steve Barbieri Jnr. In 1950 he converted the fish & chip shop into an American style ice cream parlour which he called the Chrome Rail. Unfortunately, as one Dundonian remarked, "he was years ahead of his time and the business did not catch on". He subsequently moved to a pub and restaurant on the corner of Peter Street and the Seagate, taking the name Chrome Rail for his new enterprise.

21, Wiliam Kidd & Son, stationers

William Kidd who had worked for Frederick Shaw, a bookseller, set up his own business at 3 Union Street in 1871. On Shaw's retiral, Kidd purchased the firm and moved to 112 Nethergate. As a consequence of the rapid development of the business and thus the need for increased accommodation, Kidd built the handsome block in Whitehall Street known as the 'Palace Buildings' and moved there in 1885. Among the books published by Kidd were Maxwell's History of Old Dundee, Allen's Guide to Navigation, and numerous guide books to Dundee, Arbroath, etc.

The firm was also known for selling foreign stamps. In 1955 Kidds had not long settled here, having sold their shop in Whitehall Street (between Justices and Draffens) to Draffens who used it for their linen hall.

27, John Mitchell, butcher
This business was operating as long ago as 1850 in Butcher Row. In 1875 it had moved to 16 Victoria Road but by 1880 it had moved again, this time to Ladywell Place at the foot of the Hilltown.

33, Restaurant Wilson Ltd
This restaurant was what was termed a silver service restaurant and specialised providing High Teas. It was also frequently used by parties on bus tours. It was opened here in 1927 by Robert Wilson, at first under the name of Wilson's Restaurant, until in 1938 it became Restaurant Wilson. By 1943 it had branches in Reform Street and the Wellgate. In 1947 it became a public company and two years later opened branches in Dunked and Crieff.
See also Reform Street and Wellgate

41, A. L. Swan, newsagent
This was run by a Miss Swan who also sold sweets.

43, Robert Taylor & Sons, coal merchant
This firm of wholesale coal merchants had been started in 1860 by Robert Taylor. In 1907 it was operating from Yeaman Shore and in 1909 it became a Public Company. The company owned a number of ships, including the Alice Taylor, named after Robert's daughter. These ships were used to bring coal from England to Dundee and Montrose. When Robert died in 1917 the firm was handed over to his sons, James, David, William, Robert Jnr, and Albert. In 1933 one of Taylor's grandsons, Cecil Taylor (son of William), set a record by driving from Lands End to John o' Groats in 22 hrs. After the premises purchased for the site of Greens Playhouse in 1934, the firm moved to this address and later to Reform Street.

45, B. C. Vincent, butcher
Vincent boasted this store had the first refrigerated shop window in Dundee. It was later taken over by Wilkies, the butchers, who had their main store in the Overgate. Vincent had another shop in Clepington Road.

50, James Hardie & Son, chemist
This firm was originally set up by by Alexander Hamilton and John Hardie in 1854 in the Nethergate. His son James Miller Hardie became a partner in 1906 when his father died. In 1909 the firm, who had by this time moved 68 High Street was acquired by Henry James Hunt. In 1922 Hunt moved the firm to 26 High Street. When in 1925 Mr Hunt died the firm moved to these premises but still operated under the James Hardie name.

48, Smith Hood, coal merchants
This business had been established by James Hood, who was born in Edinburgh in 1849. Hood went to the USA and returned from there to Dundee where, in partnership with a Mr Smith, he established a shop at this address in 1861. He subsequently left the partnership and set up business on his own. The firm was acquired by Allied Coal & Shipping Ltd of Glasgow in May 1942. but William Hood (the grandson of the founder) and David Younger remained as directors. The shop sold not only coal but all kinds of fuel.

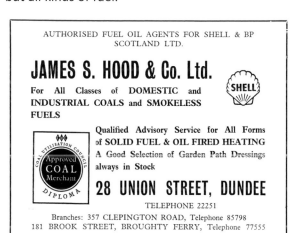

46, Scottish Medical Supply Ltd
This was a small shop opened in 1934 that sold among other things a wide range of insoles and surgical goods.

38, Mrs Agnes Whyte, restauranteur
The Horseshoe Restaurant which had been opened by Willliam Whyte in 1938 was a well-known lunchtime meeting place for businessmen where, during the war, queues would wait for a seat to become available. When Mr Whyte died in 1942 the

business was carried on by his widow, Agnes. The restaurant was presided over by Mrs Whyte, a rather stout elderly widow who was always seated behind the counter by the door, assisted by her daughter, Gertie. The food was simple and usually had a menu with little choice, but in the days of rationing that did not matter.

36, Carse of Gowrie Dairy Co.

These premises were actually run by the Dundee Pasteurised Milk Company, known to all as "the DPM". This firm was set up in 1923 and had a number of shops throughout the city. Its main depot on Mains Road was later turned into a public park. It was reputed to sell the best apple pies in Dundee.

34, Allan M. Robertson, flesher

This firm was set up in the 1870s by Alan Robertson. He became prominent in the butcher trade and in 1901 was elected as the President of the Dundee Master Butchers Association. He died suddenly in October 1920 and his wife Annie took over the running of the business. After the end of World War Two an accountant, Tom Craig, was brought in to advise the business and he eventually bought the firm in the early 1950s. In 1974 he was succeeded by his son David Craig.

30, Strathtay, fishmonger

In 1955 this business was actually owned by Robertsons, its neighbours at 34 Union Street. Although separated by a pend and with a separate entrance the shop was connected to Robertsons by a basement that linked the shops below street level.

28, John Roger & Son, game dealer

John Roger opened his shop here in 1933. This firm also sold poultry meat and their premises backed on Couttie's Wind where an occasional hen could be seen running wild before meeting its end. Skinned rabbits hung in the window and pheasants and grouse were hung outside on occasion.

24, Janmac, butchers

This shop actually changed hands in 1955. At the start of the year it was the Carlton Restaurant owned by Leo Ferrari who was born in a small village near the Swiss /Italian border. He came to Dundee in 1920 and in 1928 set up business at this address.

It was taken over by two Angus farmers, one of which was George Yull Mackie who was later to become Lord Mackie of Benshie, a prominent Liberal politician. Together, they set up in 1955 what they claimed was the first fully self service butchers in Scotland. It was certainly ahead of its time in Dundee, featuring refrigerated shelves full of plastic wrapped meat and poultry.

22, A. Harris, tobacconist

This firm, which also operated a lending library, was located at 7, Union Street until 1949 when it moved to this address.

18, J. R. Ingram, bakers

James Ingram, an Aberdonian started this firm in 1913 when he took over the bakery firm of William Wallace. The firm was successful and in 1919 had taken over Lamb's restaurant at 56 Reform Street. Ingram took an enterprising approach to the business and by 1930 was exporting shortbread to Australia, New Zealand and East Africa. In May 1936 Ingram retired and sold the firm to Samuel Houghton who had been born in Manchester. Ingram subsequently died in 1942.

Houghton had started his career with James Keiller & Sons and had acquired Dundee bakers Rough and Fraser in April 1936. Houghton took the business to new heights, winning three gold and two silver medals at the 1951 Scottish Master Bakers exhibition in Glasgow. He died in March 1953 after which the business was taken over by Mr Peter Gillies from Glasgow, at which time the firm had 15 shops throughout Dundee. The firm carried on producing high quality food, winning medals at the national and international level.

16, Nicoll & Peter, grocers

This firm was established in 1820 as 'Italian Warehouseman and wine and spirit dealer.' In 1917 they opened up at this address. By 1955 it was an old fashioned shop that was known for the range of salami that it sold. It was owned by George F. Brown, who had taken the firm over from George Peter.

14, John R. Gow & Sons

This firm was set up in 1860 by John R. Gow and subsequent to his death run by his sons. In 1955 the business was run by Dr Evelyn Walker (nee Gow) who had taken over the business in 1934. A talented woman she had a degree and a PH D gained at Oxford University and was a ballistics expert called upon by the police as an expert witness. She designed fishing rods and fishing bags, baits, lures and flies.

Dennis Collins recalls that Evelyn Walker and her mother, who were both usually dressed in dark green costumes, often wore hats decorated with feather sprays suitable for salmon flies. Dr Walker ran the shop for 32 years and retired in 1966, at which time she sold the business to Gordon Johnson.

8/10, Margaret Ritchie, florists

This shop was acquired in 1950 by Margaret Ritchie from John Hunt & Sons florists, of which she was a director.

Union Street South

This street led to the Tay Ferry harbour and was home to a number of shops and cafes that were aimed at those waiting to cross the Tay to Fife or were returning from a visit to the Swimming Baths.

23, Easy Eats Cafe
Previously the Craig Pier Cafe the name was changed to the Easy Eats Cafe in 1954.

21, Angus Garage Company
This was the showroom for this well established local car firm that in 1937 had developed the City Underground Garage in Crichton Street. It had been started in Broughty Ferry but moved to this showroom in 1934. It also had the Dundee agency for Bendix Washing Machines and featured one of these in its shop window.

19, J. W. Sutherland, tobacconists
See 44, Castle Street.

16, W. W. Croal, grain merchants
This shop which also sold pets and pet food was run by Joyce Croal who was a pioneer water skier.

15, The Dog Food Shop
This pet shop which had first been opened in Tay Street in 1934 was owned by Croal's. It moved here in 1936, at first under the name of "The Field & Orchard", later becoming the Dog Food Shop. Horseflesh was sold here every Tuesday and Friday.

14, Mrs G. Nicol, confectioner
See 15, Nethergate

12, P. Forte, confectioner
This was a traditional small café selling sweets, ice cream and had a café. It capitalised on its position on the route to and from the swimming baths by providing "shivery bites" of hot orange drinks and biscuits.

9, Stuart Patrick, tobacconist.
This was a shop that was ahead of its time in opening on Sunday afternoons to sell its wide range of magazines and newspapers. It was also unusual at that time, in that its shop door was always open to encourage passers by into the premises. One of Patricks's first shops was at 314, Perth Road where he ran a lending library. "2 pence per book per week" was the advertising slogan.... "Zane Gray and other Wild West books, romantics etc". Another lending library that he had was at 5, Barrack Street. Patrick also had a newsagents at 18, Castle Street.

D C Thomson

D C Thomson

Wellgate

The Wellgate, as its name implies, ran from the gate in the city wall near the Ladywell at the foot of the Hilltown into the Cowgate. As it was one of the two main accesses to the city centre from the north it was a very important shopping street.

1, Style & Mantle, costumiers

This was a London based firm which opened its first branch in Dundee in 1928 at 79 Murraygate. In 1952 after a car crashed into its shop window it moved to this address.

3, Boots the Chemist

See 2, Reform Street

7, Home & Colonial Stores

Home & Colonial had been at one time one of the largest retail chains in the UK. Founded by Julius Drewe and John Musker in London in 1883, by 1885 it was trading as the Home & Colonial Tea Association. In the 1920s it bought Maypole Dairies and merged with Liptons to form a company with three thousand branches. In 1961 it changed its name to Allied Suppliers. In 1983 the company was taken over by Argyll Foods who in 1988 merged with Safeway UK.

10, William Hunter, drapers

William Hunter, the son of a crofter, and was born in Tealing. His first job was an apprentice to a draper in the Wellgate. He set up on his own in 1860 at 35 Reform Street. The early success of the firm was based upon the purchase of goods from bankrupt businesses. By 1882 William Hunter, as the firm was now named, had moved to 15 / 17 / 10 Wellgate selling mainly clothing but also a wide range of goods from dog carts to india rubber dolls. In 1884 he became Lord Provost of Dundee.

In 1890 the business could afford to take seventy employees in horse brakes to Clunie Castle for a picnic dinner in the Castle Hall. After the death of William Hunter in 1925, Mr A. M. Strachan, their London buyer, became managing Director. Mrs A. M. Strachan became chairman until 1936 when she died and was succeeded by Albert J. Strachan, her son. In 1959 the business was sold to Alexanders Stores of Glasgow but continued to operate their Wellgate store under the Hunter name until, in March 1971, it was closed to allow the redevelopment of the Wellgate for a new shopping mall.

18, Dundee Bedding Company

This firm had been set up in 1910 by John Anderson, a native of Linlithgow. It first opened in Temple Lane but soon moved to 18, Kirk Entry, off the Wellgate. Anderson died in 1936 after which his son carried on the business.

16, D. T. Smith, sunshade specialist

This shop dealt primarily in blinds.

21, Elena Mae, photographic dealers

This firm had been founded by Thomas Cook, a native of Dundee,who used his army gratuity to set up in the photographic trade. He named the business after his wife Elena Mae. Elena Mae also had shops in Reform Street and Castle Street and although they specialised in photographic equipment they also stocked items such as binoculars, calculators and cassette recorders. This branch was set up in 1954.

23, MacMillan & Munro, confectioners

This was a branch of a Glasgow firm who were chocolate and confectionery manufacturers with shops throughout Scotland. In 1953 the company moved their Dundee shop from the Cowgate to this address.

25, Watts (Dundee), musical supplies

Opened as Watts Salons in 1919, this shop sold both sheet music and musical instruments as well as radios and gramophones. It also organised instrumental classes for children and Norrie Robertson recalls being taken to the shop to learn the intricacies of playing the chanter.

33, Menzies & Sons, drapers

Born in Strathmiglo John Geddes Menzies first came to Dundee in 1880 but in 1890 returned to Fife to take over his father's business as a handloom weaver in Dunshalt. He returned to Dundee in 1900 and opened a small drapers business in Princes Street. In 1926 the firm became a public company with John G. Menzies and his two sons, William Menzies and John A. Menzies as directors.

By 1930 he had 70 employees engaged in making shirts and in 1926 opened this shop in the Wellgate. Later the company opened a further store in Dundee at 56 Overgate, a branch in Aberdeen and in 1944 another in Perth. When J. G.Menzies died in July 1935, William, John and their sister Miss B. G. Menzies took over the business. William died in November 1955.

37, Why Pay More Stores, clothiers
This Edinburgh firm had branches in Glasgow and Aberdeen, and opened this shop in 1954.

43, Cable Shoes
The first Cable shop in Dundee opened in 1909 at 78, High Street selling Saxone Shoes, which were made in Kilmarnock, and Sorosis shoes made in America. It opened a shop at this address in 1938 and another at 99, Overgate in 1940. It sold shoes aimed at the more mature lady.

45, G. A. Johnston's Stores, grocers
See 193 Overgate

47, Fullotone, radio specialists
This London based firm was originally set up in 1919 by Albert and Charles McDougall as The Cabinet Gramophone Company to sell clockwork gramophones. It both made and sold radios and gramophones and by 1955 had started to rent out television sets. It opened its Dundee branch at this address in 1953.

51, Graftons, costumiers
This shop was owned by Morrisons Associated Companies, a Glasgow firm that owned about 200 fashion stores. This shop was very much aimed at young people and sold cheaper clothes.

57, S. C. W. S., furnishing department
See Stores.

65, Hugh Logan, stationer
Hugh Gray Logan, newsagent, stationer and tobacconist, had been at this address since 1945.

67, James Young, fishmonger
James S. Young opened this fish shop in 1931. He had another shop at 250 Hilltown.

69/75, Henderson & Co., house furnishers
Established in Glasgow in 1901 this firm was owned by Louis Hyman, the proprietor of Henderson & Kinton. In 1928 they allegedly introduced hire purchase to Dundee. They opened this shop in 1932.

68, William Martin, ironmonger
An old established Dundee ironmonger, Martin remained in this shop until the 1970s when it was taken over by the City Council for the redevelopment of the area.

60, West Riding Wallpaper Co.
This company was originally a mail order firm based in Leeds but advertised in Dundee from 1918 onwards. In 1926 the company opened a shop in these premises.

58a, Christofano Cardosi, restaurateur

This shop was opened by Cristofano Cardosi in 1931 as The OK Fish Restaurant. There it stayed until Mr Cardosi retired in the mid 1970s due to the redevelopment of the Wellgate. Mr Cardosi,who had come to Dundee in 1926, was the Italian consul in Dundee before World War Two but like many other Italians from the city was interned in Inverkeithing after the opening of hostilities.

58, Miss Dallas, hosier

Miss Dallas's business was known as "The Stocking Shop".

54, Mrs S. Christie, tobacconist

This was actually a newsagents that also sold small ware of various kinds.

52, James Millar, clothier

An old established business Millars was founded in 1842 and had another shop in the Overgate. The shop specialised in college and university scarves, blazers and ties. James C. D. Millar owned the shop up to his death in October 1949 but the business was still trading under his name in 1955.

50, Edward Piggot, butcher

This shop had been founded in 1903 as Piggot Brothers by Adam and Edward Piggot. Adam died in 1930 after which the business was carried on by Edward who became a President of the Dundee Master Butchers.

48, Adamson Smith, furniture dealer

A relative newcomer to this address in the Wellgate, Adamson Smith moved to this shop from his previous premises at 4 Wellgate.

46, Chas Stephen (Dundee), chemist

Charles Stephen who qualified as a chemist in 1891, was in 1904 selling Edison Phonographs from his chemists shop at this address.

44, James M'Kenzie, small ware

in 1916 M'Kenzie set up at this address as a dealer in small wares but in 1934 he was advertising as a draper. He died in 1946 and the business was continued by a partner trading under the same name.

42, A. Harris, tobacconist

See 57, Overgate.

40, Mina Robertson, milliner

Mina Robertson was in business here in 1940 and also had a branch in High Street Lochee.

34, Menzies & Sons, drapers

See 33 above.

28/30, Aberdeenshire Meat Co.

This firm was founded in the late 1870s by a Mr Murray who by 1878 had set up shops in Arbroath and at this address. James Smith came from Fraserburgh to work with Murray around 1885. He took over the company when Murray died. Smith ran the firm until he died in October 1925. after which Mr Joseph Roy became managing director.

26, Stewart Lyall, grocer

This licensed grocers business was started by Stewart Lyall in 1916. When he died in 1924 his wife, Mary Speedy Lyall carried on trading under this name. In 1955 the firm was being run by her daughter, Mary Speedy Bowen Lyall who had assumed control after her mothers death in 1951.

24, Radio Rentals

This firm was founded in 1930 in Brighton by Percy Perring-Thoms. It rented out radio sets and grew and expanded throughout the UK. At its peak it had more than two million customers and over five hundred shops. By 1955 it had opened a branch at this address by which time it was renting television sets for these were, at this date, quite expensive to buy.

22, Grafton's Sportswear

See 51 above

20, Angus Butchers

This business opened at this address in 1951. This was at a time when meat rationing was still in force. The shop sold horseflesh for human consumption and whale meat, neither of which were rationed.

18, Andrew G. Kidd, bakers

See 36,High Street.

10, Nelson Cream Ice Co, confectioners

In 1926 this firm was operating from 45, Nelson Street In 1955 it was being run by George Diamond and also had a branch at 66 Nethergate.

8, Restaurant Wilson

See 33, Union Street

4, Greenlees & Sons, bootmakers

This was originally a Glasgow firm started in the 1800s and traded under the name Greenlees Easiphit. From 1904 it had a branch in the Murraygate but opened a branch here in 1932.

2, Claude Alexander, tailors

This Scottish clothes chain based in Glasgow opened a branch here in 1943. It was taken over by United Drapery Stores in 1950 but in 1955 was still trading at this address under the Claude Alexander name.

Whitehall Street and Crescent

Whitehall Street and Whitehall Crescent were designed together as a major urban redevelopment scheme. This was planned by the City Council by means of the 1870 Improvement Act. Work commenced in the early 1880s and went on for the next 20 years.

Whitehall Street

1, Draffens, warehousemen
See Stores.

9, Thomas Justice, ironmongers
See Stores.

15, Thomas Justice, house furnishers
See Stores.

40, Cooper & Co. Stores Ltd, tea merchants
Coopers grocery firm was based in Glasgow and had branches throughout Scotland. They opened at these premises in 1915. In the early 1960s it was one of the first shops in Dundee to sell Sperry & Hudson pink trading stamps. They were eventually taken over by Allied Bakeries.

30, Henderson & McKay, silk mercers
In February 1901, D. S. Henderson & J. McKay took over the business of John Easton, silk mercer. Henderson had previously been the head of the finance department at Moon & Langlands, (latterly Draffen and Jarvies) for the previous 30 years. McKay had served an apprenticeship in Perth before working at the Bon Marche in Paris. This firm opened their shop here in 1928 and made bespoke dresses and gowns for the wealthy woman. Thay were taken over by Draffens in April 1961.

24, Larg & Sons, music sellers
This shop in the 1950s was a mecca for all aspiring musicians and also pioneered television in Dundee. The business was founded in Montrose by Alexander Larg, originally from Forfar, who in 1897 opened a shop at 8, Whitehall Street selling pianos and American organs. In 1901 Larg's moved to 24, Whitehall Street by which time they were selling gramophones and records. As the firm developed Alexander and his son David had, in 1918, opened a branch in London. When Alexander died in 1928, David took over the London business and his brothers, Robert G. and A. W. Larg took over the Dundee and Montrose businesses. When R. G. Larg died in 1945, the business went to Eric Larg, an outgoing man who drove a yellow Rolls Royce.

14, Nicoll & Smibert, restaurateurs
This firm of bakers and confectioners was started around the end of the 19th century at 4, Nethergate by T. D. Smibert and James S. Nicoll. By 1955 they had a number of branches in the city one of which was at this address. This was at first run as a sweet shop but with an additional access through its cellars to the adjoining basement function suite & restaurant of the main shop .

12, I. J. Collins, clothiers
I. J. Collins, who had been a tailor's cutter with James Morton and Son, tailors, in 1905 purchased the recently built No.12 Whitehall Street and set up his own business. As the business expanded the adjacent premises at No.14 were purchased. Although for a while there were two main doors the interior was undivided. The workrooms for the tailors were on the top floor of a building at the top of Crichton Street. At one time there were a staff of almost thirty. By 1938 there was no need for the double shop, and No.14 was rented to a succession of tenants, the tailoring business continuing at No.12. The business was owned by two of the founders sons, David and Lewis, until 1961 it was sold.

8, McGregor's Bookshop
This shop was originally known as the Bookmart and was taken over by J .McGregor in 1942. By the 1950s the shop was run by Miss McNab and was the best bookshop in the city. It had a good-sized basement stocked with books and had office accommodation on a mezzanine floor.

Whitehall Crescent

3, C. F. Eadie, confectioner
Mr Charles F. Eadie, a Dundonian, bought this business from Arthur Spark in December 1949 and was still in charge in 1955.

9, McKay Brothers
This firm was a mainstream travel agent who specialised is bus tours around the United Kingdom and Ireland. McKays also sold tickets for London

theatre shows. The shop had a very fine wrought iron gallery above the ground floor that can still be seen today in the premises occupied by the Solicitor's Property Centre.

15, Thomas Justice, cabinetmakers
See Stores

17, Cantrells, fishmongers
This store also sold game, some of which hung outside the shop. It was established in 3 Craig Street in 1885 by George Cantrell. When he died in 1903 the business was carried on by his widow, Ann Cantrell (nee Lyall) who sold the business to Robert McDonald in 1925. McDonald died in 1946 after which the firm was run by his son Angus. The shop was closed in December 1980 by Angus McDonald. His reason was the change in pedestrian flows away from the area "due to the development of the Overgate and the Wellgate shopping areas."

19, George Young, tobacconist
This shop had been occupied by a series of tobacconists over the years but in 1955 it was occupied by George Young.

21, Smith Hood coal, merchants
See 48,Union Street.

42, Gestetners Ltd., duplicators
This firm which sold duplicating machines was founded in London in 1879 by David Gestetner, a Hungarian immigrant who became a wealthy inventor but spent six months in jail for tax evasion. Gestetners first opened a branch in 7 Dock Street in 1925. In the 1940s they moved to this address and in 1955 the shop was being managed by Archibald Hood.

40, G. Paton & Son, seed merchants
Established here by 1922, the firm was an enthusiastic competitor in flower shows throughout Scotland.

38, Camerons (Dundee), fishmongers
This firm had been established as a fishmongers in 1911 by a Mr Cameron and W. D. M'Farlane. In 1922 a company was set up by W. D. M'Farlane, fishmonger, and J. Grafton Lawson, a solicitor, to take over the firm. In 1930 the shop caused a stir when a shark was exhibited in the shop windows as a publicity stunt.

34, Peebles Bros, grocers
This firm had first been established by David Peebles in 1886 in Whitehall Street but in 1897 had moved to Whitehall Crescent. Peebles was a pioneer and protagonist of an Early Closing Day in Dundee. The firm expanded and branches were opened in Albert Street, Broughty Ferry, Monifieth, Carnoustie and Tayport. When Peebles died in November 1948 the business was taken over by his son, David Adam Peebles. These premises are remembered by a number of Dundonians as being very old fashioned.

32, Keith Scott, outfitter
This business was originally established in 1890 by Keith Scott who came from Fettercairn. He started as a hatter and hosier in a small shop in the Overgate but within less than 10 years had gained major contracts for police uniforms in Fife and Dundee. By 1896 Scott was also operating from premises at 12 High Street beneath the Town House, but vacated these in 1901 when he established a shop in Whitehall Place. By 1907 he had opened a branch in Reform Street and by 1923 he also had a shop in the Murraygate. When Keith Scott died in 1949 the firm was taken over by his son, Mr Frederick Scott. It was later purchased by Douglas Wilson.

28, Gordon Cleaning Co., dyers
This firm originated in Huntley, Aberdeenshire, and opened a branch at this address in Dundee in 1935.

26, James Farquharson, draper
This shop was opened here by J. S. C. Farquharson in June 1928.

22, The Toy Shop
This shop was a magnet for schoolchildren and had originally been set up in 1906 by Archibald Webster. The Toy Shop was a specialist toy shop that at one time had been visited by the Queen Mother to buy toys for her daughters, Eilizabeth and Margaret. The premises were very narrow but extended to three floors. The shop attracted young boys with a working Meccano model of a crane in the window and a basement that was stuffed full of boys toys. In the 1950s, the shop was run by the widow of the original owner, Mrs Mary Webster and their son Richard. Richard would deliver and set up Hornby train sets and tracks at private houses.

As Websters was in business as a toy shop throughout the year, some thought it unfair for Draffens, Smith Brothers and Phins to open toy departments each December for the Christmas business and then in January to sell at a discount those toys that were still unsold.

16, Lawsons, warehousemen
See Stores

8, The Silk Shop, drapers
This shop sold fabrics for dressmaking and curtains.

4, J. W. Sutherland, tobacconists
See 44,Castle Street

9 POSTSCRIPT

We have seen in the preceding pages how shopping in Dundee has developed from the Middle Ages to the Millennium. Over a large part of this period most people existed at a subsistence level, growing much of their own food, and making most of their clothes.

As Dundee grew so did a prosperous middle class and this, in the latter part of the 18th century, stimulated the creation of shops as we know them today. However, the enormous increase in the population in the 19th and the major part of the 20th century, firmly established Dundee as the regional shopping centre.

However things began to change in the last quarter of the 20th century. Up to then Dundee had been full of optimism about the future of its city centre. But a feeling of uncertainty began to arise in the 1970s when, for the first time in two centuries, the population of the city and its catchment ceased to grow.

In addition Dundee's shopping centre had now to compete with Aberdeen, Edinburgh and Glasgow. Not only that but within the city itself the centre had also to compete with the newly established out of centre superstores and the retail parks at East and West Kingsway.

Better communications at a national level saw nationally and internationally based retail chains expanding into Dundee and ousting many local shops. After the Millennium the growth of commercial globalism saw UK based chains taken over by companies based abroad, often in tax havens. Many others were pulled into retail conglomerates such as Philip Green's Arcadia group who own, among other chains, Burton's Top Shop, Miss Selfridge, Dorothy Perkins and Wallis.

The massive expansion of the Tesco, Asda, Morrison and Sainsbury chains over some 25 years, saw these food giants not only dominating the food market, but directly competing with the city centre for the sale of both food and a range of non-food goods, including kitchenware, electrical goods and clothing.

In spite of all this retail floorspace continued to increase against the background of a fairly static population. Even more significantly the City Council committed itself to one of the largest and most far reaching development proposals ever to be contemplated by the local authority, namely the approval of a master plan for the Central Waterfront which envisages a vast expansion of the city centre.

But in the first decades of the 21st century even as developers continued to expand the city's retail floorspace, shops began to find their very existence threatened by a revitalised mail order sector, and more importantly by a rapid growth in online sales.

Many other things have changed, some for the better. The city centre's shopping environment has been greatly improved by new paving, lighting, and street furniture that is unique to Dundee. Within Dundee's shops there are goods in profusion, and the range of things for sale is amazing by the standards of the past. But although it is always easy to cast a golden glow over the past - after all one was younger then - there are grounds for thinking that shopping in Dundee is now a quite different experience.

For example, although, apart from the Overgate and Wellgate, most of the buildings which house the shops have remained the same, the businesses that occupy these premises have not. The town centre is now dominated by chain stores, and the locally owned shops of the past are hard to find. Shops selling furniture and purveying electrical goods have almost all departed to the out of centre retail parks, as have the grocery stores that were once so common in the city centre. Most of the shops are relative newcomers.

Whilst most of these modern shops have well designed interiors they have, unfortunately, become anonymous selling machines, often owned by corporations based in tax havens located thousands of miles away. Recently a commentator in a national newspaper remarked that "there is beginning to be a real disenchantment with the present nature of shopping. For many it has zero individuality and is becoming just a chance to worship at the shrine of brands".

These kind of changes are, of course, not peculiar to Dundee but can be seen in most shopping centres throughout Scotland and England as they are a reflection of the way in which British society has changed in a world dominated by electronic communication.

However the biggest change for shoppers in Dundee is that the city centre, once the unquestioned hub of the city, is now only one of a number of destinations in the city for shopping.

So much for what has happened up until now. How shopping in Dundee is likely to evolve in future is very difficult to judge. Even the seemingly unstoppable growth of Asda,Tesco, Morrison's and Sainsburys has been halted in its tracks. One recalls the old saying that "Predictions are very unreliable, especially when they are about the future". What follows is therefore a very personal view of how things might evolve as we move towards the end of the first quarter of the twenty-first century.

The 21st century has been characterised by some major trends which seem likely influence the future of shops and shopping in Dundee.

One is the growth in retail floor space and particularly in out of centre stores. Given the general expansion of urban areas and the decentralisation of population that has taken place since the middle of the 20th century, the popularity of the use of the car boot as a mobile shopping basket seems unlikely to change in the foreseeable future.

Another is the growth in online shopping. both at a national and international level. This is not surprising as online retailing saves consumers both time and money and offers exceptional choice. Online sales are also increasingly attractive to manufacturers, who see on line sales as offering increased profit margins in an increasingly competitive world.

In future consumers will increasingly be able to shop online and have their purchases delivered to their doors. It is already the case that some people avoid buying food from shops altogether, using the growing home delivery systems run by the major supermarkets, and fast food restaurants. Others of a different persuasion are able to use organic food delivery schemes. Either way these trends will reduce the demand for shops.

At a broader level, it seems unlikely that real incomes will rise in future as rapidly as they did in second half of the 20th century. Indeed in the recent past the wages of those in work have been depressed, whilst the low level of interest rates has reduced expenditure by the elderly who form an increasing proportion of the population.

Unless there is radical social and economic change all of these trends are likely to persist and one is driven to conclude that the demand for shopping floorspace is likely to decline, rather than grow. Things could be radically changed if there were a significant increase in the city's population arising from, say, a decentralisation of one of the Scottish Government's departments from Edinburgh to central Dundee.

However, at the local level, much will depend on the way in which individuals, and the City Council react to this situation. If they want to support the city centre it will be important to maintain its uniqueness by retaining the constraints upon the range of goods sold in out of centre locations and encouraging the sale of personalised products such as arts and crafts. More of the variety now present in Exchange Street would do much to make shopping in Dundee a more attractive experience. A rating system that is based upon turnover rather than rents would also help in ensuring that there is a wide range and variety of shops in the city centre. The city may even have to contemplate ways of ensuring that parking charges are the same in the city centre as in out of centre shopping plazas.

Along with this, more people should be encouraged to live in the city centre. The development of the central Waterfront may well offer a great opportunity in this regard and hopefully bring more tourist expenditure to the city centre.

How far, and where, all this might go is uncertain, but given the basic gregariousness of human beings, it seems unlikely that people will wish to live in isolation with all that they need delivered to their homes from remote warehouses.

But, if we do not want this kind of a future then all of us will have a part to play. There is, after all, little logic in bemoaning the number of empty shops in the city centre while buying goods on-line. If Dundonians wish to have a vibrant city centre full of shops, then they must work on the principle of "Use them or lose them".

Acknowledgements

This book could not have been written without the active support of a wide range of organisation and individuals. Chief among the organisations has been D. C. Thomson Ltd and in particular Murray Thomson, whose assistance and advice has been invaluable. Thanks are also due to a number of people at D. C. Thomson, in particular David Powell, Barry Sullivan and Terry McCallum.

One of the great official resources available to anyone who is interested in the history of Dundee is the local Section of Dundee City Council Library where Eileen Moran, Deirdre Sweeney, Maureen Hood., Gillian Malloy and Carol Smith were all extremely helpful, and a pleasure to work with. That was also true of the staff of Dundee City Archives, especially Ian Flett and his successor, Martin Allan. I would also wish to thank Stewart Murdoch and his colleagues at Dundee Leisure and Culture for their help and assistance. Thanks also to SUAS for the use of their maps of medieval Dundee. The photographic resources of the University of Dundee Archives section were also of great assistance.

When researching the history of Dundee over the last three quarters of a century a sometimes neglected resource is that contained in the memories of individual Dundonians. So many of these were of great help in putting this book together that it is impossible to name them all. However, the contribution of a number of these was crucial.

Norrie Robertson was of great help in so many respects, but particularly in pointing me towards individuals who might be able to help and coming forward himself with important items of information. Especial thanks are also due to the late Dennis Collins, for his help and guidance, particularly in respect of Dundee in the mid 1950's.

The section of the book dealing with the major department stores is overarched by the story of the individuals who ran these concerns all of which were very much family businesses. It is no surprise that the assistance of the present day descendants of these families was vital in enabling their story to be told. Of great help in respect of Cairds were Margaret Chalmers, Iain Caird and Pat Caird. Richard Hynd, Michael Hynd, and Frances Simpson gave patient advice in regard to Draffens and Kate Leslie and Joan Cowley did the same in respect of Smith Brothers. I am also grateful to Iain Wilson and Diane Anderson who gave great assistance on the life and times of G. L. Wilson.

Other contributions of note were made by Stephen Allardyce, Liz Barrie, Betty Baird, Sheila Boath, Allan Braithwaite, Jim Buist, David Craig, Andrew Cronshaw, Scott Henderson, Ian Johnstone, Sheila Potter, Sandy and Liz Melville, Mel Mitchell, Margaret Reed, Stewart Robertson, Averil Skea, Joyce Smart, Ian Smith, May Strachan, Bill Walker, Vera Winslow and Margaret Wright.

The Italian community in the city were an important part of the retailing history of Dundee. My contacts in this group were universally helpful and, it must be said, extremely entertaining. In this respect I would like to mention in particular Silvia Delnovo, Dino Barbiera, Sandy Cabrelli and Lawrence Sterpaio

Finally a special thanks to Jim Howie, known to many as a collector of postcards and a regular contributor to the Craigie column. However, he is much more than that and his interest and knowledge of the history of Dundee were most helpful in gaining an appreciation of the recent past of Dundee.

Index

Note: Individuals have been indexed by surname except where they were running a business in which case they have been indexed by the name of the firm.